Classroom Culture and the Construction of Learning Opportunities

An Ethnographic Case Study of Two EFL Classrooms in a Higher Education Setting in China

李英春・著

This is dedicated to my mother Zhenzhi Liu, who passed away just before I embarked upon my PhD journey, with all loving memories.

Abstract

This study seeks to gain an in-depth understanding of EFL (English as a Foreign Language) teaching and learning in two classrooms in a higher education setting in China. A specific focus has been placed on discerning the interrelationship between classroom cultural life and the construction of learning opportunities.

The two classrooms or the two cases under examination are led respectively by a British teacher and a Chinese teacher. They have been approached as two cultural entities comprised of basic classroom cultural components. Language learning is understood to be situated in its institutional and wider sociocultural context, it is a co-constructed process by classroom participants and classroom interaction is seen to play a central role in this process. Learning opportunity is seen to be essentially learners' access to activities that have *perceivable* or *potential* effects on the development of their language knowledge and skills.

The study employs an ethnographic case study approach with the use of multimodal data collection and data analysis methods. It is revealed that the two EFL classrooms under scrutiny demonstrate very different classroom cultural characteristics and that these are closely associated with the construction of learning opportunities in the two classrooms. That is, the pedagogical goals of the EFL classrooms, participants' demographic and dispositional features, their interactions along with the other classroom cultural components all contribute to the construction of learning opportunities. Despite the cultural differences as shown in these two EFL classrooms, they are both deemed successful by their participants in the sense that abundant learning opportunities are constructed in both classrooms.

With the acknowledgement of the heterogeneity and diversity of classroom cultures, this study is not meant to make generalizations for classroom realities either within China or more broadly, it is intended to demonstrate how a focus on classrooms as cultures can reveal the very different ways in which learning opportunities are constructed through the study of two EFL classrooms in contemporary China.

The study has contributions and implications for both EFL classroom pedagogy and classroom research. Pragmatically, it is hoped that the "positive classroom cultural traits" synthesized in this study can be of referential value for teachers in the development of positive classroom cultures for their learners. Theoretically, this study calls for a holistic understanding of classroom cultural life and an emic perspective on the construction of learning opportunities in the classroom reality. Learning opportunity, as illustrated through this study, can be a valuable unit of analysis in classroom research. It is proposed that more ethnographic case studies can be conducted on classroom cultures. The examination of multiple cases of classroom cultures or the longitudinal study of a single case of classroom culture can shed more light on the understanding of classroom realities and their impact on the construction of learning opportunities.

Acknowledgements

My deepest gratitude and thanks go to my supervisors, Ms. Sarah Rich and Prof. Gert Biesta. Ms. Sarah Rich has provided me with her encouragement and support in many ways throughout the whole PhD project besides giving much valuable input into this work; Prof. Gert Biesta has greatly influenced me with his bright ideas and pithy comments, making the whole learning experience as enlightening as rewarding.

I am grateful to the School of Education and Lifelong Learning, University of Exeter, U.K., for offering me SELL Studentship over the years and the Hardship Fund in the last phase of this research, so that I could complete this PhD project.

I am much obliged to Mr. Song Lin, who has given me financial as well as emotional support in my pursuit of this life's goal.

I would like to extend my thanks to the administration and teaching staff of Shenyang Normal University, Liaoning, China, for their assistance during the research process. Ms. Yixun Yan, Mrs. Melanie Brown Gao and the participating students have generously shared their language teaching and learning experiences with me.

I am grateful to Mr. Ian Moor and Mrs. Angela Moor, who have given me help in my life, guidance on my spiritual belief, and wise advice on my academic work.

I would like to express my thanks and love to my father and all family members and relatives who have given me all the support they could provide while I was studying in the UK.

To those dearest friends who have been encouraging and supportive, I shall always remain thankful.

Classroom Culture and the Construction of Learning Opportunities

• Contents •

· Table ·

• Figure •

· **Box** ·

• **Acronyms** •

BERA:	British Educational Research Association
CA:	Conversation Analysis
DA:	Discourse Analysis
CHC:	Confucius Heritage Culture
CLT:	Communicative Language Teaching
CREDE:	Centre for Research on Education, Diversity and Excellence
EFL:	English as a Foreign Language
ELT:	English Language Teaching
ESOL:	English for Speakers of Other Languages
G-T:	Grammar-Translation Method
IA:	Interaction Analysis
IATEFL:	International Association of Teachers of English as a Foreign Language
IELTS:	International English Language Testing System
LO:	Learning Opportunity
MOI:	Medium of Instruction
NCEC:	National College English Curriculum
NCEM:	National Curriculum for English Majors
NNS:	Non Native Speaker
NS:	Native Speaker
SLA:	Second Language Acquisition
TESOL:	Teaching English to Speakers of Other Languages

Chapter **1**

Introduction

This chapter is intended to provide an introduction to my research project and this book. I introduce in this chapter the rationale for the current study, my research aims and objectives, my research questions and research subjects before I explain the significance of the study and the structure of the whole book.

1.1 Personal reflexive experience and rationale for the study

This is an EFL classroom at a tertiary institution in China. The Chinese teacher is holding a textbook in her hands while ardently explaining vocabulary, grammatical rules and sentence structures through the lines of the texts; in the meantime, her students are preoccupied with note-taking. Almost every one of them is listening attentively to what the teacher is saying; although some are busily scribbling on their textbooks, some are flipping through dictionary pages to look up certain English words, and some are conversing in a hushed voice to exchange information that is in doubt. Teacher and students rarely make eye contact over classroom conversations. After explaining the text line by line and giving it verbatim translation from English to Chinese, the teacher and the students start to do language exercises based on their textbooks. In order to practise the English language knowledge in question, the teacher plays the role of a model and students mimic in chorus. Once in a while, the teacher would single out a student to answer certain questions, the student then would either provide an answer in a low voice or stand still in embarrassment not knowing a definitive answer to the question before the teacher supplies the right answer.

The above represents a familiar scene to me in my 20 years of formal schooling in the Chinese educational system. Irrespective of the subject being taught, the teacher was always the person who stood in the front doing most of the talking in class and students were, by and large passive and reluctant to air their personal views in front of their classmates, if they did have any in mind. Moreover, there was rarely any peer interaction between and among students in class and students were mostly listeners or onlookers. In other words, the teacher was the provider of knowledge and expected her students to follow and take back what has been delivered in class; students in return expected to sit in the classroom and take in as much as they could. In the English language classroom, learning for the students was realized mostly through the painstaking knowledge transmission and persuasive speech on the part of the teacher, combined with students' strenuous efforts spent on all kinds of written language exercises with an unquestioning acceptance of what the teacher said and what the textbook contained.

The majority of students resigned themselves to the teacher- dominated language classrooms because the students saw them as a necessary means to ensure their educational success in a system driven by the acquisition of language "facts" to be reproduced in examinations. Nevertheless, this classroom style was not unanimously enjoyed by all the students. There were always some students, including me, who secretly cast doubts on the EFL classroom practices and China's language educational system in our private conversations regarding the benefits of such practices and such an educational system for learners' foreign language learning.

When I started my university education, I had my first encounters with native English speaking teachers (widely referred to as "foreign experts" or "expatriate teachers" in China) for the first time. These teachers brought the language learners, including me, a novel classroom experience and completely different classroom dynamics which led me to further reflect on the nature of the traditional classrooms I had encountered up to that point and continued to encounter at the university. These expatriate teachers tried to get students to talk and enthusiastically directed the language activities towards a free-style communication system. Much of the class time was spent on students' pair works and group works; the teacher assigned students many tasks to complete and expected them to speak up in the class.

The Chinese students of English showed a variety of responses towards the expatriate teachers' organization of the language class after their initial excitement and curiosity waned. On the whole, my fellow students welcomed the coming of expatriate teachers as they believed that these expatriate teachers could provide them with a source of authentic use of English language. In fact, many students including me did enjoy the classroom activities designed by the expatriate teachers as we were encouraged to talk with the teacher and our fellow classmates in class. However, there were also students who experienced disorientation in class due to a multitude of reasons. Some regarded the classes as unsystematic because of the absence of textbooks, some criticized these classes as being chaotic due to the use of group works, and some held the opinion that they didn't learn much from expatriate teachers' teaching and these classes couldn't be of help in respect of ensuring their success in the national language exams.

The experiences of classes led by expatriate native speaker teachers triggered considerable debate amongst students, which were centred on the pros and cons of what was typically described as a "Chinese classroom teaching style" versus a "Western classroom teaching style". For some students, the central concern was whether one style of teaching could be seen as superior to the other. Some of my classmates condemned the Chinese educational system as a complete failure due to its overriding emphasis on testing which they blamed for producing "dumb English language learners" who could not speak English, and they believed the solution was to let the Western classroom teaching model replace the Chinese language teaching model. Others believed that the traditional Chinese educational system and teaching approaches had advantages over the Western one as the Western language teaching model was not of much use in terms of fulfilling the curricula objectives.

These may have stood for two extremes of opinions. For many of us, including me, more than anything else, the experiences of different teaching styles left us with an unanswered question: Which language teaching approach is better for us language learners to learn the foreign language?

After graduating and later taking up my career as a university language teacher, I experienced a reversal of roles in the language classroom-from being an EFL language learner to an EFL language teacher, which gave me a different set of insights into the question of which approach could help language learning but also made the answer to this question more elusive. I found that I, as the language teacher, could initiate and experience different classroom dynamics in different classrooms, regardless of the fact that I was a Chinese teacher of English and my students were all Chinese students. In addition, I noticed that sometimes one classroom might be less "interactive" than another; but this did not necessarily mean students in the former ended up with lower language achievement than those in the latter, judging from their overall

4

performances in classes and in formal exams. Meanwhile, I also discovered that while some of my "expatriate" colleagues have accomplished good results in their students' language learning with communicative language teaching methods, others felt disappointment when being silently resisted by their Chinese students in the language classrooms.

All my past life experiences as a language learner and a language teacher prompted me to constantly weigh the merits and demerits of the Western language teaching methodology and the traditional Chinese classroom language teaching methodology.

It seems to me that the underlying assumption for the advocates of "a communicative language classroom" is that verbal interactions lead to the production of language learning opportunities which can then contribute to the development of learners' language knowledge. In other words, the reasoning for the encouragement of classroom verbal interactions is that verbal interaction is correlative with language learning. However, a number of questions were still unanswered in my mind.

Since a Western teacher's language classroom is usually perceptibly more "interactive" than a Chinese's teacher's, does this then establish that a Western teacher's language classroom provide more learning opportunities than a Chinese teacher's classroom can provide and thereby lead to better language learning? Why, then, have many Chinese teachers and students indicated clearly their preference of traditional Grammar-Translation language teaching methodology over Western Communicative Language Teaching methodology?

At an educational philosophical level, do the different approaches to classroom language teaching as demonstrated by Chinese teachers of English and Western teachers of English simply mirror the divergences in Chinese and Western educational philosophies and legacy? There has been abundant research evidence suggesting that the classroom behaviour of Chinese teachers and Chinese students are partly the manifestation of

5

what Watkins and Biggs (1999) call the Confucian Heritage Culture (e.g. Boyle, 2000; Brick, 1991; Cortazzi & Jin, 1996; Gao & Watkins, 2002; Ho & Crookall, 1995; Hu, 2003; Watkins & Biggs, 1999).

According to Sullivan (2000), the varied definitions of the purposes of groups can be related to two approaches to knowledge. The broader context outside the language classroom in the Chinese society is that hierarchy and sustained relationships are greatly valued, knowledge is transmitted from the ancestor to the descendents through observation and reflection. Great respect is paid to canonical doctrines and those stay in authority. On the other hand, the Western' perspective is that knowledge is based on reason, observation, critical analysis, and Aristotelian logic; in the pursuit of knowledge, debate and dialectical interchange are greatly emphasized. But I remained unconvinced that these two approaches to knowledge were an adequate way of understanding the relationship between different approaches of language teaching and their effects on language learning.

In an eagerness to gain more insights into the "Western teaching approaches", I came to the U.K. at the beginning of 2003 for further pursuit of knowledge. It turned out that to actually witness and experience highly interactive classroom environment in a genuine English context has provoked my further questions.

From my experience, compared with classrooms in British universities, EFL classrooms in Chinese institutions appear far more authoritarian. In British university classrooms, I observed that an interactive classroom milieu which typified the classrooms I experienced in Britain meant that teacher and students could enjoy a more or less symmetrical relationship. That is, that these appear to exhibit characteristics of pedagogical democracy (Finkelstein & McCleery, 2002). However, I am left wondering whether pedagogical democracy is only achievable if there is a symmetrical relationship between the teacher and the students as displayed through their more or less equal share of class talk? Moreover, if pedagogical democracy is synonymous with successful teaching, does it afford participants more and better learning opportunities? Most importantly, is it possible to implement this pedagogical democracy within the Chinese education setting?

To sum up, what I have experienced and observed as a language learner and a language teacher in China, and later as a postgraduate in a British higher education institution has proved that the search for the answers to the series of questions in my mind demands a thorough understanding of classroom teaching and learning, and that this is an appropriate and worthy focus of my PhD study.

1.2 Purpose of the study and research design

The chief aim of this research is to gain a better understanding of classroom teaching and learning, specifically, an understanding of how learning can be facilitated in classrooms. My objective is to interpret the varied effects of patterned classroom events on the construction of learning opportunities within classroom contexts in China in search of solutions to optimize classroom language teaching and learning.

Language learning is regarded as a situated activity within its context (Boekaerts, 2002; Breen, 1985; Candlin & Neil, 2001; Duff, 2003; Freeman & Johnson, 1998; Gibbons, 2003; Hu, 2003; Seedhouse, 2004; Tudor, 2001); language classrooms as the primary site for language learning to occur have been approached from different angles. A cultural approach to language classrooms (Allwright & Bailey 1991; Beales et al. 1967; Breen, 2001; Cortazzi & Jin, 1996; Holliday, 1999, Holliday, 2002; Spindler, 1967) is the approach that has been adopted in the current study.

In this research project, language classrooms are approached as multi-dimensional cultural entities. Classroom interactions, by their very nature, are perceived as inherently central to the process of language learning while classroom learning is regarded as being situated at various levels and is co-constructed by participants.

With the view that classrooms are cultural entities, I have designed this ethnographic case study for the investigation of the relationship between classroom culture and the construction of learning opportunities in two classrooms in a higher education institution in China. Specifically, my research questions are:

- What are the characteristics of the two EFL classroom cultures under scrutiny?
- How are learning opportunities constructed in the two EFL classroom cultures?

My data collection has been a multimodal processes. Participant observation, interview, field-note, audio-recording, and collection of documents and texts have been employed as data collection methods. Data analysis, started alongside with data collection has been an iterative and recursive process in which ethnographic analysis methods and conversation analysis have been applied. To ensure the validity of this research and its findings, I have used multiple triangulations including the triangulation of research methodologies, the triangulation of data collection methods, the triangulation of data analysis methods, the triangulation of data sources and the triangulation of perspectives.

1.3 My research subject

To find out the relationship between classroom culture and the construction of learning opportunities, I have chosen two EFL classrooms as my research subjects for investigation. The two classrooms are located at the School of Foreign Languages in a Chinese provincial Normal University, led respectively by a British language teacher and a Chinese language teacher. The choice of my research subjects is grounded in their reputation as two very successful classrooms at the School.

While it is my intention to treat these two classroom cultures as individual cases, and the focus is on deepening an understanding of the ways learning opportunities are constructed in each, there is a degree of comparison at times. Nonetheless, this study is meant to be more interpretive than comparative or contrastive. The objective of this research is not to measure the merits of one EFL classroom culture against the other; instead, this study has been carried out to reveal the relationship between EFL classroom cultures and the construction of learning opportunities through the illustration of how learning opportunities have been constructed in these two EFL classrooms.

1.4 Significance of the study

This research supplements the current research literature on language classroom and language learning; it has yielded new insights into how we approach classroom reality and learning opportunity. There is little research, to my knowledge, that has been conducted in Chinese language classrooms using an ethnographic case study approach. Besides, while learning opportunity has been widely used in classroom research as a key concept to study the relationship between classroom interactions and language learning; little research has been found to use "learning opportunity" as an incision point in the study of classroom realities. The theoretical perspective that language classroom can be viewed as cultural entities comprised of basic components as applied in this study makes possible a holistic understanding of classroom interaction and language learning; the definition of classroom interaction and categorization of learning opportunity made in this research can be valuable for later study on classroom interactions and learning opportunities.

This study can help to deepen the understanding of classroom teaching and learning and shed new light on the construction of learning opportunities. It has proved the symbiotic and reciprocal relationship between the two. To enhance the construction of learning opportunities in language classrooms, we have to view language learning as a co-constructed process. Classroom teaching is for classroom learning and informed by classroom learning; classroom learning is dependent on classroom teaching and influences classroom teaching. In the close inspection of classroom teaching and learning, this research has brought to the fore learners' roles in the whole process. The meaning of learning opportunity, as unveiled in this research, is subject to learners' idiosyncratic interpretations rather than to those of the teachers. This has foregrounded the need for language educationalists and educationalists in general to get to know learners' needs and make efforts to meet these needs in their classroom teaching.

1.5 The structure of this book

Chapter 1, the present chapter, presents a general account of my research project. I introduce briefly the rationale for the current study, its aim and objective, its methodology and research subjects, and its significance. I also describe the structure of the whole book in this chapter.

The purpose of Chapter 2 is to contextualise the study by first providing an extensive review of the conventional EFL classroom practices in China with relation to its philosophical bedrock of Confucian Heritage Culture. It is followed by the discussion of China's endeavour for more effective EFL classroom pedagogy in the modern era such as the advocacy of communicative language teaching methodology. I then outline China's EFL educational policy and explain contemporary Chinese language educational system and its perceivable effects on the existing EFL classroom language teaching practices and language learning approaches. Finally, I report on how perceived dissatisfaction with both traditional teaching approaches and those advocating a more communicative approach to EFL teaching in China have led to considerable debate and disagreement as to the best or most appropriate methodology for foreign language education in China.

Chapter 3 provides a theoretical framework for this study. I first give a critical review of the ways in which researchers have attempted to understand the impact of classrooms on learning. I consider two major orientations in attempts to describe the significance of classroom experiences to learning-one has viewed language classroom as an arena of interactions, the other has viewed language classroom as a cultural entity. I discuss the implication of each for how learning opportunities are best understood to come about. With reference to the previous research, I expound on the theoretical framework for this research project in which classrooms are conceived as multidimensional cultural entities and language learning opportunities are seen as constructed in the interplay of classroom cultural components.

In Chapter 4, I provide details of the design of the study. I first give an overview of the methodologies applied in previous classroom research and I describe how these have informed my research design. I then give a detailed account of the ethnographic case study design I employ and give the rationale for my choice of different research methods. Following this I describe my data collection procedure and recursive data analysis process. Finally, I reflect on practical problems anticipated, encountered and solved when carrying out this research, discuss ethical issues that arose and how these were addressed and report on the perceived limitations of the research.

Chapter 5 presents a rich description of the two EFL classroom cultural lives in the two classrooms under investigation. I describe in detail the cultural characteristics of the two EFL classrooms here. Participants' demographic and dispositional characteristics, classroom cultures' physical settings and pedagogical goals, their norms of behaviours and interactions are unfolded with the aid of descriptive data.

After the description of two EFL classroom cultures, I provide an account of how learning opportunities are constructed in each of the classrooms in Chapter 6. The major focus of this chapter is on how learning opportunities are defined and afforded in the two EFL classroom cultural entities. In the final part of this chapter I consider how the insights gained from this analysis contribute to a broader understanding of learning opportunities and extend the initial understandings of these presented in my theoretical framework.

Chapter 7 summarizes the key findings from this study and the contribution of this research to knowledge. I reiterate my research questions which are concerned with classroom cultural characteristics and learning opportunity construction. I then give a recapitulation of the cultural characteristics of the two EFL classrooms in this study and how learning opportunities are found to be constructed in them before I explicate the contribution of this study to knowledge at conceptual, theoretical and practical levels. I conclude this chapter with the implications of this research and my recommendations for future investigations.

Chapter 2

Shifting Perceptions of Effective Classroom Practices in China

This chapter is to provide the contextual information for the current study. I first expand on the perceptible effects of Confucius Heritage Culture (Watkins & Biggs, 1999) on EFL classroom teaching and learning in this chapter with a description of its influence on participants' perceptions of their classroom roles and classroom behaviour. Then I give an introduction to the traditional classroom teaching methodology, the classroom dynamics generated; China's language testing system and the learning approaches adopted by language learners.

Following this I reveal the current EFL tertiary educational system and the relevant language educational policy. Because of the growing dissatisfaction with traditional EFL classroom practices, CLT, a Western language teaching methodology, has been introduced into China's EFL classrooms to outperform the traditional language teaching methods. Parallel with the import of CLT has been the import of the notion "pedagogical democracy" which promotes students' participation in classrooms. Commendable as they are, I exhibit how CLT has been received in China and raise questions regarding the viability of "pedagogical democracy" as an educational ideology in a Chinese context at the end of this chapter.

2.1 EFL classroom teaching and learning traditions in China

EFL classroom education in China has its own established traditions although these do not deviate far from the norm of classroom education in other subjects. In the EFL classrooms, language teachers and language learners have their defined roles to act which can be traced back to the influence of the ancient Chinese educational philosophy; the language teachers have their preferred classroom teaching methodology and the language learners have their adopted learning approaches to conduct language teaching and learning under China's national language testing system.

2.1.1 CHC, participants' roles and their classroom performance

The stereotypical teacher-student relationship in Chinese classrooms have been extensively reported (Chen, 2005; Dooley, 2001; Rao, 2002; Watkins & Biggs, 1999) as it is controversially regarded as the source of less than interactive classroom dynamics and one of the causes leading to the production of English learners who lack linguistic competency. The teacher is regarded as knowledge provider and authority in the classroom while the students are regarded as knowledge receptacles and subordinates; knowledge is transmitted from the teacher to the students for the teacher's task is to "give" and the students' task is to "receive". Students are generally obedient, passive and unwilling to air personal views (Dooley, 2001; Watkins & Biggs, 1999).

The establishment of these roles may be attributed to one aspect of their classroom context that merits particular attention-the educational traditions of Chinese society in which participants have been educated and socialised. These traditions are very likely to influence what participants expect to find in the language classroom, for example, how the teacher should carry out language teaching tasks, how the students interpret and interact with what is proposed to them by their teacher, in their course books, or in other teaching-learning materials (Tudor, 2001). These educational traditions are very often linked with Confucius Heritage Culture (CHC) in China (Watkins & Biggs, 1999). Scollon (2000), for example, has shown that Chinese students' participation patterns in classrooms can be related to their underpinning philosophical assumptions concerning classroom communication.

In fact in China, Confucius' educational philosophy has been the overarching canon for Chinese teachers and students to comply with in their classroom life for centuries. The following quotes are taken from *The Analects*, which is a record of Confucius' words and discussions he has held with his disciples regarding a multitude of things such as education and politics.

When talking of his preferred teaching style, Confucius made the following remark,

> "I transmit but do not innovate. I am truthful in what I say and devoted to antiquity."

Speaking of learning approaches, he said,

> "By three methods we may learn wisdom:
> First, by reflection, which is noblest;
> second, by imitation, which is easiest;
> and third by experience, which is the bitterest."

It is phenomenal how these educational philosophical sediments are still influencing participants' beliefs in and perceptions of classroom organization, classroom power relations, and classroom interaction patterns. Fundamentally, these educational philosophies have influenced greatly on classroom participants' understanding of how learning should be achieved. In this legacy-rich CHC context, participants' dispositions have been cultivated through years of schooling that position them towards certain classroom attitude and behaviour.

According to Confucius' educational theory, knowledge is appreciated as something proved to be correct by ancestors, and it mainly comes from two authoritative sources-the teacher and the textbook (Jin & Cortazzi, 2002). The teacher in this sense is a symbol of knowledge (Zhong & Shen, 2002) and as such, the teacher is commonly not open to challenge. When the teacher is the symbolic representation of "truth" that is not open to challenge; he or she has been naturally endowed with this supreme power of authority within the territory of the classroom.

The students, considering "the easiest way to learn is by imitation" (see the above quotes), are ready to sit in the classroom and take in what is said by the teacher. They tend to associate "true knowledge" with authoritative textbooks and teacher's lectures. Students voluntarily imitate what their teacher says because they believe their teacher is their role model. They mainly see themselves as receivers rather than negotiators or discoverers in this learning process. They learn by internalisation of the content of their textbooks and by emulation of their teacher's words. Therefore, the role of the students is to command the knowledge that teacher delivers and learn by following the role model of their teacher.

Thus it can be said that teaching and learning for Chinese teacher and students is a process of knowledge transmission from the antiquity to the present; learning is a process of observation, reflection and imitation. All these establish participants' roles and the dynamics they are going to generate in the traditional Chinese classroom.

Apart from being influenced by Confucius' educational philosophy, participants' role-relationship is strengthened by Confucius' moral legacy. Both the teacher and the students see themselves as part of a "relational hierarchy"; this role-relationship is deeply rooted in the Chinese delineation of social hierarchy. Teacher, as the authority, puts great emphasis on students' self-discipline and proper behaviour in classrooms, rather than on their free expression of opinions and independence. Students are taught not to challenge the teachers, but to respect, obey, listen, and follow their instructions (Salili, 1999). It is characteristic of Chinese students to show their respect for their parents and teachers, to regard self-effacement and conformism as virtues (Hayhoe, 1989). Many Chinese students display almost unquestioning acceptance of the knowledge delivered by their teachers to show their filial piety.

In some cases, students' passivity and reticence is partly caused by their fear of committing mistakes or offending others. In Confucian code of morality, a man of perfect virtue is cautious and slow in speech (The Analects, 479-221BC). When it comes to English language learning, it is particularly obvious that students are reluctant to air their views in English language in classrooms because the possible embarrassment caused by making linguistic mistakes inhibit students' desire to partake in oral practice.

It can be seen from the above that Confucius philosophical and moral legacy have shaped teachers' and students' perceptions of their classroom roles and teaching and learning process, which largely prescribe their classroom behaviour.

2.1.2 G-T method and teacher- centred classroom dynamics

In the short history of EFL education in China, there have been a series of language teaching methods being practised in classrooms such as the "Direct Method", the "Audio-Lingual" method, the "Grammar-Translation" method and the recent "Communicative Language Teaching" method. Most of these language teaching methods have been but transient and transitional, but the "Grammar-Translation" method or "G-T" method has been and remains the dominant EFL teaching method in many language classrooms in China.

This traditional method has been particularly resilient in China's EFL classrooms and there are many teachers of English who still consider G-T method as both practical and effective in China even after the Communicative Language Teaching approach has won recognition in the rest of the world (Hayhoe, 1989). G-T method involves translating texts from the foreign language into the mother tongue, coupled with explanations of unfamiliar words and grammatical rules. Precisely as its name suggests, Grammar-Translation method focuses on learning the rules of grammar and their application in the translation of passages from one language into the other. What matters most is accuracy rather than fluency. University teachers of English in China have long been used to making grammar-translation method their chief classroom language teaching method for they are keenly interested in the accuracy in language forms and tend to focus on grammatical knowledge and specific syntactic constructions in English. In reality, this method has almost become a habit being consciously and subconsciously used by many Chinese teachers of English in their EFL classrooms.

As a result, traditional EFL classrooms are characterised with teacher-centred classroom dynamics. In many an English class, teachers would make efforts in explaining English grammar and analyzing sentence structures, making clear the differences in vocabulary choices; only a small proportion of class time would be spent on students' oral activities in which students practise orally what they have learned, while most of the class time is occupied by teachers' lengthy and elaborate explanations of linguistic knowledge.

Apart from the influence of CHC on students' reticence in classrooms as I have described earlier, the concern with the precision of their language output is another cause that leads to students' apparent passivity. The students are reluctant to present their own ideas until they have mastered sufficient knowledge to be able to make informed judgments. They are reluctant to stand out and express their views unless they are sure of the accuracy in their linguistic output. Consequently, students appear to be passive, teacher dependent and lacking in initiative in classrooms.

2.1.3 The language testing system and EFL classroom pedagogy

For many EFL teachers and learners in China, the higher and ultimate goal of learning English language-to become competent users of this language has very often been equated with and reduced to the short-term goal of achieving good exam scores in national language tests. "Achievement is measured with examination" has always been a constant feature of China's EFL educational policy (Postiglione, 1999).

Before even starting their university life, students' English skills have to be tested in National College Entrance Examination, which is a standardized examination for recruiting tertiary students across the country. The scores students achieve in this national examination can determine which rank of the university they are enrolling after high school and the rank of the university they are enrolled in can have a powerful effect on their future job choice and even their status in Chinese social hierarchy.

After they become university students, they have to undergo the national tests designed for university students in their four years' university life. English is a compulsory subject for all university students in China and passing certain national English tests has become a prerequisite for students to obtain their degrees in many of the Chinese universities.

The National English Testing System for university students is designed to examine the implementation of the National College English Curriculum and to evaluate EFL classroom teaching and learning at tertiary level. The National English Language Testing System for university students includes Test for English Majors Band 4 and Band 8 (TEM4 & TEM8) for English major students; College English Test Band 4 and Band 6 (CET4 & CET6) for non-English majors, as illustrated in table 2.1 on the next page.

It can be seen from table 2.1 that these tests, no matter whether they are for English majors or non-English majors, all include such basic component parts like listening, reading, writing; vocabulary and grammar.

The scores of these tests have been considered as the most important indicators of EFL learners' linguistic competence; the certificates that prove language learners have passed these tests can be their passports to desired job positions after graduation. The considerable significance attached to National English Testing System for individual development might be because written examinations are an important mechanism for the identification of talent and for the allocation of people to occupations in a country with a high commitment to economic development and modernisation (Paine, 1992). In the mean time, teachers' language teaching efficiency and universities' achievement in EFL teaching are also evaluated on the basis of their students' pass rates in these standardized tests. The importance of these tests then is manifested through classroom teaching methodology and participants' classroom performances.

Table 2.1: National English Testing System for University Students in China

National English Testing System for University Students in China		
Types of Tests		**Components of Tests**
TEM (Test for English Majors)	Band 4 or TEM4 (Passing is usually obligatory for BA degree)	Part 1: Dictation; Part 2: Listening Comprehension; Part 3: Cloze; Part 4: Grammar & Vocabulary; Part 5: Reading Comprehension; Part 6: Writing
	Band 8 or TEM8	Part 1: Listening Comprehension; Part 2: Reading Comprehension; Part 3: General knowledge (of the English-speaking countries); Part 4: Translation; Part 5: Writing
CET (College English Test)- Test for non-English Majors	Band 4 or CET4 (Passing is usually obligatory for BA degree)	Part 1: Listening Comprehension Part 2: Reading Comprehension Part 3: Vocabulary and Sentence Structure Part 4: Cloze Part 5: Writing
	Band 6 or CET6	Part 1: Listening Comprehension; Part 2: Reading Comprehension; Part 3: Vocabulary and Sentence Structure; Part 4: Writing

Some universities have taken very harsh measures by making certain English qualification as one of the requirements for students to graduate and win their degrees (for example, passing TEM4 or CET4 is obligatory for graduates to get their BA degrees, as shown in table 2.1). Because of this, many teachers feel driven to adopt enforcing measures in EFL classrooms to ensure their students' "good performance" in standardized national tests. Thereby, high pass rate of national exams has become one of the key pursuits of a university language classroom.

Precisely because exam pass rate overrides other concerns, tests and examinations inevitably influenced EFL classroom teaching and learning in Chinese universities. They are frequently conducted in EFL classrooms and strongly influence the content and methodology of EFL classroom teaching; the increments of English knowledge are frequently measured with tests in all forms. Chinese teachers of English keep their eyes firmly fixed on textbooks which are the blueprints for national tests in order to fulfil the goal of ensuring good pass rates of their students.

On the part of language learners, they know too well that they need better exam grades or more certificates in English qualifications to secure further educational or professional opportunities. Thus students in most of the class time are preoccupied with note-taking or answering questions as posed by their teachers. They are very attentive to what the teacher has to say, always ready to take notes of explicit explanations of English grammar and vocabulary (Hu, 2003) which are the indispensable component parts in national standardized tests. The striving for high exam scores is one of the reasons why Chinese students rely heavily on memorization (Chen & Chang, 2005).

To sum up, in a traditional EFL classroom in a Chinese university, participants' classroom roles are clearly defined; the teacher is the authority and knowledge provider, the students are subordinates and knowledge receivers. The textbook is also regarded as a source of authoritative knowledge. English language teaching is carried out in teacher-centred classrooms in which Grammar-Translation language teaching method is practised; language learning is achieved with students' heavy dependence on their teachers as well as their textbooks through imitation of teachers' language behaviours and memorization of textbook content. National English Testing System dictates EFL classroom teaching and learning methods for it is the standard based on which language teaching and learning accomplishments are measured.

2.2 Opposition to the traditional EFL classroom pedagogy

In recent years, there has arisen increasing discontent with and complaint about the established language teaching and learning traditions. The most obvious dissatisfaction is that many people including language teachers and language learners consider the traditional EFL classroom pedagogy as ineffective.

The "end product" of this EFL classroom pedagogical apparatus, the university graduates, show an average low competency when they try to put this foreign language into use in their job positions in public and private sectors. Some graduates, who have achieved high scores in exams and obtained many certificates of English qualifications, very often find it difficult to translate some technical information into English or explain information related with daily life in English; sometimes they find that they are unable to communicate freely with people coming from English-speaking countries.

This has attracted employers' criticisms of their newly-graduated employees' English level, which in turn has elicited these graduates' accusations against the EFL classroom educational traditions in China. Language teachers and students believe it is China's tertiary EFL teaching and testing system that is to be blamed for producing graduates who lack a comprehensive grasp of English knowledge and skills.

The most acute problem with tertiary EFL classroom pedagogy, as many language teachers and students see it, is the text- and test-oriented classroom language teaching and learning. Since the entire classroom activities are based on participants' textbooks, sometimes students can be ill-informed of the daily usage of English. When the value of EFL classroom pedagogy has been lessened to "English teaching and learning for national tests", both the teacher and the students may put their language teaching and learning emphasis only on textbooks and on what is relevant to the national tests while largely overlooking the practical use of the target language.

The G-T method and teacher-fronted classroom dynamics are also believed to share the blame. The G-T method, which has been favoured by language teacher and students because of its effectiveness in enhancing students' performances in exams, is believed to result in students' ignorance of the functions of the English knowledge when they concentrate too much on the forms of the language. With G-T method in use, many Chinese EFL classrooms have been characterized by an extremely high proportion of teacher-initiated interactions; the amount of students' oral output in EFL classes is indeed limited (Fang, 2005). To some language teachers and students, the inadequacy of EFL classroom interactions implies the shortage of communication opportunities in the target language, which results in Chinese students' unsatisfactory communicative ability in the target language.

As a response to these accusations and oppositions made regarding language teaching traditions, many language educationalists keep searching for ways of improving and transforming EFL classroom pedagogy in China, especially with regard to classroom organization and language teaching methodology.

2.3 Towards more effective EFL classroom pedagogy in the modern era

The last 20 years has witnessed drastic changes in many aspects of Chinese people's social and cultural life. Along with the rise in economy comes the nation's great thirst for English language talents. English is perceived to be essential for the development of the country's economy. To sustain China's increasing presence in international affairs and growing importance in the global economy, there has been a clear need to raise the national level of English proficiency (Hu, 2005). Learning English therefore has become almost a "national mission" (Cortazzi & Jin, 1996; Hu, 2003) and the Chinese government has officially announced that English learning is for the whole nation (Jin and Cortazzi, 2002).

Given that higher levels of education are accepted as critical to the economic success of a society (Rosenberg, 2004), paramount importance has been attached to English language learning at tertiary level in China. The primary concern of the Ministry of Education in China is that tertiary students should develop an adequate language competency, so that after graduation they will be ready to serve China's speedy economic growth.

However, the dramatic changes experienced in Chinese society in the modern era have posed new challenges for English educators as well as English learners.

One conspicuous challenge for language education practitioners is the severe imbalance between the supply and the demand of qualified EFL teachers in Chinese universities. This is partly due to Chinese universities' "expansion wave". Official figures have shown a challenging reality for language education practitioners. That is the disproportionate number of learners relative to teachers. In 2003, the number of university students has amounted to 19, 000, 000 contrasting with that of university teachers of English which is only around 50, 000 (Ministry of Education, 2003). The shortage of English teachers compels university language teachers to work under great pressure and heavy load. Most teachers would hope for a small class size in which students are homogeneous in their language proficiency level, but in reality many have to work with a class of fifty students or more whose language abilities are often heterogeneous.

The input-poor context has exacerbated the current EFL teaching and learning situation and made producing university graduates who are highly proficient in English language an almost insurmountable task. Since English is a foreign language in China, students' access to English language learning is very limited outside the EFL classrooms. The chance for them to communicate in English with native speakers is rare, as is their chance to access the English language media.

There has been continual recognition that the quality of English language education at tertiary level has not been overtly satisfactory although considerable progress has been made in the last several decades. To improve the quality of EFL teaching for better EFL learning, the Chinese Ministry of Education has been constantly making efforts in implementing a nation-wide language education reform in universities.

2.3.1 EFL educational reform in tertiary education in China

Parallel to the economic reform, there should be a national university EFL education reform (Wu, 2004) which started in the early 1980s. University EFL education reform activities embrace the amendments made in National College English curriculum (NCEC) for non-English major students and in National Curriculum for English Majors (NCEM) at Tertiary Level.

Out of the dissatisfaction with traditional EFL classroom practices, China's language education policy makers have been constantly making revisions in the NCEC. The NCEC in China issues guidelines for language teaching theory and practice for non-English major students, it is the official reference document for university English education professionals and administrators nationwide.

In the first version of NCEC which was drafted in 1985, the goal of EFL education for non-English major tertiary students was to develop a relatively high level of competence in reading, an intermediate level of competence in listening, and a basic level of competence in writing and speaking (NCEC, 1985). More emphasis has been placed on the development of students' reading comprehension ability than on the development of the other basic language skills. In the second version of NCEC (1995), the emphasis of EFL university education was still put on reading comprehension, although equally emphasized was a good command of English vocabulary and grammatical knowledge.

The turn of the century has seen great development in EFL tertiary education in China which is a natural response to the social demand for new type of English talents who have balanced language knowledge and skills. A newer version of NCEC (2004) was drafted and delivered to the whole country in which "to develop students' comprehensive language ability in English usage, especially listening and speaking skills" has been stressed as one of the most important goals to be achieved through university language teaching and learning (Wu, 2004), there were also a clearer articulation of EFL classroom teaching methods and evaluation methods in this NCEC, as shown in the table below.

Table 2.2: National College English Curriculum, 2004

1.	Goal of tertiary English education for non-English majors	We need to train students' comprehensive English language skills, especially their listening and speaking ability, so that they can communicate in English language in written as well as in oral forms to serve for the country's economic development and international communication. Meanwhile, we need to develop students' autonomy in learning.
2.	Principle of EFL classroom teaching	Teachers need to pay attention to the relationship between language and culture, and cultivate students' cross-cultural communication ability. There should be co-ordinated development of students' basic language skills including listening, speaking, reading, and writing abilities.
3.	EFL classroom teaching methods	Teachers need to develop classroom teaching methods that serve for the best interests of students. Teachers need to combine in-class and extra-curricular activities to develop students' language learning strategies.
4.	Testing and evaluation methods	The focus of language assessment is on the evaluation of students' basic English language knowledge and their ability to use this language. Language testing and evaluation should emphasize on both the result of EFL education and its process.

The reform activities in tertiary EFL education can simultaneously be seen in the amendments made in the National Curriculum for English Majors at tertiary level. In the previous version of NCEM (1990), reading and writing have been stressed as the two language skills to be achieved from university classrooms, and Grammar-Translation method was stated to be the main classroom teaching method. In the most recent version of NCEM at tertiary level (2000) (table 2.3 on the next page), for the first time the significance of developing learner autonomy in English language classrooms has been put forth. What is more, it is advocated that English language learning should be realized through a variety of classroom activities with the help of multiple teaching instruments including multimedia in the classroom and extracurricular activities which supplement in-class activities. In this sense, a multidimensional EFL classroom environment should be established.

No matter whether they are intended for English majors or non-English majors, the amendments made in NCEC and NCEM have reflected the trend and direction for China's tertiary EFL education. The shifts of focus can be summarized as follows:

- There is a shift in the goal of tertiary EFL classroom education. It is recognized that the primary goal of EFL tertiary education is to improve students' "comprehensive language knowledge and skills";
- There is a shift in classroom dynamics from "teacher- centeredness" towards "learner-centeredness". In the employment of EFL classroom teaching method, there is clear indication that learners' needs should be taken into consideration in both curricula (cf. "Teachers need to develop classroom teaching methods that serve for the best interests of students" in NCEC in 2004; "we need to change the teacher-fronted EFL classroom model into the student-centred classroom model in which teachers play the role of a guide" in NCEM in 2000);
- There is a shift of focus in language evaluation. The National English Testing System for university students is no longer branded as the sole criterion for evaluating English language teaching and learning as schools can design their own evaluation system; EFL education assessment is based on both the result and the process of EFL classroom teaching and learning.

Table 2.3: National Curriculum for English Majors at Tertiary Level, 2000

1.	Goal of tertiary English education for English majors	In order to adapt to the new demands and new situation, we need to educate foreign language professionals geared towards the 21st century. They should have a solid foundation of English linguistic and cultural knowledge and proficiency in English.
2.	Principle of EFL classroom teaching	The first and foremost task for EFL teaching is the development of students' basic language skills, which should be an on-going process throughout their 4 years' university education. We should pay attention to students' listening, speaking, reading, writing and translation skills. In the course of teaching, we should pay close attention to foster students' cross-cultural communicative competence.
3.	EFL classroom teaching methods	We need to change the teacher-centred EFL classroom model into the student-fronted classroom model in which teachers play the role of a guide. To motivate students and to maximize learning for students, EFL classroom teaching should be task-based involving activities in various forms. A diversity of teaching methods can be employed. Extra-curricular EFL teaching and learning practice is an extension and expansion of classroom activities to develop students' language abilities. Extra-curricular activities can promote participation and cultivate the spirit of cooperation, they include: reading, lectures, debates, book reports, drama, newspaper editing, interviews, and film shooting.
4.	Testing and evaluation methods	The Ministry of Education authorize the National EFL Tertiary Education Committee to implement TEM4 and TEM8 testing system. Schools can also design their own testing system to give comprehensive assessment as for students' English knowledge achievement.

These amendments made in tertiary EFL educational curricula have inevitably led to changes in EFL classroom teaching methodology. Many language education innovators have ventured to convert the traditional teacher-fronted EFL classrooms into more communicative classrooms aiming for the promotion of Chinese language learners' communicative competence. Some of them believe that the development of language learners' communicative competence can only occur in classrooms with more symmetrical teacher-student relationships than those in traditional EFL classrooms. This has ushered in "pedagogical democracy" in tertiary EFL classrooms with CLT as the classroom teaching method in practice, although these changes, as they were, spawned unexpected results and controversies.

2.3.2 "Pedagogical democracy" and CLT

Democracy is more of a political abstraction than a pedagogical one. It literally means "rule by the people" and it comes from the Greek word *demos,* which refers to "people"; and *kratos,* which means "rule" (Wikipedia, the online encyclopedia). It can indicate a form of government and the practice of the principle- equality of rights, opportunity and treatment. John Dewey sees it as much broader than a special political form for it is a social and individual way of life (1975).

"Pedagogical democracy" refers to a non-authoritarian style of education in which learning takes place not as a result of the authoritative say-so of the teacher, but as a result of the learners' own efforts and experience (Kaplan, 1997). The reasoning for the advocacy of pedagogical democracy is that it can generate productive learning and democratic values in the future citizens. In pedagogical democracy, learning is facilitated by joint productive activities among teacher and students; teaching is realized through conversation and participation. Teachers and students are involved as partners in search of truth, rather than being involved in a transmission process (Pring, 1995). There should be frequent opportunities for students to interact with each other and with the teacher during instructional activities (occasional report by CREDE, 1998).

When applied to English language teaching and learning, pedagogical democracy has got exceptional value. It implies that the teacher and the students can stand on an equal footing; it incorporates cooperative and participatory language teaching and learning.

Breen (2001a) has postulated that communication, whether between equals or unequals, requires an orientation toward interactional symmetry. In this interactional symmetry, students are more likely to see themselves as part of the language learning community that can be more or less democratic in the original meaning of this term (Breen & Littlejohn, 2000) and are more willing to assume responsibilities for learning so that the language classroom can be more productive. Language learning in such classrooms, therefore, is not just a matter of developing one's grammatical, socio-linguistic, discourse and strategic competence; it is also a group experience requiring cooperative negotiation, joint interpretation, and the sharing of expression (Breen, 2001).

The underlying presumption is that democratic or participatory classroom practices are superior to authoritarian practices and promise more efficient classroom performance. Oxford (2001) points out that the autocratic approach of teaching increases competition and dependency and does not result in excellent work by students; by contrast, the democratic or participatory approach of education produces superior student work. Many English educators in China thus draw the conclusion that since China's EFL classroom communication is dominated by teacher's one-sided control and is minimally dialogic, students are put in a disadvantageous position and their language learning opportunities are largely inhibited.

Chinese Ministry of Education have endeavoured to lead university teachers of English towards more democratic classroom practices in the tertiary EFL education reform. Hayhoe (1989) once gave an account of such a "democratic move" in China:

> English language teaching and learning, in my view, has formed sort of subculture within the Chinese educational system on a larger scale. Especially at tertiary level, English is taught in the medium of target language in classrooms, the content of the texts are taken out from the original texts, students are encouraged to think in "English", Western classroom teaching style is imitated in a certain way. Teachers and students are trying to build up somewhat "Westernized democratic" classroom atmosphere.

The imitation of "Western classroom teaching style" is embodied in the use of Communicative Language Teaching method, or CLT. Partly as a response to international trend and mainly out of the growing dissatisfaction with conventional EFL classroom practices in the formal educational system, China's Ministry of Education "imported" CLT in the 1980s as a replacement for the traditional G-T classroom teaching method. CLT was promoted extensively in a top-down manner through syllabus design and material production (Hu, 2005). However, the controversy regarding the practicality and appropriacy of CLT has existed ever since it went onto the stage of China's EFL classrooms.

In the 1970s, traditional language teaching methods such as Audio-Lingual method and Grammar-Translation method were questioned. It was argued that language ability involved much more than grammatical competence. While grammatical competence was needed to produce grammatically correct sentences, attention shifted to the knowledge and skills needed to use grammar and other aspects of language appropriately for different communicative purposes such as making requests, giving advice, making suggestions, describing wishes and needs and so on. What was needed in order to use language communicatively was communicative competence. The appearance of CLT was a natural response to this need, and it has appealed to many within the language teaching profession (Richards & Rodgers, 2001). They felt that students were not learning enough realistic usage of language for the students did not know how to communicate using appropriate social language, gestures or expressions (Galloway, 1993).

CLT created a great deal of enthusiasm and excitement when it first appeared as a new approach to language teaching in the 1970s and 1980s, and language teachers and teaching institutions all around the world soon began to rethink their teaching, syllabuses and classroom materials (Richards & Rodgers, 2001). Communicative language teaching was thought to be desirable at the time for unlike the audio-lingual method and grammar translation method of language teaching which relied on repetition and rote-learning, CLT involves students in real-life simulations that necessitate communication for the authentic usage of the target language; therefore, students are motivated to learn the target language in meaningful ways.

"The phrase-'competence in terms of social interaction' sums up the primary emphasis of CLT" (Kumaravadivelu, 2006, p. 60). The key concept in CLT is "communicative competence", for CLT aims at the engagement of learners in communication so that they can develop communicative competence (Savignon, 2002). Many language teachers would agree that the teacher's engagement of learners in overt participation is a defining characteristic of CLT (Breen, 2001).

In the classrooms where CLT is practised, there is a switch of role relations between the teacher and the students as CLT calls for language learners to play an active role and shoulder increased responsibility for their own learning (Breen, 2001; Larsen-Freeman, 1986; Nunan, 1988). Students are therefore involved in information sharing and meaning negotiation while teacher mainly plays the role of a facilitator in the classroom communication process (Nunan, 1987). Hence the EFL classroom should be a highly interactive context in which language teaching mainly serves for the purpose of enabling students to carry out social activities in English in real life situations.

There are English teaching professionals who believe that CLT can compensate the deficiencies of traditional language teaching methods in China's EFL classrooms; transforming the authoritative teacher-fronted language classroom into a democratic student-centred language classroom. Liao (2004) claims that CLT is the best classroom methodology for China. CLT has become, in some people's eyes, the panacea for China's EFL education, even the very future of China hinges on the adoption and promulgation of this approach (Zhang, 2004).

However, the actual scene in China's university EFL classrooms is that features of G-T method have endured until the present day; while features of CLT, which partly demonstrate the essence of "pedagogical democracy" have sparked debate.

Chinese language teachers have tried to change the dominant classroom teaching procedures but quickly experienced frustration and lost their initial enthusiasm after their arduous efforts of propagating CLT have been met with open resistance in the EFL classrooms. Meanwhile, Western teachers have also experienced frustration when they tried to implement CLT in the language classrooms.

Ever since the 1980s, more and more expatriate teachers who are called "foreign experts" have come to different parts of China to teach English language in a Chinese setting at different levels. The import of expatriate English language teachers is almost equivalent to the "import of Western teaching ideology and methodology" although the expatriate teachers' language teaching ideology and methodology are very often at odds with the educational traditions in Chinese society.

It is widely held that native English speakers can bring into China's EFL classrooms genuine English language learning atmosphere. Many people believe that the expatriate teachers, with their communicative language teaching approach, will help to eliminate Chinese students' passivity and "dumb English". But some students have made bitter complaints only after they enjoyed their expatriate teachers' classes for a short while, for they don't think they have learned much from the games, pair works and group works in their language classes.

Western teachers' venturing of CLT in China's EFL classrooms has thus very often ended up in their disappointment. They found the educational approach they were used to and were willing to advocate in China has been met with the apparent resistance from the passive Chinese learners (Watkins & Biggs, 1999). Many expatriate teachers have found themselves overwhelmed by disillusionment, and some of them had to adopt an eclectic position in reconciling the very different, almost contrastive Chinese language teaching tradition with their preferred communicative language teaching approach. Take, for instance, a Western teacher has described his "classroom culture shock" as he was greeted by wide-eyed wonder and silence and is led to believe that it would be a struggle to implement CLT in the Chinese EFL classroom (Schreck, 2005). Only the fortunate minority of Western teachers could have set up a communicative classroom environment where their students readily accept and welcome their teaching ideology and classroom methodology.

The major obstacles for implementing CLT has come from the negative learning approaches as seen by Western teachers (Cortazzi & Jin, 1996), for students take great interest in their exam scores only rather than in the process of language learning through active communication and participation. They do not like to participate in communicative-type activities and prefer more traditional classroom work (Rao,

2002). Some language teachers and language learners think CLT merely cultivates oral communication skills and places less stress on reading and writing (Lin, 2002); although it can create an engaging and communicative language classroom, it is virtually unavailing for them to attain good results in national language tests. Some Chinese teachers believe that it is not feasible to adopt CLT in China's EFL classrooms because China has its special characteristics including its lack of genuine English environment and its insufficiency in qualified language teachers (Zhang, 2004).

Many EFL teaching professionals in China then resign themselves to the reality that CLT as a Western language classroom methodology derived from Western classroom teaching ideology cannot be accepted as a "cure-all" for China's EFL education. Hu (2005) reports that CLT has failed to produce the expected impact on EFL education in China because essentially the assumptions underlying CLT conflict with the established educational philosophies in China's CHC sociocultural context. In a CHC context, the favoured teacher-learner roles, learner qualities, classroom etiquettes, and learning strategies are often in conflict with those required by CLT but they are highly compatible with teacher-centred methodologies such as G-T. The claim that CLT is "best for China" has been attacked as absolutist that is based on problematic assumption of CLT's universal effectiveness (Hu, 2003).

When the eulogy of CLT was quietened down and replaced with suspicion and criticism, many English teaching professionals chose to acquiesce to tradition and revert to the G-T method. It is important to note that traditional instructional practices predominate or at least exist side by side with CLT in the EFL classrooms (Hu, 2005). Both Chinese and Western teachers of English have to come to terms with their classroom reality since the effectiveness of classroom teaching methodology depends crucially on its appropriateness for the situated, local and dynamic realities of teaching and learning (McDonough & Shaw, 1993).

2.3.3 Antithesis and perplexities in EFL classroom pedagogy

The coexistence of G-T method and CLT method in China's EFL classrooms has largely reflected the antithesis latent in Chinese language educationalists' thoughts.

The G-T method is in compatibility with the Confucian educational philosophy that stresses the importance of learning from antiquity in accordance to the moral code set by the teacher and the authoritative personnel (Scollon, 1999). As such, teacher-fronted authoritative classroom dynamics is predominant. There are little, if any, students' peer interactions because knowledge procurement is realized through the cautious reflective and imitative methods by the learners. Knowledge comes from the teacher or the text, is transmitted from the teacher or the text to the learners.

Conversely, the CLT method is in alignment with the Socratic method of education that emphasizes the art of rhetoric (Scollon, 1999) and the search for knowledge is realized through dialectical questioning. Language learning in CLT classrooms is achieved through communicative classroom activities. The appeal of CLT classrooms is their democratic classroom environments in which language learners are engaged in cooperative, participatory tasks through joint interactions.

Be it authoritative or democratic, teacher-fronted or learner-centred, EFL classroom should serve for language learning; and the adoption of certain classroom methodology is for optimizing language learning. It is because of the discontent with the traditional EFL classroom and its G-T method that CLT was imported. The focal question in disagreement between G-T advocates and CLT advocates may be whether it is the transmissive classroom dynamics or the interactive classroom dynamics that produces more language learning opportunities for learners and is therefore more beneficial for their language learning.

But when neither of these methods have been completely satisfactory, many language educationalists in China are perplexed as for what is the direction for EFL classroom pedagogy in China. In search of "good EFL classrooms" that generate "good language learning", I started this investigation in two EFL classrooms. The inquiry requires a concrete comprehension of the role of EFL classroom interactions for language learning, the nature of classroom reality and classroom learning.

In the next chapter, I am going to first critically review the previous classroom research in which classroom has been approached as an arena of interactions before I explicate my perspectives on language classroom and language learning.

Classroom Culture and the Construction of Learning Opportunities

Chapter **3**

EFL Classroom and Language Learning: A Cultural Approach

In this chapter, I first present a review of previous classroom research. I describe how language classroom has been approached as an arena of interactions and how different classroom interaction patterns are perceived to have different effects on language learning opportunities. Then I explain the several leading language acquisition hypotheses, each of which relates interaction with language learning from its own angle.

After a critical analysis of the previous research, I articulate my own theoretical framework for the current study. I believe a language classroom can be best approached as a multidimensional cultural entity, which is comprised of some basic classroom cultural components including its physical environment, its pedagogical goal, participants' demographics, participants' dispositions, the classroom norm of behaviour, and classroom interactions. Then I convey the interconnections between classroom cultural entity and language learning and clarify the definition of learning opportunity which is a key concept in this research.

3.1 Language classroom as an arena of interactions in research

The language classroom, with its clearly-defined objective as assisting language learners to grasp the target language knowledge and skills, is a crucial site for learners' language learning and to some degree it has a determining effect on learners' language learning result. Classrooms are the very heart of the educational process, the business end, where education is done (Wright, 2006). Given their importance for language learning, a considerable amount of research has been undertaken in the realm of language classrooms. "Classroom research is a commitment to go into the classroom and find out what goes on in it (Van Lier, 1988, p. 14). The purpose of second or foreign language classroom research is to identify the pedagogic variables that may facilitate or impede language learning (Nunan, 1990).

There have been reports of the characteristics of the language classroom in research literature (c.f. Johnson, 1995). Since all classroom pedagogy proceeds, necessarily, via a process of interaction (Allwright, 1983), language classroom has been mostly conceived as an arena of human interactions (Prabhu, 1992)-not only the pedagogic interactions desired or elicited as a part of teaching strategy (which may or may not occur as expected) but the more elemental, inevitable interactions which occur simply because human beings, with all their complexity, are involved.

What happens in the language classroom is therefore a series of interactional events (Ellis, 1998). Language classroom research concentrates on classroom interactions that go on between and among teachers and learners in order to gain insights & increase our understanding of classroom teaching and learning (Allwright & Bailey, 1991). Hall (2002) considers such a research focus can provide the grounds for the development of an integrated theory of language teaching and learning. "It makes good sense for us to want to try to understand the contribution of classroom interaction to language development" (Allwright, n.d.) for the collective experience of language teaching professionals does lead to the belief that language learning typically has something, if not absolutely everything, to do with the nature of the interaction that takes place during lessons.

To study the relationship between interaction and language learning, researchers have observed classroom interactions between the teacher and the learners, interactions between and among the learners; some researchers have surmised language acquisition hypotheses that explain the relationship between interaction and language learning from different angles (Krashen, 1985; Long, 1983; Swain, 1985).

3.1.1 Teacher-learner interaction and language learning

Teacher-learner interaction has been mostly described as a tripartite sequential exchange between the teacher and the learner (e.g. Barnes, 1992; Silverman, 1985; Sinclair & Coulthard, 1975). Its benefits for language learning are controversial as revealed in previous classroom research.

Initially, the basic unit of classroom interaction or classroom discourse is construed to be the IRE pattern consisting of teacher's Initiation, learners' Response, and teacher's Evaluation of the response (Sinclair & Coulthard, 1975). The ubiquity of the IRE pattern is observed by researchers including Barnes (1992), Cazden (1988), Mehan (1979), to name but a few. Similarly, Silverman (1985) describes the basic logic of classroom conversational exchange as "teacher: question; pupil: answer; teacher: evaluation".

It is said that the uneven distribution of power caused by the predominance of the IRE pattern (Cazden, 1988; Kramsch, 1981; Seliger &
Long, 1983; Van Lier, 1988) has negative consequences for learners'
opportunities to learn because with the teacher in control, the language
learners mainly produce responses. Extensive teacher-initiated talk in
classroom has been found to restrict student talk severely, allowing little
opportunity for extended learner talk at the length of a clause or more so
that it has been suggested too much teacher talk time deprive learners of
opportunities and limit their involvement in more communicative language events (Anton, 1999; Gass & Varonis, 1994; Lemke, 1990; Mehan, 1979; Pica, Young & Doughty, 1987). Long (1983) points out that
this teacher-learner interaction pattern reveals the transmission model of
education; this approach to education leaves the learners little opportunity to practise genuine communicative uses of language in a full range
of functional moves or to negotiate for meaning. Allwright (1988) argues that learning is better accomplished when the verbal roles taken up
by classroom interactants (a teacher and his or her learners') are nearly
symmetrical in attempts to reach decisions by consensus rather than by
unilateral decision-making.

The derivative of IRE-the IRF pattern (teacher's Initiation, learners'
Response, teacher's Follow-up) is later found by some researchers
(Nunan, 1987; Painter, 1989) to have similar restrictive effects on learners' language learning opportunities. Van Lier (2001) exposes that
learners' opportunities to exercise initiative or to develop a sense of
control and a sense of ownership of the discourse are extremely restricted in the IRF format. Not only are learner utterances often highly
elliptical and syntactically reduced, occurring only in the response slot,
sandwiched between two teacher turns, IRF also prevents the learners
from doing turn taking, topic development, and activity structuring work.
It does not allow, to any significant extent, negotiation of the direction

of instruction. Characterized by one-sided control, IRF is only minimally dialogic, and the learners' participation in its construction is largely passive. Therefore, Van Lier (2001) concludes, prolonged use of the IRF format may have a negative effect on intrinsic motivation and cause a decrease in levels of attention and involvement. In terms of communication, control, initiative, meaning creation and negotiation, message elaboration, and a number of other features characteristic of social interaction, the learner's side of the IRF interaction is seriously curtailed.

At variance with these views, there are researchers who claim that the triadic pattern has its potential value in language classroom education. Learning opportunities can emerge from strictly controlled instructional talk (Wright & Bolitho, 1993). This discourse pattern can provide scaffolds to encourage structured participation in the target language in the classroom, particularly with beginning speakers of English (Boyd & Maloof, 2000).

The concern with the quantity of teacher talk in the language classroom has since been shifted towards a concern with the quality of teacher talk in verbal interactions. More emphasis then has been put on how effectively IREs are able to facilitate learning and promote communicative interaction in language classrooms through the kinds of questions teachers ask, the speech modifications they make when talking to learners, or the way they react to learners' errors (Nunan, 1989).

Wells (1993) points out that the quality of IREs may differ, depending on the type of question that constitutes the Initiation for the prospective nature of questions in the I-move enables teacher's use of a variety of teaching strategies (Nassaji & Wells, 2000). Brock (1986) notices that the kind of questions teachers ask can significantly affect the quantity and quality of learner interaction and the learning opportunity generated in the lesson.

The potential value of the IRF for supporting and promoting student interaction has also been confirmed in studies of language classrooms. Nassaji and Wells (2000) maintain that the F move is the most significant part of the IRF pattern, for a relatively closed question can lead to exploratory dialogue if the F-move is non-evaluative. Teacher follow-ups encourage learners' attempts to express their own thoughts and opinions on topics which open the door to further discussion and provide more opportunities for learning because learners are invited to expound upon or qualify their initial responses (Duff, 2000; Hall, 2002). When the teacher provides extending rather than evaluating feedback, the next cycle of the learning-teaching spiral has its point of departure in the third step of this tripartite pattern of classroom interaction (Wells, 1995).

Besides, the IRF pattern is thought of as the archetypal form of interaction between a teacher and a learner-a basic unit of classroom talk as a continuous stretch of classroom discourse; it has benefits for classroom learning because it provides a predictive structure of classroom interactions for the participants to follow.

One reason for this may be that teachers instinctively adopt an IRF mode of instruction because it is perceived, perhaps unconsciously, to be a powerful pedagogic device for transmitting and constructing knowledge. It can at least provide predictable lesson structures which permit both the teacher and the learners to give close attention to the academic content of lessons (Geekie & Raban, 1993). The teacher knows exactly what answers he or she seeks and learners are essentially trying to provide the information that the teacher expects them to know (Breen, 2001) so that the IRF pattern allows the teacher to monitor learners' understanding and retention of the learning material. The IRF pattern, as argued by some researchers, is important for classroom interactions; it is helpful in creating an inclusive classroom culture that values participation and learning, ultimately enhancing students' academic performances in the language classroom (Boyd & Maloof, 2000; Hall, 1998; Wells, 1993). Seedhouse (2004) thinks that with the teacher taking the lead for most of the class time, both the IRE and the IRF are interactional features that are appropriate to the core goals of education.

Based on the IRE pattern and IRF pattern, Gibbons (1998) has gone a step further to identify the SI/TR classroom discourse pattern in which Student Initiates, Teacher Recasts. He finds its effect in modifying power relations because learners are at least temporarily enabled to be in active control of learning. The importance of learner initiative in teacher-learner interactions is also emphasized by Garton (2002) for it elicits teacher's correction and provision of explanations. She also shows that the use of learner initiative can lead to accuracy in the learner's language output. Kumaravadivelu (1993) suggests that teachers should encourage learners to initiate and participate in interaction-to ask for information, seek clarification, express an opinion, agree or disagree with peers and teachers. It follows then that learners' peer interactions are found to be beneficial for language learning by some researchers although this is not without debate.

3.1.2 Learner-learner interaction and language learning

It is suggested that learners' peer interactions have important benefits from both pedagogical and psycholinguistic perspectives (Long and Porter, 1985). Pica (2000) claims that there is a need for classroom interaction that balances teacher-led instruction with learner-to-learner interaction, or peer interaction.

Pedagogically, it is argued that peer interaction is likely to encourage in-class oral interaction, which in turn can increase input (Pica,

Young and Doughty, 1987) and output opportunities in the target language. Pair and small group activities provide learners with more time to speak the target language than teacher-fronted activities, promote learner autonomy and self-directed learning (Brown, 2001; Crookes and Chaudron, 2001; Harmer, 2001; Long and Porter, 1985).

McDonough (2004) explored instructors' and learners' perceptions about the use of pair and small group activities in a Thai EFL context and he examined whether the learning opportunities theoretically attributed to pair and small group activities occur. In particular, whether learners who actively participate during the pair and small group activities show improved production of the target language forms. His conclusion is that pair and small group activities generate learning opportunities through various interactional features that occur when learners engage in the communication of meaning. The most significant pedagogical implication to be drawn is that learners can take greater initiative or assume more responsibility for their own learning through peer interactions than teacher-fronted interactions.

With peer interactions, learners are enabled to use language more communicatively across a broader range of function than they do in lessons characterized by lock-step, teacher-led classroom interactions and a communicative classroom environment may result from collaborative peer interactions (Storch, 2002). Although a communicative classroom with "genuine interactions" is a rarity, Kumaravadivelu (1993) confirms that in theory, a communicative classroom seeks to promote interpretation, expression and negotiation of meaning which help to create learning opportunities in the language classroom.

Psycholinguistically, peer interactions are found to enhance learners' self esteem and positive attitudes toward school (Sharan, 1990; Slavin, 1980). In particular, when interacting with their peers, learners may feel less anxious and more confident during pair or small group activities than during whole-class discussions (Brown, 2001; Willis, 1996).

But the value of peer interactions is questioned by some researchers. For example, Breen (1989) reports that the problem with peer interactions is whether the learners can actually learn from one another as there lies the danger that learners might teach each other errors. Breen has found that there is a gap between the intended purpose of pair and small group activities and learners' implementation of those activities. Learners often have their own ideas about how to carry out an activity, and their ideas may diverge from those of their instructors. In his report, the instructors believe that the learners should attend to language form when carrying out pair and small group activities, but the learners are oriented toward the achievement of communicative goals so they produce less target language output and use only the language forms necessary to accomplish that goal. Consequently, the language learning opportunities attributed to pair and small group activities such as those provided by negative feedback and modified output have not occurred.

3.1.3 Interactions, acquisition hypotheses, and language learning

In order to better understand English language learning and explain classroom pedagogical moments, researchers interested in the relationship between interaction and language learning have proposed various hypotheses that acknowledge the role of different aspects of interaction for language learning. Each of these theoretical perspectives on language learning has its distinctive pedagogical implications for classroom education and has thereafter introduced the application of different language teaching methodologies into the classroom.

The *Input Hypothesis* put forward by Krashen (1985) has been very influential and has provided language education practitioners with inspiration regarding the process of language learning. According to Krashen, "language acquisition" depends mostly on the amount of comprehensible input one receives. The thrust of the Input Hypothesis is that in order for language acquisition to take place, the acquirer must receive comprehensible input through reading or hearing language structures that slightly exceed their current ability (Brown, 2000).

The Input Hypothesis also states that there is a "natural order" for an acquirer to grasp a language; forced early production of the target language should be avoided as this is not deemed to be beneficial by the language acquirer. Many language learners will go through what is referred to by some as a "silent period" when learners receive comprehensible input before they can start to produce their own language structures (Shannon, n.d.).

The language classroom is credited by Krashen (1985) as having the potential to provide a rich source of comprehensible input. Put into practice, this means that learners are better served if language teachers can provide them with a volume of listening or reading, at a language level that is understandable yet challenging. That is, a certain amount of comprehensible input must be built up before the learner is required to speak in a classroom (Brown, 2000). The best classroom teaching methods are therefore those that supply comprehensible input in low anxiety situations, containing messages that learners really want to hear. These methods do not force early production in the target language, but allow learners to produce when they are ready (Krashen, 1985).

As an early attempt to demystify the language learning process, the Input Hypothesis has been received with a combination of acceptance and rejection. The concept of "comprehensible input" has been criticized as being ambiguous since it hasn't been clearly defined. Krashen's claim that "language is 'acquired' rather than 'learned'" has made him the subject of accusation for providing a circular definition of learned and acquired systems (Lightbown & Spada, 1993). There are also allegations suggesting that more empirical evidence is needed to back up his silent period assertion-his assertion that language acquirers need to go through a period of silence before they produce intelligible target language utterances.

Different from Krashen's "Comprehensible Input Hypothesis", Swain (1985, 1995) has set forth the *"Comprehensible Output Hypothesis"* stating that learners must have opportunities to produce the language if they are to become fluent, native-like speakers. Swain's Comprehensible Output Hypothesis (1985) claims that the development of a learner's communicative competence does not only depend on comprehensible input but also on the learner's output; the latter has an indispensable role to play in language learning (Yu, 1990).

According to Swain (1985), output is important because it forces the learner to develop precise, coherent and appropriate linguistic resources and it provides the learner with the opportunity to try out hypotheses to see if they work. The production of the target language enables learners to notice the gap between what they can say and what they want to say when they formulate and test out hypotheses about the target language, when they consciously reflect on the language they are producing, and when they move from semantic analysis of the target language to syntactic analysis of it. It stimulates learners to move from semantic, open-ended, nondeterministic, strategic processing prevalent in comprehension to the complete grammatical processing needed for accurate production (Swain, 1995). Thus, learners' output may lead to their language development by increasing language accuracy, intelligibility and appropriacy (Pica, 1994; Swain, 1995).

The classroom implication for this, according to Gibbons (1998), is not that language form per se should become a major teaching focus, but that it is important, at times, for learners to have opportunities to be pushed toward the delivery of a message that is not only conveyed, but that is conveyed precisely, coherently, and appropriately. In order for learners to increase their target language proficiency, they need to generate output, that is, to produce language via speech or writing and receive feedback on the comprehensibility of their language output. In classroom language teaching, there must be a focus on extended opportunities for learner talk because language learning depends on explicit attention to productive language skills (Swain, 1985). Providing learners with opportunities to use the language and skills at a level in which they are competent, is almost as important as giving students the appropriate level of input (Swain & Lapkin, 1995).

Swain has not claimed that comprehensible output is responsible for all or even most of the language competence learners develop. Rather, the claim is that sometimes, under some conditions, output facilitates language learning in ways that are different from, or enhance, those of input (Swain & Lapkin, 1995). However, this hypothesis has been yet again criticised as being flawed because there are numerous studies to confirm that we can develop extremely high levels of language and literacy competence without any language production at all (Krashen, 1994) and instances of comprehensible output are relatively infrequent (Gass, Mackey & Pica, 1998). Krashen (1998) challenges that "The Comprehensible Output Hypothesis" can hardly be supported by data and it is problematic in that output is surprisingly rare; in the case of "comprehensible output", the problem is especially severe, and there is no evidence for its efficacy.

Seeing speech modifications during communication between learners or between learners and their teachers as central to language learning (Long, 1983; Long & Porter, 1985; Lightbown 1985, Pica, 1994; Pica, Young & Doughty, 1987), the "social interactionist" perspective represented by Long's (1983) *Interaction Hypothesis* proposes that language learning is strongly facilitated by the use of the target language in interaction. This theory underlines the importance of social interaction for language learning since it can foster negotiation for meaning. In other words, successful language learning depends on the amount of adjustments speakers are able to make in order to understand each other (Long, 1983).

According to Long (1996), meaning negotiation, especially negotiation that triggers interactional adjustments by the native speaker (NS) or more competent interlocutor, impels learners to modify their own output and this interactional modification promotes language learning because it connects input, internal learner capacities and output in productive ways.

Compatible with the "Interaction Hypothesis" is the communicative approach to language teaching. In CLT, learners are involved in meaning negotiation through completing particular tasks (Zou & Cai, 2006). It is argued that when learners are given the opportunity to engage in meaningful activities they are compelled to negotiate for meaning, to express and clarify their intentions, thoughts, opinions, etc., in a way which permits them to arrive at a mutual understanding (Ellis, 1990).

Despite its popularity among CLT advocates, the Interaction Hypothesis, which puts great emphasis on interaction in language learning, has been doubted as "vague" (Krashen, 1994). There are questions ensued: Is interaction necessary or just helpful? Is it the only way to learn language or one of the ways to learn language? The Interaction Hypothesis has been criticised as attempting to deny that language learning can occur from reading and listening although it has been proved that language learning is possible without actually participating in the interaction (Ellis, 1990) and reading itself can promote language development (Krashen, 1982).

It is discernible that the previous classroom research and language acquisition hypotheses have been largely the inquests into the effects of interaction on language learning; the concealed premise is essentially a theoretical understanding of how language is learned and of the roles of "input", "output" and "interaction" in this language learning process.

By interaction, many researchers imply verbal interaction (Wragg, 1979; Hall & Verplaetse, 2000); it is this dimension of classroom discourse upon which both the interaction and output hypotheses and much classroom research have tended to focus (Breen, 2001). Swain (1995) argues that an understanding of learning processes can be enhanced by using *dialogues* as the unit of analysis in language learning.

The reason for approaching language classroom as an arena of interactions or verbal interactions is that many researchers associate these interactions with practice opportunities in the target language and it is believed that practice opportunity leads to fluency and communicative competence (Verplaetse, 2000). Through talk we learn not only the structured components of a language but also the communicative application of them (Boyd & Maloof, 2000). With exceptions, many researchers believe that learners' open participation in classroom activities lead to their language learning (e.g. Brown, 2001; Crookes & Chaudron, 2001; Harmer, 2001; Long & Porter, 1985; McDonough, 2004; Pica, Young & Doughty, 1987; Storch, 2002). The general implicit assumption in much current pedagogical literature appears to be that the relationship between pedagogy and interaction is a simple, unproblematic, and unidirectional one in which pedagogy is translated directly into interaction (Seedhouse, 2004).

There continues to be a great deal of debate, however, and more importantly, a lack of empirical evidence, on which form of interaction actually contributes to language learning (Ellis, 1990). My view is that input, output, and verbal interaction all play their respective roles in learners' language learning. In an EFL context such as China, the opportunities for language learners to expose themselves to the target language and the opportunities for them to practise the target language outside the classrooms are very limited; so are the opportunities for them to engage in verbal interactions with native English speakers. Thus for language learners to become fully competent target language users who do not only grasp the linguistic aspect of the language but also the functional aspect of the language, they will need to have and make use of the opportunities for input, output, and verbal interaction in the target language. The amount of these opportunities they are able to obtain and utilize in the classrooms is vital for learners' language development.

The contention of the leading language acquisition hypotheses and the discrepancy exhibited in previous classroom research regarding the relationship between interaction and learning opportunity have made it clear that more research needs to be done in relation to the impact of different interaction patterns on language learning in the classroom context.

For example, does oral interaction always lead to learning opportunity? Do learners' peer interactions always provide more learning opportunities for the learners than the teacher-fronted interactions do? Suppose pair work and group work do increase interaction, do they always increase learning? Given that teacher-fronted interaction still occupies a prominent place in language classrooms, wouldn't it be more helpful if research findings can suggest how this type of interaction can be best exploited for the goal of language learning rather than simply relegating it as being detrimental to language learning? Most fundamentally, how do we perceive "interaction" and "learning opportunity" as two key concepts in classroom research?

The core of the previous research and hypotheses, as can be observed, is the relationship between interaction, language learning and the language classroom. Before we make the major step of moving from conceptual proposals to methodological ones, we will need to better understand the classroom reality (Allwright, 1991). Below I am going to expound on my "cultural approach" to language classrooms and language learning in this research.

3.2 The language classroom as a cultural entity

3.2.1 "Classroom culture" as a metaphor

Previously I have reviewed how language classroom has been approached as an arena of interactions. However, the language classroom is "a unique community" (Tarone, 2006, p. 164) in which all participants contribute, all the variables are interrelated and jointly affected (Ellison, 2000), and these variables are more than just classroom interactions.

To unravel the complexity of language classrooms, researchers have referred to what happen in the language classrooms as social events (Allwright, 1988; Block, 1996; Storch, 2002), language classrooms are conceived to be social ecologies (Ellison, 2000).

According to Breen, "Classroom culture" is a more meaningful metaphor to approach classroom realities because it "addresses the interactive, social and often opaque features of the classroom which are instrumental in language learning" (Breen, 1994, p. 21). The notion of "classroom as culture" is widely endorsed in applied linguistics literature (Allwright & Bailey, 1991; Breen, 2001, Holliday, 1994) and is the approach adopted to study classroom realities in this research.

Culture, as a broad concept, has been given a plethora of definitions based upon different theoretical assumptions. It is an extremely difficult task to give a unified definition of "culture". I take the view that a social grouping can be said to have a "culture" when there is a discernible set of behaviours connected with its group cohesion (Beales, Spindler & Spindler, 1967). "Culture" as used in this thesis is a dynamic, ongoing group process which operates in constantly changing circumstances to enable group members to make sense of and operate meaningfully within those circumstances (Holliday, 1999). There can be "institutional culture", for example, when the staff and student group in a university share certain ways of speech and behaviour under the influence of various contextual factors within the university. Similarly, there can be "classroom culture" when the teacher and the students have formed certain implicit code of practice in the classroom context.

It then might be imperative to make a distinction between "classroom culture" and "learning culture". "Learning culture" refers to the particular ways in which the interactions between many different factors shape students' learning opportunities and practices (Hodkinson, Biesta, James, 2007). "EFL classroom culture", as I see it, is a special kind of "learning culture" in which learning speech and behaviours take the EFL classroom as their main site of occurrence; it embodies the intensification of the cultural experience of learning (Breen, 1985) in a particular social context-the EFL classroom.

This minimal definition of classroom culture can provide the description of those aspects of social cohesion, values and artefacts which distinguish one social group from another (Holliday, 2002). Every classroom can be perceived to have its own individual culture (Cortazzi & Jin, 1996; Holliday, 1994, 1999) and it varies from site to site. A small, operational notion of culture (Holliday, 1994)-classroom culture, allows the differentiating characteristics of groups to be discovered rather than presumed. Each classroom culture is comprised of some basic components such as the physical setting of the classroom, participants' subjective worlds, and participants' speech and behaviour. It is in the constant interplay of these classroom cultural components that a classroom culture is established and developed. The characteristics of these classroom cultural components vary from one classroom to another; consequently, the characteristics of the classroom culture vary from one classroom to another.

Viewing the EFL classroom as a cultural entity makes possible a comprehensive understanding of classroom reality. My cultural approach to the EFL classroom and language learning is concerned with participants' language teaching and learning behaviours in the totality of all relevant classroom cultural components. These elements are not isolated from each other; rather, they are interrelated as an integral whole.

In language classroom research as reviewed previously, many researchers have tended to stress the importance of classroom interactions and study one or two aspects of interactions with regard to their relationship and language learning. For example, verbal interaction has attracted most attention in language classroom research; the several leading language acquisition theories have stressed on "input", or "output", or "interaction" as being most important for language learning. Language learning and the language learning outcome, as I perceive, are achieved through a network of interactions under the function of various forces in the whole structural system of classroom culture.

For example, the particular participants, their life histories, the very processes by which participants conjointly make use of the interactional activities and the resources available, their experiences as members of their classroom cultures, all act on learners' language learning. We can't allege that a learner's language learning is dependent only on verbal interaction, or on any singular component of the whole classroom cultural system. The significance of this cultural approach to the language classroom and language learning is that an emphasis on the organic, ecological nature of language development may have a strong effect on educational research and on how we conceptualize learning and teaching process (Van Lier, 1998).

3.2.2 Classroom cultural components

3.2.2.1   The physical setting

The physical setting of an EFL classroom is the actual learning environment for the classroom cultural group; it includes the size of the classroom, the wall displays of the classroom and its furniture arrangement. Seemingly peripheral as these elements are, they have important impact on the EFL classroom cultural developing process and learners' language learning activities.

Many people, including the teacher and the learners, very often underestimate the importance of the physical environment of a classroom. In fact, the arrangement of furniture and the allocation of spaces within the classroom can greatly affect what can be accomplished within a given instructional setting (Weinstein, 1981). The physical setting of an EFL classroom culture contributes to the setting up of the EFL classroom ambience by providing conditions that are favourable for certain classroom activities and interactional patterns while inhibiting others.

For example, in a classroom in which seats are fixed onto the floor facing the teacher and the blackboard, it might not be easy for the language learners sitting in the first row to talk with the language learners at the farthest back, thereby their verbal exchanges might be limited due to seating restrictions. Learners might tend to direct their responses to the teacher who stands facing them. On the contrary, a circle or U-shaped seating arrangement might be more encouraging for interpersonal interactions and peer discussions. In addition, if the classroom furniture is not fixed onto the floor, the mobility of the classroom furniture may improve the mobility of the learners in the EFL classroom for group tasks, oral exercises, and discussions.

3.2.2.2   The pedagogical goal

The pedagogical goal of the EFL classroom addresses the exact target to be achieved for the particular EFL classroom cultural group. It can be defined by the institutional and national goal of English language education on a grand scale; it can be determined by the specific subject being taught in the language classroom on a small scale.

The pedagogical goal of an EFL classroom stipulates its educational content and its classroom language teaching and learning activities-some interactional activities may be privileged while others may be dismissed as being less useful. As Freeman states (2006), this explicit goal circumscribes how individuals participate as well as the personal goals or outcomes they are seeking to achieve in the setting.

3.2.2.3   Demographics of the participants

Demographics usually refer to selected population characteristics used in research. In my study, the demographic profiles of participants in the EFL classroom cultures include the age and gender distribution of the participant cohort, their academic backgrounds such as their language proficiency levels. I consider the demographic features of the classroom population as an integral part of the EFL classroom culture because of their influence on participants' classroom life experiences.

(Continued from Section 3.2.2)

Table 3.1: The Basic Components of EFL Classroom Culture

The Basic Components of EFL Classroom Culture		
	Components	*Function*
The physical Setting	The size of the EFL classroom, wall displays and furniture arrangement of the classroom	Contributes to the setting up of the EFL classroom ambience
The pedagogical goal	The target to be achieved in the language classroom; it may be set by curriculum, the institutional and national goal of language education and is under the influence of the teacher's language educational ideology	Prescribes classroom culture's educational content and may decide the use of certain classroom interactional patterns
Demographics of the participants	Age and gender distribution of the participant cohort, their academic background including their language proficiency levels	Form an integral part of classroom culture and influence participants' classroom performance and experience
Dispositions of the participants	Beliefs, values and expectations concerning language learning; preconceptions of the appropriate classroom behaviours	Predispose the language teacher and learners towards certain classroom behaviour and classroom cultural system
Norm of classroom behaviour	Set of routines and procedures in classroom life; including aspects such as the medium of instruction and classroom etiquette	Regulates classroom cultural life, makes EFL classroom cultural life manageable for teacher and learners
Classroom interaction	Includes interpersonal interactions and textual interactions	Is pivotal for the production of language learning opportunity and the construction of classroom culture

3.2.2.4   Dispositions of the participants

Participants have expectations and values regarding what constitute good classroom language teaching learning, and how language teaching and learning relate to broader issues of the nature and purpose of education (Allwright & Bailey, 1991). These expectations derive primarily from often hidden assumptions that are deeply rooted in participants' backgrounds and/or stem from general orientations towards learning resulting from previous educational experiences (Cortazzi, 1990). Participants' dispositions are formed from these expectations, values, and beliefs.

Participants' dispositions manifestly contribute to EFL classroom cultural traits. Our "dispositions" "dispose" us to act in certain ways. We bring them with us to our social experiences, and are inclined to make sense of our experiences, and coordinate our actions with others in particular ways because of them (Hall, 2002). Participants' behaviours in the language classroom are affected by who we are, the views we hold, and the societies we are part of (Harrison, 1990).

Because of the power relations, it is likely that a teacher's values pervade a language classroom culture. In principle, at least the teacher has the power to undermine some aspects of the classroom culture and to strengthen others (Reynolds & Skilbeck, 1976). Teacher's classroom practices are very much informed by his or her educational ideology, namely, by his or her beliefs in and attitude towards EFL education. Moreover, the teacher's beliefs, assumptions and knowledge play a major role in what counts as knowledge (Bloome & Egan-Robertson, 1993), how he or she will interpret events related to teaching, in both planning and implementation, and therefore the teaching decisions that are made and the changes that result (Aitken & Mildson, 1992; Woods, 1996).

Learners, of course, also have expectations of teachers (Nash, 1976) and how they expect classroom teaching and learning should be carried out. For adult language learners, they have fully formed personalities and minds when they start learning another language and these have profound effects on their ways of learning (Cook, 2001). They bring their whole experience of learning into the classroom life, along with their own reasons for being there, and their own particular needs that they hope to see satisfied (Allwright & Bailey, 1991). However, since the classroom culture is an ever-evolving entity, participants may also acquire new dispositional features by adapting to this changing system in the process of classroom learning.

3.2.2.5　Norm of classroom behaviour

The norm of behaviour is the code of practice for participants in the whole EFL classroom cultural system. For it to function, a classroom community realises its own values and priorities through implicitly or explicitly accepted procedures and routines (Breen, 2000). Over time, these sets of routines are accepted by participants and become part of the classroom culture. Aspects of language classroom life such as the medium of instruction, classroom etiquette, the preferred forms of classroom activities all contribute to the setting up of standardized classroom norms.

The norm of classroom behaviour regulates classroom cultural life and provides the structure for participants' classroom engagement. Once the classroom norm of behaviour is established, the EFL classroom life may become more manageable for both the teacher and the students. Nonetheless, teacher may evaluate and adjust it towards a more productive and effective classroom cultural system and learners also play a part in the adjustment process.

3.2.2.6   Classroom interaction

As I have reviewed in Section 3.1, classroom interaction has been one of the foci in previous research and language classroom has been approached as an arena of classroom interactions. In my research, I view the language classroom as a multidimensional cultural entity, and interaction is only one component of this entity, although it is pivotal for the construction of classroom culture and language learning opportunities.

Unlike in previous studies where classroom interaction has been mainly meant to be verbal or oral interactions (Wragg, 1979; Hall & Verplaetse, 2000), in my study, I give "classroom interaction" a broad definition, it includes "interpersonal interaction" and "textual interaction" (Michael, 2001).

"Interpersonal interaction" refers to the interaction that happens between people. It can be either "verbal" or "nonverbal". Verbal interpersonal interactions can happen between two parties (bilateral) or among many people (multilateral); directed from one party to the other party (unidirectional), between one party and the other party (bidirectional) or among the classroom participants (multidirectional). Nonverbal interpersonal interactions may encompass participants' eye-contact and gestures for their classroom communication.

"Textual interaction" refers to the interaction that happens between people and text, or between people via text. For example, there can be interaction between learners and their textbooks when learners seek information, abstract knowledge from their textbooks or written language learning materials. The textual interaction between people via text can be participants' exchange of information via written notes.

In this sense, the EFL classroom culture involves all of its participants in interpersonal or textual interactions of certain kinds. In their interactions with each other, teachers and learners assume particular identities and roles, they act and react, and together participants develop understandings of what is to be learned and how that can be learned.

Classroom interaction as such, needs to be put into the cultural context of the language classroom, for the forms and patterns of classroom interactions are influencing and influenced by the other classroom cultural components such as the classroom culture's physical setting, its pedagogical goal, its norm of behaviour and participants' demographic and dispositional features. We need to examine the various aspects of classroom interactions as they occur in the EFL classroom surroundings so as to gain a thorough understanding of the language classroom reality and the language learning process.

The basic components of EFL classroom culture are illustrated in table 3.1 on page 61.

3.2.3 Classroom culture and language learning

Understanding classrooms as cultures has ramifications for how we understand learning. Classroom culture as the context for language learning has intricate relationship with language learning because both the process and outcome of language learning are greatly influenced by the interplay of various classroom cultural components. Before I explicate how I perceive language learning as it happens in the classroom culture, I am going to first clarify how I define learning opportunity in this research.

3.2.3.1   Understanding learning opportunity

"Learning opportunity" in language learning is commonly found in educational literature, typically without comment or explicit definition (Crabbe, 2003). However, recently some researchers have sought for more robust theoretical understandings of learning opportunity. In particular, Allwright & Bailey (1991) and Crabbe (2003) have made attempts to define and categorize learning opportunity as I am going to discuss below.

A broad interpretation of "learning opportunity" in language learning has been given by Allwright and Bailey (1991) in which they divide "learning opportunities" into two types: "input opportunities" and "practice opportunities". The former refer to learners' activities that are connected with what they are trying to learn; the latter refer to learners' encounter with what they are trying to learn. Very often these two types of learning opportunities occur together.

These two kinds of learning opportunities may be of high-priority in language learning; but there can be far more different types of learning opportunities involved in the language learning process than the above two-way distinction.

Crabbe (2003) has defined "learning opportunity" as follows:

> The term *learning opportunity* is used to refer to access to favourable learning conditions, whether access to learning in general (as in educational opportunity) or, in the sense adopted here, access to specific conditions, such as those required for language learning. An opportunity for L2 learning, then, might be defined as access to any activity that is likely to lead to an increase in language knowledge or skill. It may be the opportunity to negotiate meaning in a discussion, to read and derive meaning from a printed text, to explore a pattern in language usage, or to get direct feedback on one's own use of language. Such opportunities are normally available in classrooms in varying quality and quantity (p.18).

he further gives the coverage of learning opportunity categories, as shown below:

Table 3.2: Coverage of Learning Opportunity Categories (Adapted from Crabbe, 2003, p. 28)

Ingredient	Activity covered by the concept
Input	Listening to and reading monologue or dialogue that can be understood with limited difficulty
Output	Producing meaningful utterances in written or spoken form, either monologue or in the context of interaction
Interaction	Speaking and writing with one or more interlocutors in real or simulated communicative situations
Feedback	Receiving information relating to one's own performance which may include indirect feedback (e.g., that one has not been understood) or direct feedback (e.g., that one has made a specific error)
Rehearsal	Any activity designed to improve through deliberate repetition specific aspects of performance, including experimentation with pronunciation, memorisation of words or word patterns, and repeated role-play of a piece of communication
Language understanding	Any conscious attention to language that is intended to lead to an ability to explain or describe or gloss an aspect of grammar or sociolinguistic conventions
Learning understanding	Any conscious attention to one's own language learning that is intended to lead a better metacognitive control over that learning, which would include a detailed representation of the task of language learning, an analysis of the difficulties encountered and an awareness of strategies to overcome the difficulties and achieve the task

By expanding the two-way "input-output" distinction and giving a specified categorization of "learning opportunities", Crabbe explains the concept of "learning opportunity" further and delineates the activities covered by each category of learning opportunities. In addition, he brings up the existence of learning opportunities that are not *directly* connected with language learning, but are *indirectly* related with language learning because they contribute to the increase of language knowledge-the opportunities for "language understanding" and "learning understanding" (see table 3.2).

While Crabbe has provided a comprehensive coverage of learning opportunity categories, there are overlappings in his categorization. For example, there might be "input" and "output" opportunities in "interaction" opportunities, similarly, "feedback" and "rehearsal" may also overlap with "input" and "output" opportunities respectively.

Drawing on the previous definitions and classifications of learning opportunities, I conceive "learning opportunity" in language learning as essentially learners' access to activities that have *perceivable* or *potential* effects on the development of learners' language knowledge or skills. In my research, I keep an open-ended approach to "learning opportunities" without giving them preconceived categorizations.

Before I probe into the language classrooms and study the construction of learning opportunities in them, it is necessary to first of all develop a clear understanding of the relationship between classroom culture and language learning because such an understanding will inform and guide me in understanding how learning opportunities are constructed in the context of a language classroom. In this "cultural approach" to language learning, I acknowledge that interaction (more than verbal) plays a central role in the development of classroom culture and language learning, language learning is situated at multiple levels with classroom culture as its immediate context, and classroom culture and language learning are co-constructed.

3.2.3.2 Interaction is central to language learning

No matter whether it is verbal interaction or nonverbal interaction, interpersonal interaction or textual interaction, the fact that interaction is a key component in the whole classroom system and its close connection with learning opportunities have been increasingly recognized (Green & Harker, 1982; Mehan, 1979; Hall & Verplaests, 2000). Evidence from SLA research literature supports the strong relationship between interaction and language learning (Klein, 1986).

Research on oral interactions in language classrooms links learners' involvement in them with their communicative and conceptual development (Baker, 1992; Cazden, 1988; Eder, 1982; Wells, 1993, Van Lier, 1998). Conversational interaction has been shown to have positive effects on language comprehension and production (Gass & Varonis, 1994; Pica, 1994; Pica, Young, & Doughty, 1987). Learners' overt participation in communicative interaction is regarded as being conducive to the development of their innate capacity for language learning (Breen, 2001)-our innate capacities dynamically merge with and are ultimately shaped by the interactional activities made available to us as social actors in our sociocultual worlds (Hall, 2002). In an EFL classroom culture where the target language is seldom used outside it and the learners' exposure to the target language is therefore mainly in it, the kind of interaction that is made available is particularly important (Tsui, 1995).

Allwright (1984) asserts interaction is significant for the creation and exploitation of learning opportunities. In a similar vein, Van Lier (1998) concludes that our interactions with others constantly provide pedagogical moments or learning opportunities. The patterns of classroom interaction represent a crucial aspect in the learning processes, for they can provide and constrain, to a greater or lesser degree, learners' opportunities to participate in and learn from classroom events (Johnson, 1995). If we learn a language in the company of others in a classroom, Breen claims, social relationships and interactions in the classroom orchestrate what is made available for learning, how learning is done, and what we achieve (Breen, 2001).

The study of interactional processes is central to an understanding of how language is learned in a formal context (Walsh, 2006). Although different from many of the previous researchers, I have given interaction a broad view and conceive it as being more than verbal, I concur that interaction is central to language learning by making possible the construction of learning opportunities. It is also central to the development of classroom culture because the characteristics of classroom culture are largely established by and manifested through classroom interactions.

What I uphold, though, is that interaction as one of the basic classroom cultural components needs to be inspected along with the other components for a more revealing picture of the relationship between classroom interaction, EFL classroom culture and language learning opportunity, and a main reason for this is because language learning is situated practice.

3.2.3.3 Language learning is situated at multiple levels

Language teaching and learning is a social phenomenon and is therefore influenced by the sociocultural context in which it occurs (Tudor, 2001). In my study, I perceive language learning as being situated at multiple levels; it is situated in the immediate interactions and the classroom culture in which it takes place, it is situated in its institutional and wider sociocultural context, and further, it is situated in the international language teaching and learning community.

To begin with, language learning is situated in classroom interactions and classroom culture. To understand what is being learned by the classroom participants, it is necessary to consider its situated nature within the process of ongoing interactions. Moreover, language learning is situated in the particular classroom culture because the EFL classroom culture is the primary site for language learning to be carried out; and as such language learning process and its outcome are under the influence of the constant interplay of classroom cultural components.

At the second level, language learning is situated in its wider institutional and sociocultural context. A classroom culture in which language learning takes place is an inherently complex and unpredictable context; it is a context where social, cultural and institutional forces interact (Tudor, 2001; Wright, 2006). Classroom culture itself is situated in and indeed shaped by socio-historically framed and locally defined contexts (Hall, 2000). For example, language teaching and learning as performed in the EFL classroom culture is supposed to first of all fulfil the institutional language education goals. To a great extent, larger institutional, social, and cultural forces outside classrooms exert an influence on what takes place within the EFL classroom culture, including the kinds of identities participants assume and the activities and resources that are made available to them for appropriation (Hall, 2002). Therefore we need to understand the language learning process with reference to the broader context of the beliefs, expectations and traditions of the relevant sociocultural system.

At the third level, language learning is situated in the international language teaching and learning community. The trend of globalization has made this planet a more compact world; which results in increasing enthusiasm for English language learning since English is the most widely spread language. Great efforts have been made to improve English teaching practices in the language classrooms for the purpose of generating effective language learning. China's "importation" of CLT as a classroom language teaching method and its recent stress on developing language learners' communicative competence in classrooms is such an example. In TESOL, we live in the professional world of interactional events (Richards, 2003). This professional world is composed of English teaching practitioners around the globe whose language classroom research is communicated and whose classroom language teaching methods are introduced.

The situated nature of language learning makes it necessary to make such a connection between the classroom as a social setting which is illustrative of, and contributes to, higher-order social forces (Freeman & Johnson, 1998). In this ethnographic study, I perceive language learning as a contextualized social process that involve a multitude of elements both inside and outside the language classroom.

3.2.3.4　Classroom culture and language learning are co- constructed

Classroom culture and language learning are fundamentally social phenomena and whatever happens in the language classroom is indeed a co-production (Allwright, 1988). I believe classroom cultural development process and language learning process in the classroom are co-constructed in which both the teacher and the learners have their own roles to play.

The participants in the language classroom, including the teacher and the learners involved in pedagogical events, both have a share in the negotiation of the classroom cultural development and language learning process. The teacher may play a leading role in that he or she may control the content and the structure of an EFL classroom culture; learners nonetheless may interpret and respond to what the teacher says and does in their own ways.

The teacher, as the leader of an EFL classroom culture, can have vital importance in the development of an EFL classroom culture and the process of language learning. He or she manipulates classroom interaction through his or her agenda and controls the social system of interpersonal relations (Cazden, 1988) in the language classroom. In the EFL classroom culture, asymmetric relationship can very often penetrate the "expert-novice dyad", the teacher influences and even transforms the learners with regard to their language learning beliefs and approaches while guiding them through the language learning process.

But learners have their own parts to play in the classroom cultural reality by giving the EFL classroom culture and language learning their own input. A large proportion of apparent mismatches between teaching and learning could be explained if language learning is perceived as being the product of both teacher's and learners' contributions (Slimani, 2001). The learner's role, however compliant, is still crucial in classroom culture building process and language learning process. For instance, "even the mere presence of a participant constitutes a contribution to the management of classroom interaction, since it will affect the behaviour of others, however subtly" (Allwright, 1983, p.159). Learners' contributions to the language classroom cannot and should never be ignored. It is widely agreed that learners actively engage in the creation of what occurs in classrooms and affect classroom events as much as they are affected by them (Pintrich et al. 1986; Wittrock, 1986) so that they may partially determine the characteristics of classroom dynamics and their own learning outcome.

Based on shared goals, shared resources and shared patterns and norms for participation in the language classroom, teacher and learners therefore co-construct the language learning context and the language learning process. The language classroom culture then is the result of multiple constructions (Block, 1996) by the classroom participants; the language learning process depends on the strength of each individual's contribution (Wright, 1987).

In this chapter, I have explicated my theoretical framework in which I adopt a cultural approach to EFL classroom and language learning, which can be encapsulated in the following box:

Box 3.1:   A Cultural Approach to EFL Classroom and Language Learning

A Cultural Approach to EFL Classroom and Language Learning

- An EFL classroom can be viewed as a multidimensional cultural entity, it is comprised of basic classroom cultural components;
- Classroom interaction is one component of classroom culture, its relationship with learning opportunity needs to be studied in its classroom cultural context;
- Classroom interaction, as a component of classroom culture, is central to classroom cultural development and language learning processes;
- Language learning is situated in classroom interaction and classroom culture in which it takes place, it is further situated at multiple levels;
- Classroom cultural development and language learning processes are co-constructed by the teacher and the learners in the language classroom.

To look into the construction of language learning opportunities in their classroom cultural context, I carried out an ethnographic inquiry into two EFL classroom cultures in search of a thorough understanding of the patterned classroom lives and their implications for language learning. In the next chapter, I will elucidate on my research design against the background of an overview of the methodologies applied in language classroom research.

Chapter 4

Conducting Ethnographic Research in Two Classroom Cultures

The aim of this chapter is to introduce the methodological framework for the current study. I first present an overview of applied methodologies in classroom research and a discussion of their strengths and limitations, which serve to inform my decision with regard to the research design for the current study.

I then present my research design in this chapter: this study has used an "ethnographic case study" approach in which the two EFL classrooms are treated as two cultural entities and two cases under close examination. Data collection has been a multimodal process with the combined use of data collection methods such as participant observation, interview, audio recording, field notes, and collection of documents and texts. Data analysis has been an inductive and recursive process to achieve revealing and valid results. Ethnographic data analysis methods in conjunction with conversation analysis method have been used in data analysis and data interpretation. Following the presentation of my research design, I describe the practical difficulties and ethical concerns involved in this research process. I am aware of the limitations of the current study such as the "representativeness" of the two cases and I address this in the last part of this chapter.

4.1 An overview of applied methodologies in classroom research

Below I give an overview of the methodologies as they are applied in previous classroom research and discuss their relevant advantages and disadvantages before I present my own methodological framework for the current research project in two EFL classrooms in China.

Reflecting the great diversity of researchers' theoretical backgrounds, a wide range of methodologies have been applied to classroom research since the early 1960s. Chaudron (1988) classifies these research methodologies into four categories: psychometric studies, interaction analysis, discourse analysis, and ethnographic analysis. In Chaudron's classification, psychometric studies typically involve the use of the so-called experimental method with pre- and post- tests for both control and experimental groups. Interaction analysis involves the use of analytical observation schemes and focuses on the social meanings inherent in classroom interaction, while discourse analysis focuses on the linguistic aspects of interaction. The last category of research methodology in Chaudron's division, ethnography offers interpretive analyses of the events occurring in the classroom (Nunan, 1990).

Widely-influential as it is, Chaudron's (1988) classification of classroom research methodologies has been debatable. For example, Nunan (1990) considers that the four categories may be reduced into two-the psychometric and the ethnographic; the demarcation between which is in alignment with that between quantitative and qualitative research traditions. Some researchers are more inclined to use quantitative research methodologies because they think that certain educational phenomena are quantifiable and controllable; while others are more inclined to use qualitative research methodologies for descriptive and interpretive strength. There are also researchers who use combined research methodologies for the production of more descriptive and precise research results. Concerning the classification of classroom research methodologies, no agreement has been reached yet so far in research literature.

Some researchers have approached the language classrooms using experimental research. Associated more with research in science than in social science, experiments in educational research have both a pragmatic usage-"engineering particular forms of teaching and learning"-and a theoretical implication-"developing domain specific theories by systematically studying those forms of learning and the means of supporting them" (Cobb, Confrey, Disessa, Lehrer, & Schauble, 2003). In experimental research, through the manipulation of variables, the researcher is able to exercise control over an educational context, so that relationship among the variables can be exposed (Wolf, 2005).

Experimental research in the language classroom, in many cases, is used to reveal the causal relationship between certain variables-such as the effects of certain instruction techniques on language learning. Take, for instance, Long et al. (1984) have engaged in an experimental study on wait time in L2 classrooms in Hawaii, the preliminary results of which indicate that increasing wait time has a beneficial effect on the quality of learner responses. Experiments are also used to test language acquisition theories and in the quest for innovative ideas. Ellis (1990) has used classroom experiments to prove one of his main hypotheses: the most productive interaction-the kind most likely to result in language learning is one in which topics are selected by the learners and not the teacher.

Experimental research has the advantage over the other methodologies in classroom research in that experiments are designed to collect data in such a way that threats to the reliability and validity of the research are minimized (Nunan, 2004); another advantage for the use of experiments in classrooms is its efficiency in researching the causal relationship between pedagogical variables. The use of experiments makes it possible to investigate whether instruction in feature "x" leads to the learning of "y". Nonetheless, experimental research in classrooms may not always warrant the extrapolation of research outcomes to broader population (Ellis, 1990) across classrooms because the experimental conditions are human controlled instead of being naturalistic; and experimental research may not always be ideal for the study of pedagogical variables that cannot always be easily controlled such as participants' psychological factors.

Action research has been first developed as a tool to help teachers reflect on their own teaching practices in the 1970s (Stenhouse, 1975) and later as a research approach to meet the specific needs of professionals in the teaching of a foreign language (e.g. Nunan, 1990; Wallace, 1998). It typically involves small-scale projects in the teacher's own classroom. It seeks to increase the teacher's understanding of classroom teaching and learning and to bring about improvements in classroom practices (Kosnik & Beck, 2000; Platt & Platt, 1992; Wallace, 1998). It consists of collecting data in one's everyday teaching and of analyzing the data in order to come to some decisions about what the future practice should be (Wallace, 1998).

Action research has become increasingly used in language classrooms in recent years. In mainland China, Perrement (2005) has found that action research revolutionised the traditional Chinese pedagogy in the EFL classroom by enhancing language teachers' critical thinking and analytical skills in a bid to boost "quality education". In England, Price (2003) has been concerned about excessive teacher talk so he used action research to discover ways of increasing learners' learning opportunities in class.

There is no doubt that the dual identity of being a "language teaching practitioner" and a "reflective action researcher" can raise the language teacher's awareness of improving his or her classroom practices. However, for an action research project to be completed, the amount of time that has to be committed by the "teacher researcher" can be significant; what is more, the teacher researcher's intense involvement in the research may potentially lead to biased research findings.

In classroom research, *discourse analysis* (DA), *conversation analysis* (CA) and *interaction analysis* (IA) have been extensively used to study classroom talk. Although it is questionable whether they are methods of data collection and data analysis or distinct research traditions (Nunan, 1990), DA, CA, and IA have been regarded more as research methodologies in their own right in recent years when they are being increasingly used in language classroom research (Seedhouse, 2004).

DA has been employed and found to be quite effective in the investigation of language teaching and learning for it embraces the analysis of oral and written communications that are textually constructed (Hicks, 1995) (e.g. Barnes, 1992; Cazden, 1988; Mehan, 1979; Sinclair & Coulthard, 1975). Being the study of "talk-in-interaction", CA is an approach particularly for the analysis of oral interactions (Whetherell, Taylor, & Yates, 2001) to discover how participants understand and respond to one another in their turns at talk, with a focus on how sequences of action are generated (Atkinson & Heritage, 1984; Hutchby & Wooffitt, 1998). In IA, various observation schemes with their sets of pre-established categories have been developed in order to describe certain verbal behaviours of teachers and students (Chaudron, 1988).

Although DA and CA have been used widely and have helped to produce insightful findings in language classroom research, they are criticized for not being able to adequately account for the dynamic nature of classroom interaction and not adequately accounting for the range of contexts in operation in a lesson (Walsh, 2006). IA's dependence on quantitative measurements is criticized because the essence of communicative intent has been reduced to numerical codification (Kumaravadivelu, 1999).

To interpret and evaluate practices in the language classroom, *case study* and *ethnographic study* have been perceived to be powerful for they are both methodical ways of identifying and accessing language classroom instances and events. Ethnography in the language classroom has developed research methodologies for investigating classroom and institutional cultures which make up the social educational context with a strong emphasis on studying the behaviour of certain groups of people (e.g. Spradley 1980; Hammersley & Atkinson 1995; Long 1983; Van Lier, 1988, 1990).

Ethnography and case study as two popular research methodologies are similar in ways. They both involve the use of multiple data collection methods and data sources, this is especially useful for the depiction of complexity in the language classroom. The weakness for both is that the findings derived are sometimes criticized for their lack of generalizability; ethnography as a naturalistic study has been criticized for its lack of control in the variables in question.

There are fundamental differences between the two, however. Case study can utilize both qualitative and quantitative data and methods (Nunan, 2004) whereas ethnography is essentially concerned with the cultural context and cultural interpretation of the phenomena under investigation using mainly qualitative methods (Wolcott, 1988). According to Cohen (2003), the central difference between ethnography and case study lies in the study's intention: case study is outward looking, aiming to describe the nature of phenomena through detailed investigation of individual cases and their contexts; ethnography is inward looking, aiming to uncover the tacit knowledge of culture participants.

Each of the above diverse range of research methodologies has its own incision point and exploration procedures for different research projects. The research methodologies applied may reflect how the researchers as the "project conductors" intend to discover the answers to their research questions, in other words, the application of research methodology is based on one important principle-"fit for purpose".

> Different projects will have different purposes and audiences, and that it is these purposes and audiences which should determine the research methodology and design (Nunan, 1989, p.10).

Informed by the previous researchers' use of various methodologies to fit for different purposes of their projects, I designed this ethnographic case study which I am going to explain below.

4.2　My research design

4.2.1　The choice of my subjects and my research questions

The aim of this research is to gain a better understanding of classroom teaching and learning because I have been concerned with the construction of language learning opportunities in different classroom contexts. The objective of this research project is to observe and interpret the impact of the patterned classroom life on the construction of learning opportunities.

Towards this goal, I have chosen two EFL classrooms at the School of Foreign Languages in a provincial Normal University in China as the targets of investigation. I have chosen this university because I used to be one of the English major students studying on campus for four years in this institution less than 10 years ago; this has enabled me to have some insider's knowledge of the institutional ethos, its curriculum design and staff profiles although things might change over time. The familiarity with the institution and its teaching staff has also proved to facilitate my access to my research field. The choice of the two EFL classrooms has been based on the recommendations given by the Head of the School and other faculty members at the School because these two EFL classrooms are regarded as "model" classrooms with exemplar classroom practices.

My research questions are:

1). What are the characteristics of the two EFL classroom cultures under scrutiny?

2). How are learning opportunities constructed in these two EFL classroom cultures?

To answer research question 1), I have got some subquestions:

- What are the physical settings of the two EFL classroom cultures?
- What are the demographic and dispositional features of the two EFL classroom cultures?
- What are the norms of classroom behaviour for the two EFL classroom cultures?
- What are the interaction patterns in the two EFL classroom cultures?

To answer research question 2), my subquestions are:

- What are participants' perceptions regarding the effects of certain classroom practices on language learning?
- What classroom cultural characteristics contribute to the construction of learning opportunities in the two EFL classrooms?

- Are learning opportunities only constructed in a more "participatory" or "democratic" language classroom?
- Are there different types of learning opportunities constructed in the two EFL classroom cultures?

4.2.2 My ontological and epistemological orientations

Based on the perception that the two EFL classrooms are best approached as two cultural entities for the study of the construction of learning opportunities as I have described in my theoretical framework in Chapter 3, I believe ontologically, what happens in the language classroom is a cultural world set up with basic components; and the reality of this cultural scene is the product of multiple perceptions (LeCompte & Preissle, 1993). This world of the language classroom is fundamentally different from the natural world for participants have their own intentions and emotions which have impact on each other and on their educational context (Hargreaves, 1972; Ely, 1991). Thus a language classroom is composed of subjective and intersubjective realities that are worked out, changed and maintained. These realities are not trivial background for the tasks of teaching and learning a language. They continually specify and mould the activities of teaching and learning (Breen, 1985).

The epistemological orientation for this research is that I believe the social realities in these two EFL classroom cultures are comprehensible in the form of multiple, intangible mental constructions, socially and experientially based, local and specific in nature (although elements are often shared among many individuals and even across cultures) (Denzin & Lincoln, 1994). I believe that the understanding of these social realities should be based on empirical evidence of naturalistic events.

In order to unveil these realities in the search for answers to the above research questions, I have contrived this "ethnographic case study" design for the current research project.

4.2.3 An ethnographic case study

In this study, I have jointly employed ethnographic research methods and case study methods. With the two EFL classrooms approached as two cases of "classroom cultures", an "ethnographic case study" design, I believe, can assist the generation of an analytic description (Van Maanen, 1988) of classroom reality from both emic and etic perspectives and help to bring about illumination on the relationship between classroom reality and language learning.

In the study of life in language classrooms, one of the challenges that face the researchers is how to contrive a methodological framework that bolsters the endeavour to account for the various forces on classroom performances-a framework which recognizes and accommodates the complexity and density of classroom interaction as well as incorporates a consideration of the context in which the classroom is situated (Cray, 1999). Therefore, it is incumbent upon classroom-based investigators of language learning to propose an anthropological approach (Breen, 1985).

Ethnography is concerned with who people are, how they behave, and how they interact with each other (Woods, 1986). It studies people's behaviour in naturally occurring, ongoing settings and focuses on the cultural interpretation of people's behaviour (Hymes, 1982) in an attempt to codify and build a theory of particular culture (Framke, 1969). It emphasizes on the emic, or participants' attitudes, beliefs, behaviours, and practices; as the objective of ethnography is to come to a deeper understanding of how people in particular contexts experience their social and cultural worlds.

While emphasising "interaction" and "social context", (Lowenberg, 1993; Nunan, 2004), my goal in this research is to provide a descriptive and interpretive account (Hammersley & Atkinson, 1995) of what participants do in the two EFL classroom cultures, the meanings that classroom interactions and classroom cultural context have for them regarding the construction of language learning opportunities. My emphasis is on highlighting the need to contextualize the actions and contributions of participants in which language development takes place (cf. Freeman, 1992; Holliday, 1994; Van Lier, 1988, 1990). Towards this end, ethnographic methodology enables me to systematically document language teaching and learning interactions in rich, contextualized detail (Watson-Gegeo, 1988).

Case study is an intensive study of a specific individual or a specific context (Trochim, 2006). There can be single case study design or multiple case study design in which cases are analyzed and compared. In TESOL, a case typically refers to a person, either a learner or a teacher; or an entity, such as a school, a university, a classroom or a program (Faltis, 1997; Johnson, 1992, Nunan, 1992). Case study has been exploited in classroom research for many purposes, one of which is to focus on the details of classroom life, which is exactly the focus of the current study.

In my research project, the two cases are the two EFL classroom cultural entities, through which I aim to expose how language learning opportunities are constructed in contextualized social interactions. The careful examination of these two cases can help me to gain an in-depth understanding of classroom realities; the comparison of these two cases can render research findings that are informative and revealing for classroom language teaching and learning.

I believe the combined use of ethnography and case study can enhance the robustness of this research design. Ethnographies are sometimes case studies when they are reconstructions of cultures (LeCompte & Preissle, 1993). The "ethnographic case study" design both affords an emic understanding (Agar, 1985; Pike, 1967) of the two cultural lives and allows an etic view of the two cases. With an "emic" or "insider" perspective, I can experience and describe the cultural realities as a member of the classroom cultural groups (Van Lier, 1988), thereby gaining insights into what practical significance these two classroom cultures have for their participants' language learning. With "etic" or "outsider" perspective, I can stand detached conceptualizing the two cultural systems of the two cases; comparing and contrasting their "cultural characteristics".

Traditionally, ethnographers must engage in an extended period of observation, maybe months or even years, to understand a group of people. However, the essence of ethnographic study is to record and interpret the real life of a cultural grouping. Extended engagement in the field may be one of the means to ensure the achievement of a detailed description of a social group's cultural life. In recent years, more time efficient methods have been applied in ethnographic research, some researchers have even developed "rapid ethnography" (Millen, 2000) to achieve the understanding of a particular culture in a reasonable amount of time. A collection of research techniques such as constraining research focus and scope and using key informants are intended to serve for this purpose.

In this research, I have employed a combination of research methods to achieve an ethnographic description of the two classroom cultures. Although the time spent in the field was not extensive (about two months), my knowledge of the institutional culture was comprehensive (I have been studying and living on campus in this institution for four years when I was a university student) and my actual involvement in my participants' in-class and out-class cultural activities has been intensive in the field work, which enabled me to witness, understand and interpret participants' authentic speech and behaviours in the natural setting of their cultures.

The "ethnographic case study" design has mandated the use of investigatory strategies that are conducive to cultural reconstruction. Both ethnography and case study involve mixed methods of data collection and data analysis. In order to inspect the complexity of classroom realities with hope of success in this research, I have implemented a multimodal data collection process and a recursive data analysis process.

4.2.4   A multimodal data collection process

Ethnography is essentially multimodal or eclectic (Hammersley, 1990, Dicks, et al., 2006) and case study also relies on multiple sources of evidence (Yin, 2003). My "ethnographic case study" design therefore requires the use of an assemblage of data collection methods. A multimodal data collection process can serve for the benefit of providing a "rich" description of these cultural realities as well as reinforcing the validity of my research findings through triangulation.

In November, 2004, I went into my research field-the two EFL classrooms and carried out the fieldwork over 8 weeks. Aiming to capture participants' actions, interactions, and their interpretations of these actions and interactions in their particular education contexts, I went into the two EFL classroom cultures and collected data using methods including participant observation, field-notes, semi-structured and informal interviews with individuals and focus groups, audio-recording, and the collection of documents and texts (the data collection schedule has been attached in Appendix 13).

4.2.4.1   Participant observations

Whatever the methodology of research involved, it is clear that observation of classroom is a central part of classroom research (Van Lier, 1988). *Participant observation* in the classroom, as a data collection method, is valuable in that it combines participation, observation and introspection (Denzin, 1989). Positioned myself as a participant- observer, I have observed 64 classes (each class lasts 60 minutes including a 10 minute break) in the two EFL classrooms. I closely observed, recorded, and engaged in participants' daily life. As a participant observer, I have been involved in participants' talks before their classes commenced, during their break, and after their classes.

Through exposure to and involvement in their day-to-day classroom activities (see Appendix 13), I have examined how interactions and language learning were socially organized in the two EFL classrooms and have learned participants' cultural ways of living (Stephen, Schensul, & LeCompte, 1999) These participant observation experiences have granted me access to the insiders' world (Jorgenson, 1989).

I have used an "open-ended" approach in this naturalistic, interpretive inquiry; one of the most important strategies in my participant observation was that I saw ideas, information, and patterns as they emerge rather than using a prescribed observation scheme. The quantified, fixed-category checklist observational schemes, in my opinion, cannot catch the complexity of classroom interactions and cannot address the intricate relationship between classroom interactions, their classroom cultural context and language learning process. The observed classroom events in this research were audio-recorded supplemented with the use of field notes.

4.2.4.2   Field Notes

Field note in this research project has acted as a source of data that feeds important contextual and supplementary information for classroom observation. It has functioned like a microscope, assisting me in magnifying some of the "observable" as well as the "unobservable" details of a class, thereby facilitating the later reconstruction and reflection of the class scene (Swann, 2001). Two journals of field notes have been produced by the end of the fieldwork; they have helped me immensely to notice and discover the subtleties of the two EFL classroom cultures.

Particularly, I have used field notes-

- to keep track of what has been observed in the two EFL classrooms; specifics such as date and time of the observation, place of the class, instrument used in the class have been preserved in field notes;
- to record my comment on interactional episodes in the classrooms at different levels (including the interpersonal and textual interactions) and at different times (in class, during the break, outside the classroom);
- to record my reflections and personal random thoughts on the overall classroom climate or incidental events;
- to record my remarks on teachers' organization and management of the class;
- to record occurrence that other means of data collection may otherwise not have addressed, such as a language learner's absence from the class and their after-class events.

4.2.4.3   Interviews

An extremely powerful tool in my research has been the use of interviews. Research interviews are attempts to understand the world from the subjects' point of view, to unfold the meaning of people's experiences, to uncover their lived world prior to scientific explanations (Kvale, 1996). Interview in qualitative research is regarded as a major tool of data collection (Wengraf, 2001). In my data collection process, I have used *semi-structured interviews* and *informal interviews* with individual participant and focus group participants for the exploration of participants' subjective perceptions and interpretations of classroom interactions, classroom cultural reality, and language teaching and learning experiences (A sample interview guide for informal interview and a sample transcript of semi-structured interview have been attached in Appendices 14 and 15).

According to Robson (2002), a semi-structured interview is an interview where questions are pre-determined but can be modified based on the interviewer's perceptions of what seems most appropriate. Questions are prepared as guidelines and can be changed or added. An unstructured informal interview is an interview where the interviewer has some general interests and concerns, but lets the conversation develop within this area.

On separate occasions, I planned and conducted semi-structured and informal interviews with the individual participants including the Head of the School, the EFL teachers and with the individual language learners. I also conducted semi-structured interviews with focus groups. The interviews conducted in the first month of my field work were mainly to find out participants' dispositional features, the interviews conducted in the second month of my field work were mainly to cross-check my preliminary findings and further investigate participants' perceptions of their classroom events which have enabled me to gain a "native" knowledge of participants' classroom cultural experiences.

I have designed some open-ended questions in the semi-structured interviews in order to provide a framework for participants to respond in a way that represents accurately and thoroughly their points of views about the classroom realities and their language teaching and learning processes. For informal interviews, I designed an interview guide in which there are some interview topics for participants to answer. These semi-structured interviews and informal interviews have permitted flexibility and eliminated the possibility of any pre-judgment (Nunan, 2004); the interviewees meanwhile have been given a degree of power and control over the course of the interview so that they were able to speak for themselves (Sherman & Webb, 1988).

The informal unstructured interview has been used as an auxiliary interview method. These informal interviews were carried out before and after a class; in the classroom and outside the classroom-at places of convenience such as students' cafeteria and their dormitory rooms or at teachers' homes. These informal interviews have very often provoked my further thoughts on the observed classroom events; they have shed new light on my understanding of their cultural experiences of language teaching and learning.

As a participant observer, I have established good rapport with my research subjects as time proceeded. The friendly relationship and the open-ended questions or topics transferred the interviews into conversational communications between me-the interviewer, and the interviewee-either an individual participant or a focus group. Seemingly casual conversations as they appear to be, the interviews conducted in this research project have been indispensable in finding my participants' dispositions about EFL classroom teaching and learning in general and their attitudes toward the particular EFL classroom interaction patterns specifically.

The selection of the focus group was convenience sampling based on participants' availability and accessibility. These interviews have produced speedy results, as participants tended to provide crosschecks on each other and thus they excluded extreme views, although I was wary not to let any one group member dominate the interview process and have tried to elicit points of views from all the group members. With focus group interviews, it was relatively easy to assess the extent to which there was a relatively consistent shared view among the participants (Patton, 1990) regarding the impact of certain classroom cultural characteristics on their language learning.

Depending on the availability of the participants at the time of the interview, the numbers of learners in these focus groups ranged from 6 to 8. The average interview time was around 30-40 minutes; there were 21 interviews in total with individual participant and focus groups from the two EFL classrooms. Most of the interviews have been administered in Chinese language for the reception of articulate responses except for the interviews with the British teacher which have been administered in English since she is a native speaker of English.

4.2.4.4   Audio-recording

Audio--recording has been vital for both data collection process and data analysis process in this research. The taped record of classroom events made possible the repeated and detailed examination of particular classroom incidents, especially the verbal interactions between and among participants. In the close inspection of these verbal interactions, I could have discovered new layers of their meaning for learners' language learning without making immediate judgments. The audio-taping of interviews supply participants' perspectives and personal accounts of their cultural lives in the classrooms. Audio-recording has also helped to produce transcripts which form a large and important part of my data corpus for data analysis.

A mini cassette recorder was used to record classroom speech events and interviews, altogether 37 mini audio cassette tapes (120m) of data have been generated. To avoid later confusion, I specified on the cassette labels the date, place, participants and gave a brief introduction of the content of each recording. A large part of the transcripts were produced immediately after the audio-recording for the reason that I could easily have recalled the classroom events after the participant observation sessions or interview sessions in the research field.

Video recording as a data collection method has been dismissed for the avoidance of obtrusiveness. Video recording can be very useful for capturing participants' facial expressions and gestures, which might add to the understanding of participants' classroom behaviours. But in Chinese culture, the appearance of a video camera can easily arouse participants' suspicion which might hamper this "naturalistic" inquiry.

4.2.4.5   Collection of documents and written texts

Apart from the aforementioned data collection methods, *collection of documents and written texts* has been an additional data collection method for my research. The documents collected include NCEC; NCEM; National Guidelines for TEM4 and TEM8 Tests; Introduction to SYNU; Introduction to School of Foreign Languages, SYNU; Course Design for English Majors at the School of Foreign Languages, Official Document of Pedagogical Guidelines at the School of Foreign Languages. Information gleaned from the documents included the national and institutional language education policy and guidelines, the background information to the School of Foreign Languages and the University in this study, and the relevant information on the National English Testing System.

The written texts collected over time included learners' assignments, their textbooks, exercise books, test papers, the portfolios designed and used for teacher-learner extracurricular communications, and teachers' instructional journals.

Seemingly peripheral to my research, the documents and written texts have been an invaluable source of data. The documents collected such as NCEC and NCEM have provided contextual information for the understanding of life in the two classroom cultures; the texts collected such as portfolios have been analysed, which has helped to shed light on the understanding of teacher-learner interactions in Ying's EFL classroom. To a great extent, these documents and texts exposed aspects of participants' classroom cultural life that were otherwise unperceivable through classroom observations.

4.2.5 An inductive and recursive data analysis process

4.2.5.1 Data analysis methods

In qualitative inquiry, there are multiple practices, methods, and possibilities for data analysis (Coffey & Atkinson, 1996). In this study, I mainly employed ethnographic analysis of the two cases so as to reproduce the two "classroom cultural lives" and account for their implications for the construction of learning opportunities; I used conversation analysis when I explored the influence of verbal interactions on the construction of language learning opportunities.

Ethnographic analysis has been used to understand participants' beliefs, expectations, values and social relationships as they are disclosed in their classroom cultural events, the data of which have been generated with the use of participant observations, audio recording, field notes and interviews. Through these ethnographic analyses of the two classroom cultures, I could have gained the anthropological interpretations of participants' classroom cultural lives as they live and experience. In these ethnographic analyses of the two classroom cultural lives, particular attention has been paid to the triangulation of participants' perspectives to ensure the validity of my research findings.

Considering interaction is central to the construction of EFL classroom cultures and language learning opportunities, and verbal interaction is the major form of interaction in both EFL classroom cultures, the analysis of verbal interactions is of crucial importance in this study. To analyze verbal interactions, I employed conversation analysis.

The employment of CA has first of all helped to reveal which "cultural" or contextual aspects the participants are orienting to in the details of their talk (Schegloff, 1992; Seedhouse, 2004). According to Schegloff (1987), much CA work "can be seen as an extended effort to elaborate just what a context is and what its explication or description might entail" (p. 221). The orientations that participants display to each other through their verbal interactions have formed part of their "classroom cultural context"; and the conversation analysis of participants' verbal interactions has assisted with the understanding of their cultural context.

As Moerman comments:

> All actions are socially situated and all situations are structured. Culturally contexted conversation analysis thus permits a description that while never complete, is sufficient for showing the nexus between cultural rules and individual intentions (Moerman 1988, p, 57).

Although unlike Moeman, I don't think CA itself is sufficient for "showing the nexus between cultural rules and individual intentions", I have tried to gain an emic perspective in the analysis of participants' verbal interactions to reveal their individual intentions and how these could relate with their classroom cultural backgrounds. CA in this study has been helpful for it provides an emic explanation of how the participants understand and make use of their classroom cultural context through their verbal interactions. The task of CA analysts is to develop an emic perspective to uncover and describe the organization and order of social action in verbal interaction (Seedhouse, 2004).

CA has been highly important in my close examination of the construction of language learning opportunities through the sequential verbal interactions in situ. In this study, the use of CA has helped me to identify the practical significance of structural verbal interactions for the teachers and learners. The linguistic world to which the learner has access, and in which he or she becomes actively engaged, is full of demands and requirements, opportunities and limitations, rejections and invitations, enablements and constraints-in short, affordances (Van Lier & Matsuo, 2000). The study of the turns participants take in verbal interactions have enabled me to see how opportunities for learning are generated.

With CA as a data analysis method, I tried to make sense of verbal interactions in language classrooms as they occurred in the context. Verbal interactions analyzed include participants' "interruption" and "invitation", "question and answer", "evaluation and repair", all of which have been examined in great detail. There have been no attempt to "fit" the data into preconceived categories; evidence that such categories existed and were utilized by the participants was demonstrated by reference to examples from the data. Using CA, I aimed to account for the structural organization of the verbal interactions as determined by the participants; to track down how participants interpret each other's actions and to develop an understanding of the progress of these interactions.

In the analysis of classroom talks, I have also calculated time spent respectively on teacher talk and learner talk in the two EFL classrooms with the audiotapes in hand to reflect part of the classroom cultural characteristics.

4.2.5.2   Data analysis procedure

Data analysis in this study has been an inductive and recursive process with insights and generalizations emerge from my close contact with the data. It started with data collection and guided further data collection; it has been an ongoing process that constantly involved the "visiting" and "revisiting" of data as patterns, categories, and themes emerged and evolved for data interpretation. The premise underlying the current study is that through direct observation of daily activities in classrooms, interviews with language teachers and language learners, together with the analysis of data of other sources such as texts, a holistic picture of the two EFL classroom realities and language learning phenomena can be derived. When this picture is apprehended through cultural and linguistic filters (ethnographic analysis and conversation analysis in this study), an unprecedented understanding of the factors that impact on language learning for these learners will emerge (Ellison, Boykin, Towns, & Stokes; 2000).

Thanks to the multimodal data collection process, I could have approached the two EFL classroom cultures and the language learning processes in them from different angles and at different levels. The data in bulk warrants the substantiality and the specificity of the classroom events; the transcripts generated from the recorded material enable me to get direct and quick access to classroom episodes. Chinese language that was used in interviews has been translated into English during the transcription process.

My data corpus is composed of the transcripts and audiotapes of the observed classes and interviews, field-notes, and the collected documents and texts. The analysis of data has demanded my sensitivity to the subtleties of these two EFL classroom cultures. In order for my data corpus to be more manageable, I first divided the data into two large parts: one part was the data for "the British teacher's classroom culture" and the other was for "the Chinese teacher's classroom culture". I then delved into "the perceivable" in order to find out "the hidden" about these two classroom cultures and their participants' language learning.

Next I started with a succession of "coding" procedures as codes of different levels emerged from the data. I first assigned some broad categories to segment data masses into chunks; these categories included "classroom environment", "participants", "classroom and extra-curricular activities". Under these broad categories, there arose subcategories including "the physical setting of the classroom", "the pedagogical goal of the classroom", "participants' demographics", "participants' dispositions", and "participants' interactions". Then the data was further segmented into smaller unites of analysis. For example, under "participants' dispositions", there were subcategories of "teacher's dispositions" and "learners' dispositions" which were further subdivided. Under "learners' dispositions", there were subcategories "learners' expectation of the class", "learners' expectation of and attitude toward their teacher", "learners' preferred language teaching and learning methods", "learners' preferred classroom activities and interaction patterns". These coding procedures have helped to construct a framework for data analysis in the shape of a "coding tree" with the broadest category of classroom phenomena on top and the narrowest category of classroom phenomena at the bottom. In the coding process, I tried to make these categories as exhaustive as possible.

I then re-examined the categories and subcategories that I have assigned to the chunks of data and tried to detect the links between them-to establish themes as they emerged. The initial categories and subcategories were revised, combined, or subdivided as I took into account the relevant macro- and micro-contextual influences that stand in a logical relationship to participants' classroom behaviours and classroom events. At this stage, the triangulation of data sources and participants' perspectives has become particularly important. Themes related with "interaction, classroom culture and language learning opportunities" became apparent as I was trying to boil down the observed phenomena to two EFL classroom cultural models and exhibit their influences on language learning.

When applying CA to analyze the verbal interactions between classroom participants, I have referred to the conversation analysis procedures as delineated by Seedhouse (2004). Specifically, my analysis of the verbal interactions has involved the following procedures:

First of all, I carried out an inductive database search before the establishment of regularities and patterns in the verbal interactions. Consistent with my "open-ended" research approach, no preconceived hypotheses were borne in mind in the process of analysis of verbal interactions. After action sequences were identified, the next step of CA in this study was to give detailed analysis of single instances of the phenomenon for the purpose of explicating the emic logic of the organization of the verbal interactions. I paid particular attention to the examination of sequences of verbal interactions, adjacency pairs, preference organizations, and organization of repairs. In this close examination of the sequential organization of verbal interactions, I could detect the relative role relationships of the participants and their orientations towards language teaching and learning and towards the classroom culture. Thirdly, I attempted to explain the relationships between the single instances that show regularities in verbal interactions and the broader context in which these verbal interactions happened, with particular emphasis put on the construction of language learning opportunities in these sequential "talks-in-interactions".

While transcription systems are widely used in conversation analysis, I have deliberately adopted simplified transcription without the usage of transcription symbols for the following reasons. Essentially, the use of transcription conventions is to show how features of verbal interactions that are often missed out in more basic transcripts can be analytically useful. But transcription conventions are created and applied by humans. It is possible even for experienced professionals who follow the same transcription convention to produce different transcriptions of the same recording material, the result of which is that different accounts of the reality might be generated.

What is more, there exist different systems of transcription conventions. The most commonly used system of transcription in conversation analysis was probably the one developed by Atkinson and Heritage (1984). But the employment of transcription symbols may make the text difficult to read. To enhance the readability of this book, I have tried to present my own transcriptions in a way that is easily accessible to audiences outside the community of language researchers for the future dissemination of this research.

4.2.5.3 An inductive and recursive process and data interpretation

Data analysis in my research has been an inductive process. The primary purpose of the inductive approach is to allow research findings to emerge from the frequent, dominant or significant themes inherent in raw data, without the restraints imposed by structured methodologies. It has involved sifting and sorting through pieces of data to detect and interpret thematic categorisations, search for inconsistencies and contradictions, and generate conclusions about what is happening and why (Thorne, 1997).

Data analysis in my research has also been a recursive process. It started alongside the fieldwork, and has continued ever since. The process of data analysis has not been seen as a distinct stage of my research project that should be segregated from data collection and data interpretation; rather, it has been a reflexive activity that informed my data collection and data interpretation; which reciprocally compelled revisiting data and further data analysis.

Preliminary data analysis was carried out concurrently with fieldwork and the transcription process as some pre-eminent categories showed up. Informal and initial data analysis in the field was of assets for it could guide subsequent data collection (Hoepfl, 1997). The early data analysis, being synchronized with my fieldwork, has impelled the constant adjustment in ensuing data collection for the production of revealing and valid research findings. I learned from the initial data analysis as to what to watch for, notice, or ask during the next visit to the research field. At this level, data analysis has helped fieldwork towards the production of useful information (Coffey & Atkinson, 1996).

For example, the initial data analysis made immediately after each session of fieldwork in the first couple of weeks has permitted me to seize the nuances of classroom contextual implications for language learning and obligated additional interviews. Meanwhile, some initial themes and tentative findings derived from the first few weeks' observation in the classrooms have suggested additional focus of observation. The focus of participant observation was initially placed on the general dynamics of the language classrooms, when preliminary characteristics of classroom interactions and classroom cultures were found after the first few weeks, additional foci of observation were placed on different aspects of classroom interactions such as teachers' initiation of classroom interactions and invitation of students' participations, students' reaction towards teachers' comments and repairs, and participants' interactions outside the classroom in the course of my fieldwork. The pre-liminary data analysis that I carried out conjointly with data collection has impelled the change of focus in observations from the general to the specifics of classroom interactions and classroom cultures, and changed the nature of the observations from being completely open-ended at the very beginning to being necessarily selective over time.

To validate the tentative findings, I have had to collect relevant documents and texts for a complete understanding of participants' cultural experiences of the EFL classrooms. The whole data analysis process thus has involved the constant checking, revising, corroborating themes, revisiting data and further analysis of data.

Data interpretation in my research has been like a "dual translation" process (Thomas, 1993): I first "translated" the categories and themes that I had identified through data analysis process into two classroom cultural realities with their distinctive characteristics; I then "translated" these two classroom cultural entities into the construction processes of learning opportunities with the illustration of classroom episodes.

4.3 Piloting and technical issues

Before I went to China to carry out the fieldwork, I piloted my data collection and analysis methods in the UK so as to check their practicality and avoid potential technical problems. The trial of these methods proved to be invaluable. Ideally, this should be done "in the field", but most of us are not lucky enough to get such a chance (King, Keohane & Verba, 1994). Due to the limited time I could stay in my research field, a better option for my trial has been to test the data collection instrument, data collection and analysis methods when I was in the UK.

I observed and audio-recorded one of my supervisor's classes, which was not only a good practice of my observation skills, but also a test of my audio-recording instrument. The sound effect of the mini cassette tape recorder which I intended to use in my field work turned out to be satisfactory; it has captured the classroom participants' voices very clearly. Considering that the size of most classrooms in China's universities is larger than that of classrooms in the UK, I decided to connect the mini cassette recorder with an external microphone which can be adjusted to broaden the recording range and improve the sound quality in my fieldwork.

The "piloting" also involved a series of interviews with three students in my supervisor's class to try out my interview questions, practise my interview and qualitative analysis skills. After I have gained first hand interview and qualitative analysis experiences, I have got a better knowledge of the things that I should notice during interviews and data analysis. I kept these in my research diary, refined my interview approaches and further practised data analysis skills in the UK to be prepared for the real fieldwork in China.

The "piloting" of my data collection instrument, data collection and analysis methods and skills ahead of fieldwork has helped me a great deal to avoid potential problems and I was enabled to make use of my time in the field effectively. However, there did arise an unexpected problem once I was in the research field when the extreme cold weather (minus 29 degrees Celsius) at the time (November-December in Northeast China) of my fieldwork on one occasion has caused the batteries in the cassette recorder to stop working properly; luckily, the spare batteries I bought from the school shop prior to the observation sessions helped to prevent data loss.

4.4 Validity and credibility of the research

Qualitative research has been the target of criticism for its generation of "soft data" which raises the doubts concerning its validity and credibility. In my research, I have taken measures to safeguard the validity and credibility of my research findings. Multiple triangulations (LeCompte & Preissle, 1993) have been the measures used to enhance the validity of this research.

I achieved multiple triangulations in my research with the combined use of triangulation of research methodologies, triangulation of data collection methods and sources, triangulation of data analysis methods and triangulation of perspectives, as I explain below.

1). Triangulation of research methodologies. My "ethnographic case study" design, by combining the strengths of ethnographic study and case study, has been most helpful in revealing the "cultural characteristics" of the two cases in their depth and complexity;

2). Triangulation of data collection methods. Data collection in my research has been a multimodal process to amass large corpus of data for the later reconstruction and thick description of classroom cultural scenes. I have used a wide range of data collection methods including participant observation, field notes, semi-structured and informal interviews with individuals and focus groups, audio-recording, and the collection of documents and texts;

3). Triangulation of data sources. The multimodal data collection has produced multiple sources of data for a faithful depiction of the classroom cultural realities. Data sources include transcripts, recorded tapes of observed classes and interviews, journals of field notes, curricula, teachers' instruction plans, learners' written assignments, textbooks, exercise books, etc.;

4). Triangulation of data analysis methods. I have used ethnographic analysis in conjunction with conversation analysis to study the classroom cultural context and the contextualized verbal interactions for a more in-depth understanding of language learning;

5). Triangulation of perspectives. The analysis of classroom cultural realities and classroom talks using multiple perspectives-teachers' perspectives, learners' perspectives, researcher's perspectives made me evaluate and discover classroom cultural realities and the construction of learning opportunities in them from different angles.

As a participant observer, there have been dilemmas involved towards the goal of ensuring the validity of this research. I had to remain "objective" while acting as a "native", I had to be "open-ended" while being necessarily selective. Besides, I had to be present at the site while trying to avoid being obtrusive.

One of the dilemmas was-How to be "objective" while trying to act as a "native" in the EFL "classroom cultures" under study? When observing, there were times that I was inclined to make judgments with my personal values about the classroom setting and the classroom practices under investigation. Bearing in mind the differences between my "ideal classroom culture" and the observed "real classroom culture" as constructed by the classroom participants, I had to diminish the interference of my subjective world. I sought to maintain a distance from the other classroom participants so that I could gain a more objective view of the reality being investigated (Scott & Usher, 1999), and refrained from full participation for the sake of the attainment of the "whole picture". In my field notes, I have separated my description of the two classroom scenes from my personal judgment using "colour-coding". In addition, I frequently solicited opinions from many of my research participants as a research "check-up" procedure.

During data analysis and interpretation process, I have also tried to guard against the syndrome of "going native". To decode the participants' interactional activities and their cultural behaviour, I should have the empathy to understand classroom events as participants see them; namely, I should develop an "emic" perspective. However, the more I am involved and being empathetic, the greater the danger that my perspectives will be taken over by my research subjects (Thomas, 1993). The solution lay mainly in that I, as the researcher, had to distance myself to do a critical and objective analysis of the two EFL classroom cultures and combine the "etic" with the "emic" perspectives. The frequent revisiting of data has provided some guarantee that analytic conclusions will not arise as artefacts of intuitive idiosyncrasy (Heritage & Atkinson, 1984). The multiple triangulations and "follow-up" researcher-participant communications as I have discussed previously are also precautions I have taken to conquer this problem.

The second dilemma I faced was how to be "open-ended" while being necessarily "selective". On the one hand, I should keep an "open-ended" approach to observe and try to take in as much detail as possible; on the other hand, I had to be necessarily selective in my observations to prevent the recording of minutiae. As an attempt to avoid recording trivia as well as to fend off my susceptibility to personal bias and assumption, I have kept a researcher's diary in the "field" to keep a track record of and reflect on my research activities and evolving thoughts.

Another issue in the field was related to the "obtrusiveness" of my presence in the two classroom cultures. It was my concern that my presence in the two EFL classrooms as an observer researcher shouldn't affect the daily routines of my participants' classroom life or cause alteration in their classroom performance. Video recording has been dismissed as a data collection method for this reason. In order to make my presence as unobtrusive as possible, I made efforts to establish good rapport with the teachers and students and informed them of the purpose of my research. As I have become a familiar presence for them after the initial few sessions, they almost accepted me as a member of their classroom cultures which made possible the observation of "naturally-occurring" classroom events. My goal was to observe events at which I was physically present but to refrain from causing changes in the activities being studied (Sherman & Webb, 1988).

Credibility of my research has been enhanced through my "insider's knowledge" of the institution and my intensive interactions with the participants when I was doing the fieldwork and after I have completed the fieldwork.

The fact that I used to be a member of the institutional community in the study has left me in an advantageous position in sharing a common knowledge with my participants regarding their institutional context and has facilitated my understanding of some classroom cultural realities.

My intensive and prolonged interactions (Lincoln & Guba, 1994) with the participants in the field-inside their classrooms, in their cafeterias, in students' dormitories and sometimes in the teachers' homes over an eight weeks' time period also helped to produce an authentic description of the EFL classroom cultures and establish the trustworthiness of my research findings.

After the fieldwork in the tertiary institution in China, there have been continual "follow-up" communications between me as the researcher and my participants via e-mails and online talks when I came back to the UK which has been a "respondent validation" (Barbour,

2001) process. My participants have helped me to check certain data collected, confirm the interpretation of classroom episodes and ascertain some research findings.

4.5 Ethical considerations for the research

This research has been conducted in compliance with the qualitative research ethical framework and guidelines (cf. BERA Ethical Guidelines, 2004), and I have given due consideration to the benefits and entailment of this research for my participants.

Before commencing fieldwork, I have sought approval with regard to my research plan from both my supervisors and the Ethics Committee at the School where I have enrolled in the PhD programme-the School of Education and Lifelong Learning in the University of Exeter, the United Kingdom. After I was granted consent to my research activities, I went into my research field-two EFL classrooms in a provincial institution in China and carried out this research.

The entry to the actual research field was gained through its "gate-keeper", the Head of the School of Foreign Languages in the tertiary institution in China. I presented him the signed research ethics approval document and the introductory letter from the School of Education and Lifelong Learning in the University of Exeter; I explained to him my research purpose and what was likely to be involved before he acknowledged the benefits of my research project for the school's EFL education programme and gave me his consent to carry out this research project in the institution. Thereafter the Head of the School together with the administration team of the School allowed my entry to the classroom sites and authorized my access to the School documents.

I then obtained my participants' "voluntary informed consent" before my observation sessions in the two EFL classrooms. I paid visits to the two EFL classrooms beforehand when I explained in detail the nature, the purpose, and the procedures of my research project to my participants. This was to show my respect for my participants and to expedite the smooth progress of the research after they agreed to cooperate with me and willingly displayed their daily classroom life and activities in front of me. I have let my participants know that they would not be pressurized into participating in this research and they had the rights to withdraw at any time of the project although all of them have generously shared their perspectives and classroom cultural life experiences with me throughout the whole research process.

The seeking of informed consent has been an ongoing process along with the progress of my research project. Before the audio-recording of classroom activities, interviews and our informal conversations, I have informed my participants of the use of data I was to collect and gained their approval. It has also involved negotiating access to their extracurricular activities and access to their residence (students' dormitories and teachers' homes) for observation and interview purposes.

During data collection, I assured my participants that data collected would be stored securely and would not be divulged to third party without their consent to protect their confidentiality, which is also in line with the Data Protection Act. In the presentation of this research report, I have given my participants pseudonyms to protect their anonymity.

After the field work, my participants have been offered access to my research results, which was realized through our regular contact via e-mails and online talks. This was an attempt to accomplish reciprocity between me as the researcher and my participants. The reciprocity achieved has served both as an ethical virtue on my part-a form of recognition of and gratitude to my participants' cooperation; and as a validity and credibility check for my research findings.

4.6 Limitations of the current study

A big challenge for me to confront in this research has been its generalizability. The question posed here is "to what extent can my research results be extended to other classroom groups?"

Given China's geographical vastness and regional diversity, the classroom practices and the classroom cultural realities may not be hugely representative for the practices and realities in other classrooms located in other regions. What is more, the individuality of a particular classroom as a particular "case" makes it impractical to make rash generalizations for "one of the problems with L2 classroom research is that there is such a tremendous variety of L2 classrooms" (Van Lier, 1988, p. 5).

The pedagogical practices and participants' performances revealed in this study may not stand for all EFL classroom realities across China. However, my research questions are to discover the cultural characteristics of the two EFL classrooms and the construction of learning opportunities within them. It is my intention that through the close examination of these two cases, new and valuable insights can be drawn for the understanding of the interrelationships between classroom interactions, classroom cultures and learning opportunities. Albeit I can't make generalizations about language classroom realities in China based on what I have found in this study, I hope that the theoretical understanding of classroom culture and language learning that I have derived from this study can be of value for the understanding of language learning in other classroom contexts.

In Chapter 5, I am going to describe the cultural characteristics of the two EFL classrooms under study in order to answer my first research question, which meanwhile paves the way for the development of a theoretical understanding of classroom culture and the construction of learning opportunities.

Chapter 5

Portraits of Two EFL Classroom Cultures

This chapter presents a detailed description of the two EFL classroom cultures in this study. I first disclose the institutional context in which the two EFL classroom cultures and their participants are located in terms of its goal of English education, its pedagogical guidelines and its mission statement. I then give a portrayal of the two classroom cultures, using qualitative data as a descriptive and interpretive aid (Since each of the Chinese students in Esther's class has adopted an English name, I will use English pseudonyms to denote these participants). To do this I draw upon the classroom cultural components framework developed in Chapter 3. That is to say, my reconstruction and presentation of the two classroom cultural scenes are achieved through the unfolding of their physical settings, their demographic and dispositional features, their norms of classroom behaviours and their interactional patterns.

5.1 The institutional context and its commitment to innovation

In this research, the institutional context is set at the School of For-eign Languages in a provincial Normal University in China. The School, originally the Department of Foreign Languages at the University, has become increasingly popular among EFL learners in the region because it is regarded as being capable of producing graduates with high lan-guage competency and good employment prospect. As a result, the size of the classes is constantly enlarging and the School of Foreign Lan-guages has become one of the largest departments at the University.

Following the completion of a major renovation, the School has become very well equipped with language teaching facilities and teach-ing resources: there are 9 language labs and 1 multimedia language classroom; the language teaching staff include 15 expatriate teachers teaching 5 different foreign languages at the School (English, Japanese, French, Russian, and German), 10 of whom are native English speakers. With imbalance in gender ratio a commonplace phenomenon in China's Normal Universities, there are much more female than male students at the School.

English as a foreign language is a major subject greatly emphasized at the School and the majority of students studying at the School of For-eign Languages are English major students. The goal of English lan-guage education at the School of Foreign Languages at this Normal University is mainly to train students to become qualified secondary school language teachers and administrators after their graduation. The first line in the School's document (School of Foreign Languages, SYNU, n.d.) regarding its aim is that "students are expected to first of all have a good command of the theoretical knowledge of a foreign lan-guage", followed by the statement that "they are also expected to have foreign language communicative competence". This may partially reflect the fact that in many Chinese universities, gaining the theoretical knowledge of a foreign language (English in this case) is still the foremost target to be achieved, although achieving communicative competence of a foreign language is clearly stated as one of the school's goals, it is only secondary.

While following the national English educational curricula (see Section 2.3.1), the School has its own pedagogical guidelines that act as the overarching principles for its classroom participants, which find expression in the form of a mission statement.

The mission statement for the School has been put in a condensed four word statement: "*think, learn, lead, and link*" (Mission Statement of the School of Foreign Languages in the School's official document of Pedagogical Guidelines, n.d.). This mission statement also "informs the teaching, researching and community engagement in the School and the School is committed to innovation" (ibid).

During an interview, the Head of the School explained the School's Mission Statement as this:

> We need to reflect on our own practices so as to improve them, we need to learn from others and each other to improve; with our reflection and active learning, we can thus be in the vanguard of educational improvement and reform, while making efforts to link ourselves with the other communities. In aiming at language pedagogical improvement, the School and each member of its staff should keep an open mind to innovative ideas and methods (Interview data, 11/2004).

The School's commitment to educational reform and innovation is manifested prominently in its guidelines for teachers' classroom practices: in order to improve its language teaching quality, the School stresses the strengthening of the language teaching team and encouraging its commitment to innovation. It has put emphasis on "enhancing teachers' performance" (School of Foreign Languages, SYNU, n.d.) rather than on "enhancing students' performance" in the classrooms, perhaps in recognition of the fact that most classes are still very much teacher-fronted.

In the Guidelines for Teachers' Classroom Practice at the School of Foreign Languages (2005), it is advocated that:

- Teachers can refer to the national English educational curricula for university students, while using a variety of teaching methods in the classrooms;
- Teachers should have a loving and tolerant attitude toward learners in all kinds of teaching activities;
- Teachers should guide and inspire learners to learn with their own initiatives and advocate autonomous learning;
- The process of language teaching and learning is equally important as the outcome of language teaching and learning;
- The School is in favour of "democratic teaching".

In light of the discussion on China's educational reform in chapter 2 (see Section 2.3.1), what is stated in the Guidelines for Teachers' Classroom Practice at the School of Foreign Languages (2005) can be seen to reflect its commitment to innovation. However, the School also shows a continuing adherence to educational traditions as disclosed in its goals of English education above. To some degree, the School has preserved the same educational traditions which were existent when the researcher was studying there almost 10 years ago. For example, theoretical knowledge of the English language is emphasized over communicative competence in the language and teacher-frontedness still predominates in many of its classrooms. But it can be seen that a new language teaching and learning environment which has combined conventions and innovations has been established through the School's advocacy of teachers' flexibility in classroom teaching methodology and teachers' tolerance towards students, its advancement of autonomous learning and democratic teaching, and its emphasis on the process of language teaching and learning.

Under the influence of these institutional pedagogical guidelines, the members of the two EFL classroom cultures have established two pedagogical enterprises with their own characteristics as will be discussed below.

5.2 The EFL classroom culture in Esther's class

In this research project, one of the two EFL classroom cultures is led by Esther, a British language teacher. Her EFL classroom has been recommended by the head of the School as a "model EFL classroom" led by an expatriate teacher; it has also been credited as a "learner-friendly" language classroom among the language learners. Below I shall depict Esther's classroom culture in detail.

5.2.1 The physical setting and pedagogical goal of Esther's classroom

Esther's language classroom is set within an enclosed space of rectangle shape with four walls on each side; there is a long blackboard on the front wall and a teacher's table is put in front of the blackboard. No wall displays are put up on the wall. Directly facing the blackboard and teacher's table are five rows of long benches and tables fixed to the floor with an aisle in the middle. The size of the classroom is actually big but appears to be small with all the prearranged furniture in it. The immobility in the classroom layout has presented the class members with a defined language teaching and learning area.

The subject being taught by Esther is *"English Conversation"*, its pedagogical goal being to develop learners' English oral skills and enhance their communicative competence through communicative activities (School of Foreign Languages, SYNU, 2004).

5.2.2 Demographics of the classroom culture in Esther's class

The cultural group in Esther's EFL classroom is comprised of a native English speaker as the language teacher-Esther, and her 33 sophomore students as the language learners.

While Esther is only one of the thousands of expatriate teachers working in China's higher institutions and one of the 15 expatriate teachers at this School, she is exceptional because of her outstanding qualifications, her length of language teaching experiences in a Chinese context and her familiarity with Chinese language and culture, which I will elaborate on below.

In modern day China, thousands of native English speakers are recruited each year to become English language teachers working in institutions across the country. This high demand for native English speakers as language teachers results in a great shortage of their supply. It is for this reason that many recruiters are not very particular about the qualifications of these "would-be English language teachers" who are native speakers of the language. In most cases, there are only two criteria for the successful job applicants to meet: one being that they are native speakers of English, the other being they are Bachelor Degree holders. It is not uncommon to see many native English speakers employed as language teachers in China who have bachelor's degree in fields other than language pedagogy. Esther stands out among these "qualified" expatriate teachers in China -she holds a Bachelor's Degree in Education which she gained from a British university and she used to be a researcher in pedagogical theories in one of the higher institutions in Northern England. Besides, she has two years' learning experience in a higher institution in Northeastern China. Her qualifications are therefore seen as well matched to the language teaching position in this Chinese university.

While many expatriate teachers would leave China after a few years' life and work experiences, Esther had been teaching English at tertiary level in Chinese higher institutions for seven years at the time this research project was conducted and she has intended to continue living and teaching in China. Her years of language teaching experiences in the Chinese context have won her a good reputation among her Chinese students who generally agree that her language classes are sources of good fun and valuable English language knowledge, as I was told by some language learners on campus in my casual talks with them.

Chinese language has been recognized as notoriously difficult for Westerners (Watkins & Biggs, 1999) and many expatriate teachers simply shy away from learning the Chinese language when they stay and teach in China for they don't observe this as relevant to their job of English language teaching. For Esther, it is her strong interest in Chinese language and culture that has drawn her to start an English language teaching career in China. While English is her native language, Esther is remarkably proficient in Chinese language as a foreign language. The fact that she is married to a local Chinese man and that she has been working in China for more than seven years may help to account for her good knowledge of Chinese culture, customs, and even local dialects.

At the time when the field work for this research project was carried out, Esther was teaching a class of 33 sophomore Chinese students, among whom only three were boys. These language learners come from different parts of the province, have diversified family background but are roughly of the same age, mostly being 18 or 19 year-olds. Having undergone six years of formal English education in their junior middle schools and high schools before they entered this university, their English levels are more or less of the same intermediate proficiency level. All of these students are English majors studying for the Bachelor's Degree in English Education, and they are supposed to become secondary school English teachers after four years' university education.

The demographic features of Esther's EFL classroom culture- participants' age and gender, their previous language teaching or learning experience, their languages and language proficiency levels are illustrated in the table below.

5.2.3　Dispositional features of Esther's classroom culture

The dispositional features of the classroom culture in Esther's class are mainly shown through Esther's beliefs in "communication" as the pivot of language education and the language learners' unconcealed welcoming attitude towards her class and ready acceptance of her educational ideology. Esther's communication-centred language educational ideology may be representative of Western language teaching values to a great extent; whereas the language learners have displayed dispositional features that might be seen to deviate from the stereotypical dispositions often ascribed to Chinese students who are mostly conceived to be passive and receptive (see Section 2.1.1). These will be discussed in detail below.

120

Table 5.1: Demographics of the Classroom Culture in Esther's Class

Demographics of the Classroom Culture in Esther's Class			
Participants	Age & Sex	Previous language teaching or learning experience	Languages and their proficiency levels
1 language teacher- Esther (British)	37 years old; Female	Once a researcher in pedagogical theories in a higher institution in England; One year's Mandarin learning experience in a Chinese university; Seven years' English language teaching experience in Chinese higher institutions	• Native language- English; • Foreign language- Chinese (highly proficient)
33 language learners (Chinese)	18-19 year-olds; 30 girls & 3 boys	Six years' English learning experience in Chinese junior middle schools and high schools plus one year's living and learning on campus at this Chinese university- altogether seven years' English language learning experience	• Native language-Chinese; • Foreign language-English (intermediate proficiency level)

5.2.3.1   Esther's communication-centred EFL educational ideology

The central theme that pervades Esther's EFL educational ideology is her belief that English language education is for communication and classroom activities should centre on communication; as she has expressed in many interviews:

> Researcher: What do you think is the purpose of EFL classroom education?
>
> Esther: Communication.
>
> Researcher: What do you hope your students can achieve through your English language teaching?
>
> Esther: I hope they can learn to be critical and analytical in the learning process, which is lacking among Chinese students; most importantly, they should be able to communicate without too much difficulty in English after a certain period of EFL classroom education (Interview data, 11/2004).

This communication-centred EFL educational ideology has guided Esther's classroom activity organizations and language assessment standards. With the awareness that this is a rather big class, it is impractical if not completely impossible to let everyone of them have the opportunity to speak up in front of their classmates, Esther insists that there should be adequate classroom participation: "I would try to involve them in various group and pair works and I expect them to participate in class" (Esther in interview, 11/2004). Towards her students' mistakes, Esther has shown her tolerance for she is more inclined to put emphasis on language learners' "fluency" instead of "accuracy" as long as they can get their messages across. Her classroom assessment is mostly contingent upon learners' classroom oral performance.

The following figure sums up the axial status of "communication" in Esther's language educational ideology:

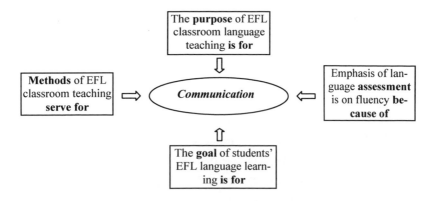

Figure 5.1:   Esther's Communication-centred EFL Classroom Educational Ideology

5.2.3.2   Esther's class-a group of "atypical" Chinese students

In Esther's class, students appear to be open to and accepting of the sort of language education ideology put forward by Esther. Moreover, they are in eager anticipation and have high hopes for Esther's language classes. with their positive orientation towards classroom participation and their open welcome of error correction in class, they appear to be "atypical" within the context of the normative picture of learners as passive non-contributors represented in many discussions of Chinese learners (e.g. Cortazzi & Jin, 1996; Watkins & Biggs, 1999).

Almost all the students hold a positive attitude towards Esther's classes even before they meet in the language classroom-more than 90% of the students interviewed expressed their overt welcome on the basis of their understanding of the style of Western classroom teaching they have got from some television programmes. Moreover, Esther's good reputation at the School arouses students' anticipation for her classes, as students expressed in interviews:

Echo: I've seen how western teacher teaches her students on television; they are very free, I like that free style of communication.

Abigail: I think foreign teachers are more appealing to us (than Chinese teachers). We can get in contact with some fresh elements (in the classroom).

Wendy: We all look forward to her (Esther's) classes; she (Esther) is one of the best foreign teachers in our School. We are really happy to have her as our foreign teacher (Interview data, 11/2004).

With respect to English language learning, a majority of these Chinese students have high hopes for Esther's classes. In line with Esther's communication-centred educational ideology, they hope to achieve communicative competence in English as well as a general knowledge of British culture and idiomatic usage of English language by attending Esther's class, which they said in interviews:

Cathy: I hope after some time, I can speak fluent English. It is ok as long as I can communicate with others without language barrier.

Echo: I prefer an expatriate language teacher's class over a Chinese language teacher's for I think I can achieve more from Esther's class in learning more about the idiomatic usage of English language.

Heather: In Esther's class, I can get to know more about their (British) culture, etc. [sic] (Interview data, 11/2004).

Although Chinese people's sensitivity to open criticism and humiliation, or "face-losing" is frequently commented on (e.g. Bond,

1986), these students appear to have a very open attitude toward critical opinions from their teacher and their fellow classmates, as one of the students expressed:

Tracy: I hope they will correct me when I use English wrongly. This is what I've expected (Interview data, 11/2004)

This group of language learners are thus "atypical" in that they are oriented towards classroom participation.

Esther has noticed this and commented in one of the interviews:

Researcher: Generally speaking, most Chinese students are very shy on public speaking occasions. Are these students the same?

Esther: No, they are not typical. They enjoy, many of them enjoy acting, they enjoy being in the front, and doing things in front of the class. I think it's part of Confucian thinking to have people have respect towards their elders and to venerate their teachers, so to some extent, that is very true in Chinese classes that students expect their teachers to convey information, and it is the students' responsibilities to absorb it. But in this particular class, I think students are more eager to speak themselves. They are very active and very motivated (Interview data, 11/2004).

Overall, these students are willing to use their own initiative in classroom participation. The great majority of these students expect themselves to be active participants in Esther's classroom activities. Over 70% of the students interviewed aim at active participation for the reason that such opportunities for interaction with native English speakers are rare and they are eager to develop their oral competence in Esther's classes. More than 20% of the interviewed adopt a "respond-when-being-called" attitude which they attribute to their lack of language skills and introvert personality rather than their unwillingness to speak; only a few-10% of those interviewed claim to be on the reserved side and to be inclined to "watch and listen to" what Esther and their fellow students do and speak.

The "exceptional" expatriate teacher-Esther along with her "atypical" Chinese students have established their procedural structures in their EFL classroom cultural system, which is reflected in their syllabus, medium of instruction, and preferred classroom activities.

5.2.4 Norm of behaviour in Esther's classroom culture

Each week, Esther and her students meet twice for a total of four hours' contact time. They maintain relatively predictable classroom routines in their language classes-the syllabus is mainly designed by Esther each time before they start class, the medium of instruction is both English and Chinese, classroom activities are in various forms but individual presentation and group works are indispensable.

1) The use of a self-made syllabus.

Unlike her Chinese counterparts at the School, Esther has got no pre-assigned textbooks or syllabus. Her so-called "syllabus" is one that is consisted of materials she collects and tasks she devises before each of her classes; it is an assembly of information ranging from "hot" topics that are closely-related with students' daily life to the introductory knowledge in connection with British culture and tradition. For example, her teaching material can be articles downloaded from the internet; can be everyday English idioms purposefully chosen; can be children's literature or virtually anything that she regards as beneficial for improving her students' oral abilities that is meanwhile of most interest to them.

Esther once explained the design of syllabus in her class:

> Esther: I think it is very common in Chinese universities, expatriate teachers are asked to teach conversation class without textbooks. So usually I will try to collect some materials for them to learn English. If I happen to find some interesting topics when I surf the internet, I will use these topics for my students' discussions in class. Sometimes I also use my daughters' books in my classes because I think the level of the English language in these children's books is suitable for my students. What I am trying to do is to get them to learn English, so I always gather some materials that I think are of interest to them (Interview data, 11/2004).

2)   The use of double-coded medium of instruction.

It is a requirement at the School that English should be the Medium of Instruction (hereafter referred to as MOI) for English majors (Guidelines for teachers' Classroom Practice at the School of Foreign Languages, 2005). Using English as the primary MOI, Esther sometimes switches from English to Chinese as the secondary MOI, should a communication barrier between her and her Chinese students surfaces. She uses Chinese language as an aid to crystallize her explanations of English language knowledge and to facilitate her students' understanding of her instructions. Occasionally, she even uses Chinese language to make some amusing comments to entertain her students or attract their attention. Approximately 3% of teacher talk in Esther's class is in Chinese language. I will explain this further in the description of interpersonal interactions in Esther's classroom culture in Section 5.2.5.

3) Primary activities employed: individual presentation and group work task.

It is a routine in Esther's classroom culture to have one or two presenters at the beginning of each class. A typical class starts with teacher-students greetings followed by two or three students' individual presentations. One student steps to the front of the class at a time either voluntarily or by being called on; the presenters would deliver a speech they have well prepared before the class that lasts approximately three to five minutes. The topics of their presentations are usually self-chosen, including a wide range of issues such as stories of their life experiences and talks on a television programme that the particular presenter is interested in and thinks his or her audience will be attracted to. When presenters do find it difficult to make a decision as to what topics to focus on in their presentation, they would choose one from Esther's list of reference topics.

It is usual for the speaker to entertain a very attentive audience who would give him or her some sort of response (a burst of laughter or warm applause) once in a while. The speaker clearly enjoys his or her speech, so do the listeners. The listeners including the teacher rarely correct the speaker's linguistic mistakes in the middle of a speech, but rather they pay attention to the content he or she is trying to deliver. At the end of each individual presentation, the teacher-Esther, and the presenter's fellow classmates will either make some comment or ask some questions that they are concerned with. The individual presentation is then given a grade by Esther, and this grade will partly determine the student's final grade at the end of the semester.

Group work is another major form of classroom activities in Esther's class, there are a wide variety of group activities that appear frequently and occupy a large part of class time including role-plays, game-plays, puzzle-solving, team-competitions, group discussions, simulated interviews.

These group works in Esther's classroom culture demonstrate some consistent characteristics:

- Each time group work occurs, learners are organized into different groups, so the size of the group and the members of the group vary from time to time;
- Group members work towards a shared goal with co-ordinated efforts and collaboration;
- Almost every one of the group members shows his or her passion for the group task and contributes to the group work;
- Group members use their own initiatives and English knowledge in the process of completing the group task;
- Group members express their sense of accomplishment after the completion of their group task.

The groups are mainly informal study teams, students are either organized in ad hoc temporary clusterings by the teacher; or they voluntarily form new groups under the teacher's request. A great sense of mobility is demonstrated in group work despite the immobility of the classroom furniture for students are free to move about to sit beside their group members for the purpose of fulfilling a task.   Sometimes, groups of three to five are initiated to start discussions about a topic assigned by the teacher; a group leader is designated by the teacher or chosen by the group members to publicize their group discussion result in front of the whole class at the end of the group discussion session. On other occasions, groups are set up to compete against each other on general knowledge in English. Sometimes students can even choose a group name for their own team in order to enhance their group profile. Students are especially excited about playing games, acting in simulated interviews and role-plays. As much as or more than a third of the class time (an hour) can be spent on group work, which means that literally almost every one of the 33 students in Esther's class is involved in group tasks.

Pair work was at first used but later dismissed in Esther's classroom culture, the reason for which I will explain in Chapter 6.

In estimate, in a 60-minute-class, 33% of class time is devoted to teacher talk including her telling of personal stories and teaching of English idioms, her summary of students' errors and comments on students' classroom performance; 23% is to students' individual presentations in front of the class (of this 23% of class time devoted to individual presentations, only around 35% is allocated to the monological talks given by individual presenters; while around 65% of the time is used by the interacting audience who will comment and question on the presentations before Esther initiates an error-detection and error-correction session. I will give a detailed description of the different phases in individual presentations in Section 6.4.2), 41% to group work, and 3% to other activities such as time spent on students' changing seats when forming groups. On the whole, teacher talk occupies less than 40% of class time with more than 60% of class time goes to student talk.

To sum up, Esther's classroom culture is set within an ordinary physical setting of a Chinese university classroom, yet it is uncommon because it is made up of a unique expatriate teacher who has a notable command of knowledge about Chinese language and culture and a group of "atypical" Chinese students who have a zest for participation. These cultural members have generated an EFL classroom culture that is characterized with high interactivity in participants' interpersonal verbal interactions.

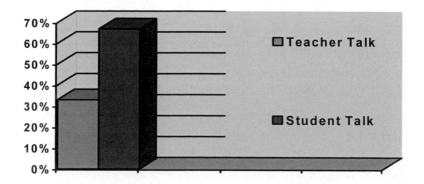

Figure 5.2:   Ratio of Teacher Talk to Student Talk in Esther's Classroom Culture

5.2.5 Interpersonal interactions in Esther's classroom culture

Interactions in Esther's classroom culture are mostly interpersonal verbal interactions, that is, oral interactions between and among people. There are not only oral interactions between the language teacher and the language learners as the two parties involved in the language educational process although teacher-learner interactions might be the most common interpersonal interactions in classrooms; there are also a great deal of learner-learner interactions in this EFL classroom. These interactions are bilateral (between the teacher and the learners or between one learner and another learner) or multilateral (among the classroom participants); unidirectional (one-way communication), bidirectional (two-way communication) or multidirectional like those in a truly communicative event.

5.2.5.1 Participants' bilateral, unidirectional verbal interactions

When a classroom cultural member addresses an issue or makes a speech in front of the rest of the class, the classroom interactions are realized through the speaker's delivery of a speech and the audience's reception of this speech. They are bilateral-between the speaker and the audience; the flow of communication is unidirectional-from the speaker to the listener.

A most conspicuous example of this may be the interaction that happens when Esther performs her managerial and instructional role in front of the class. On such occasions when Esther tries to organize some classroom activities or explains certain language knowledge, the interactions are bilateral and unidirectional-between Esther, the language teacher and her language learners, from the language teacher to the language learners.

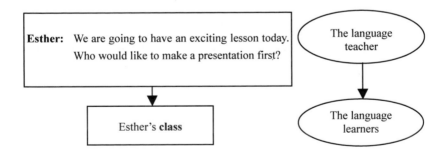

Figure 5.3: Example No. 1 of Bilateral, Unidirectional Interaction in Esther's Classroom Culture

Another example might be the interactions that take place during a language learner's presentation. When an individual learner makes a presentation in front of the class, the interactions are bilateral and unidirectional-between the presenter and his or her audience, from the presenter to his or her audience, as illustrated below:

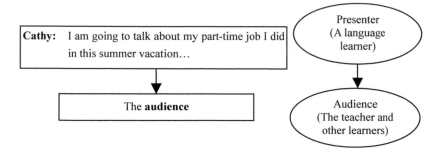

**Figure 5.4:   Example   No.2   of   Bilateral,   Unidirectional   Interactions   in
Esther's Classroom Culture**

Here "Cathy" was the presenter and she was going to make a presentation on her part-time job. While she was making the presentation, Esther was no longer the language teacher; instead, she merged with the other language learners who were listening in their seats and became a listener in the audience. The interactions in this case are thus between two parties or bilateral-between Cathy the presenter and her audience; and the interactions are unidirectional- from Cathy the presenter to her audience.

The bilateral unidirectional interactions also happen after the individual presentation. Using the above example, Cathy was bombarded with questions from her audience after her speech:

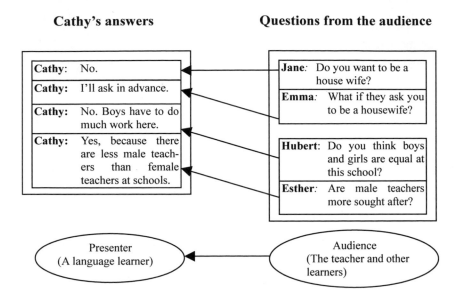

Figure 5.5: Example No. 3 of Bilateral, Unidirectional Interactions in Esther's Classroom Culture

The interactions are still bilateral-between the presenter and the audience, and they are still unidirectional-only from the audience to the presenter this time. But if there are two parties involved in a chain of verbal interactions, sometimes these interactions can also be bidirectional as either party may initiate and respond.

5.2.5.2   Participants' bilateral, bidirectional verbal interactions

In Esther's EFL classroom, many times there can be oral exchanges that are like real life conversations when two classroom cultural members are involved in a one-to-one talk in their pedagogical environment for language learning purposes. The interactions on these occasions are bilateral between the two conversationalists involved and bidirectional with a natural two-way flow of communication. One thing extraordinary about these bilateral, bidirectional interactions is that these often occur between the language teacher and a language learner.

Take, for instance, when the language teacher-Esther tells her personal story, the language learners sometimes get so absorbed that some of them would interrupt Esther now and then and ask her questions out of curiosity. Esther, then, would also ask the learners some questions. These interactions may be initiated either by the language teacher or by a language learner.

Below is such an example:

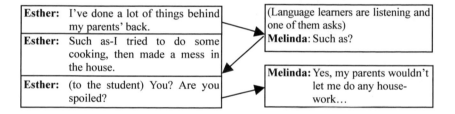

Figure 5.6:   Example of Bilateral, Bidirectional Interactions in Esther's Classroom Culture

An interesting example of bilateral, bidirectional interactions is an episode in Esther's class when the 33 language learners were divided into two large groups with one group of language learners being the "interviewers" and the other being the "interviewees" in a "simulated interview" classroom activity. The interviewers were asked to sit in the aisle seats awaiting their interviewees, holding slips of paper with interview topics in their hands; in the front of the classroom stood the interviewees. Each of the interviewees was assigned an interviewer in the first round. When the time for the three-minute "blitz interview" was up, Esther asked the interviewees to move to their next interviewers and start the next round of simulated interview. This special form of group work is actually comprised many bilateral bidirectional verbal interactions between the participants.

5.2.5.3 Participants' multilateral, multidirectional verbal interactions

Esther's classroom sometimes resembles a forum where people exchange opinions in English language on certain topics, although they are de facto learning English as a foreign language.

Below is an extract from a group discussion session when students were asked to form groups and discuss the topic "the generation gap" in their groups. The discussion group in this extract was composed of three language learners-Echo, Rose, and Peggy; Echo was the chosen "group leader". The interactions here were among the three members of the discussion group in a three-way communication as each of the members was directing her message to the other two of the group members and received by the other two members.

Extract 5.1:

Echo: Esther asked us to discuss about "generation gap".

Rose: Generation gap. Well, there is generation gap between me and my parents.

Peggy: I think there is generation gap between me and those three years younger than me. They say "three years is a gap".

Echo: Do you really think so?

Peggy: Yes. For example, I can't understand what those young singers are singing. I can't understand them.

Rose: I agree.

...

Similar multilateral multidirectional verbal interactions can also be found in inter-group competitions, group puzzle-solving and role-plays, which in part establish "high interactivity" in interpersonal verbal interactions as a prominent feature of Esther's EFL classroom culture.

Participants' verbal interactions are also enhanced with extracurricular communications. Sometimes, Esther talks with her students during break time; sometimes she would ask her students to visit her house at weekends.

Apart from the above interpersonal verbal interactions, eye contact as a form of nonverbal interaction in Esther's class is a very important ancillary tool in classroom communication. Without textbooks to cling to, Esther and her students have constant eye contact to read each other's facial expressions and this has kept the smooth flow of classroom communication and vastly facilitated the communication process, as expressed by one of the Chinese students:

> John: She would know if I am willing to talk in front of the class through our eye contact. If I do not want to, I will hold my head down, or if I do want to talk, I will look at her, and then she will read my mind (Interview data, 12/2004).

In Esther's classroom, participants' interpersonal interactions have created a language learning context which fits well the model of "democratic pedagogical environment" (see Section 2.3.2) in which cooperation and participation are greatly emphasized by the classroom cultural group.

5.2.6 Interactional symmetry and pedagogical democracy

Participants share certain practices that both define the classroom community and are nurtured by it (Fisher, 1995). As the actual classroom "cultural leader", Esther willingly abdicates her "absolute" authoritarian status and relinquishes part of her complete control of the class. She has consciously and subconsciously endowed her students with certain power in the decision-making process.

Take, for instance, before giving instructions and assignments, often Esther negotiates with her students rather than forcing them into doing something. When it is the time for individual presentation, she would ask her students: "Who will make the speech today?" When organizing a group, often she would tell the students: "please choose your group members and your group leader." Before a group discussion, she would consult her students' opinions as to the choice of topic they would like to discuss and talk about. In letting her students shoulder part of the responsibility for classroom decision-making, the students are enabled to make choices about their own language learning behaviour. The power relationship therefore has become more of symmetry between the teacher and the students.

Resulting from this interactional symmetry and the high interactivity in interpersonal verbal interactions is a "democratic" language learning environment in which the classroom cultural members have fostered a sense of cooperation and cohesion. Almost every one of its members comes to the class to hear what others have to say and to be heard by the others, this applies even to the less linguistically proficient classroom cultural members. They respect each other' speech and points of views; they manifest that everyone's ideas are worthy of being valued. They are willing to listen and speak, to interact and cooperate. With the team spirit of cooperation and cohesion, language learning has become a collective activity among the classroom participants.

I noted the following with respect to this in my field notes:

> When a student is making a presentation in front of the class, regardless of his or her presentation topic and his or her language capacity, the other students would listen attentively; at the end of the presentation, students would ask the presenter some questions showing their genuine interest before the presenter walks back to his or her seat in the company of a voluntary warm applause from Esther and the presenter's fellow classmates.
>
> In this classroom, everyone is indulged in a climate of encouragement and support, participants' speech behaviours and non-verbal cues have demonstrated that they are supportive of one another and respect each other. The teacher respects each student's voice, and the students like to listen to each classmates (Researcher's field notes, 11/2004).

Esther has also recognized this as she remarked in interviews:

> Esther: In this class, everybody values the others' views, they are willing to listen to the others, and that makes a huge difference.
>
> Esther: The solidarity they have is what makes this class so successful, they enjoy helping each other, and they have got good rapport among them (Interview data, 12/2004).

The language learners in this class meanwhile are proud of their "membership" in this classroom culture as they expressed in focus group interviews. Here I illustrate with one learner's comments for they representative of the others' opinions.

Vivien: Our teachers have commented that our class is a good class, for we are a united group and are willing to cooperate with each other and with the teachers. We feel we are a good class, too. We can excel as a model class in our grade (Interview data, 12/2004).

In summary, Esther's classroom culture is characterized with high interactivity in interpersonal verbal interactions. It is in alignment with the model of "democratic pedagogical environment". Both the language teacher and the language learners are oriented towards a communicative language learning context.

Having presented the EFL classroom culture in Esther's class, I will now turn to the description of the other EFL classroom culture under investigation-the one led by a Chinese teacher of English, Ying. Located within the same sociocultural and institutional context, the classroom culture that emerges in Ying's classroom seems to be starkly different from the one that develops in Esther's class.

5.3 The EFL classroom culture in Ying's class

5.3.1 The physical setting and pedagogical goal of Ying's classroom

Similar to Esther's class, Ying's class is set in an ordinary classroom in the same institution. There are no wall displays or decorations in this enclosed rectangular space. A long blackboard is hung up on the front wall; some chalk and a tape recorder are the language teaching instrument for Ying to use. Ying usually stands behind her table in the front of the classroom, while her students are sitting in their seats. The students are seated in rows of long benches attached to tables; and again, the tables and benches are fixed to the floor. Altogether there are eight rows of long benches and tables, four on the left hand side of the classroom and four on the right with an aisle in the middle. Students are usually seated in fixed positions which they have chosen for themselves in their first class. The immobility of the furniture partially confines and defines participants' classroom activities.

Ying's class is one of the participant classes involved in the School's programme to train qualified interpreters that are urgently needed for conferences, government agencies, and economic enterprises in China. The subject being taught is *"Interpretation"*. The pedagogical goal of this class is to train students to become "professional interpreters with accuracy and efficiency to serve in cross-cultural communications" (School of Foreign Languages, 2004).

5.3.2 Demographics of the classroom culture in Ying's class

Ying's classroom culture is comprised of a Chinese teacher of English-Ying, and her 24 Chinese language learners.

Ying was originally a graduate of this school and was offered a job position after her graduation because of her excellent academic performance. When a student, she was known for her good command of English language knowledge and near standard pronunciation; now a teacher, she enjoys good reputation for her English language teaching and her classes have been frequently observed by her colleagues as model classes. She has got more than 20 years' English learning experience and around 10 years' English teaching experience. Besides doing her language teaching job, she also has administrative responsibilities at the School, including negotiating between teachers (both Chinese and expatriate teachers) and students, and organizing language educational activities for the School.

Ying's class is of a smaller size than Esther's, although gender imbalance is also prominent in the demographic features of Ying's classroom culture. There are 24 students altogether including 21 girls and 3 boys. These students have just graduated from high schools in the province after a fiercely competitive National College Entrance Examination. They are 17 or 18 year-olds and have got six years' language learning experiences gained from three years' junior middle school and three years' high school education before university. At the time when this research project was conducted, these students have only been living and studying at the School for approximately three months, their English is roughly at the pre-intermediate level.

5.3.3 Dispositional features of Ying's classroom culture

The prior language learning and language teaching experiences plus the social and institutional context have influenced the way Ying looks at the nature of language teaching and learning, which is displayed in the dichotomy in her language educational ideology. For the language learners in Ying's classroom, the past six years of language learning experiences they received from junior middle schools and high schools have also impacted on their beliefs in and attitudes toward university language learning.

Table 5.2: Demographics of the Classroom Culture in Ying's Class

Demographics of the Classroom Culture in Ying's Class			
Participants	Age & Sex	Previous language teaching and learning experience	Languages and their proficiency levels
1 language teacher-Ying (Chinese)	36 years old; Female	A graduate of this School, more than 20 years' English learning experience; Around 10 years' English teaching experience at this university	• Native language-Chinese; • Foreign language-English (near standard pronunciation and good command of English knowledge)
24 language learners (Chinese)	17-18 year-olds; 21 girls & 3 boys	Six years' English language learning experience in Chinese junior middle schools and high schools; three months' living and studying on campus at this university	• Native language-Chinese; • Foreign language-English (pre-intermediate proficiency level)

5.3.3.1   Dichotomy in Ying's educational ideology

In Ying's student years, G-T method predominated language classrooms in China and CLT was just introduced from the West but hadn't won recognition of the language teachers and learners. Then during her ten years' language teaching experiences, CLT was first very popular among the language educationalists before it gradually lost its momentum and G-T regained its predominant status in language classrooms in many parts of China (see Chapter 2).

The shifting trends in language educational thoughts together with the educational traditions that are deeply planted in Ying's upbringing have impinged on Ying's own language educational ideology. During my interviews with Ying, she expressed very clearly that she is "a teacher of principle" for she has got her own set of beliefs with respect to EFL classroom teaching.

In Ying's language educational ideology, there is a discernable dichotomy between "tradition" and "innovation". On the one hand, Ying's educational ideology is under the great influence of the "Confucian educational tradition"; on the other hand, there are some elements that demonstrate her propensity towards "innovation" which is very much in line with the School's commitment to "innovation". Threaded through her educational ideology is her ambivalence about the process of EFL learning, learners' roles, and classroom teaching methods.

To start with, EFL teaching and learning in Ying's eyes is fundamentally a "knowledge transmission" process in which the teacher imparts what she has and the learners receive what they are given; but she also advocates "learner autonomy" and hopes that learners can be active in the learning process, which is in line with the "knowledge construction" model in which knowledge is seen as being co-constructed by the teacher and the learners.

> Ying: I should have plenty of English knowledge to give to my students, and my students should be ready to take in and try to remember what they are told (Interview data, 11/2004).

Here Ying regards language teaching as giving the language knowledge she possesses and language learning is for her students to

144

"take" what is "given". The role-relationship between the teacher and the students then is that between a "knowledge-dispenser" and "knowledge-receivers"; the learners are seen as containers to be filled with the knowledge held by teachers.

Paradoxically, Ying personally is a strong advocator of "learner autonomy" and she expects her students to assume the ownership of their language learning; she hopes that her students can be self-directed and self-evaluated in the process rather than simply listening to what the teacher says. Learner autonomy is a process whereby learners exercise control and assume responsibility of their learning by making decisions or choices (Littlewood, 1993, 1996). It is noteworthy that learner autonomy can connote a redistribution of power and it is in congruence with the "knowledge construction" model in which learners play an active role in the language learning process. In interviews and in many class episodes, Ying has repeatedly stressed the importance of learner autonomy:

> Ying: They (students) should not only listen to what the teacher says, but should also develop learner autonomy.
>
> Ying: They (students) need to know how to learn and learn for themselves. We should train them (students) to develop their own learning strategies.
>
> (Ying in interviews, 11/2004)
>
> Ying: You should be responsible for your own learning, what the teacher says is only part of education.
>
> (Ying in class, 11/2004)

Regarding classroom teaching methods, Ying believes lectures and students' exercises are effective means of language teaching, but she also aims at the innovation of classroom teaching methods.

The long term target of EFL classroom teaching for Ying is to enable her students to be qualified for good job positions so as to serve for the country's economic growth in the public and private sectors after their graduation. The most immediate target of her EFL classroom teaching is to help her students to get good scores in exams while they are at the university. She views students' academic performance in exams such as the nationally recognized TEM4 and TEM8 exams as the most important indicators of good language teaching and a successful EFL classroom. Ying considers that the conventional practices of "teacher's lectures" combined with "students' exercises" are powerful in achieving this immediate goal:

> Ying: I expect them to do really well in TEM4 and TEM8 and in various English competitions. For this reason, classroom lectures and drills are very important because they help students to get good scores in their exams (Interview data, 11/2004).

While Ying accepts that teacher's lectures and students' exercises as the essential methods of language teaching and learning; she also advances innovation in the EFL classroom teaching methods:

> Ying: I think it is necessary for a teacher to be creative when she organizes the class. In my classroom, I will try to motivate my students and engage them in all kinds of activities in class and after class (Interview data, 11/2004).

Ying's dichotomy in her educational ideology can be illustrated with the figure below:

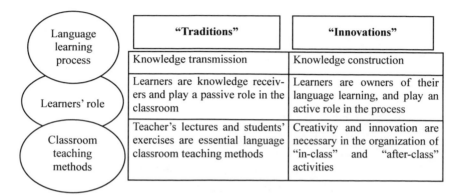

Language learning process	"Traditions"	"Innovations"
	Knowledge transmission	Knowledge construction
Learners' role	Learners are knowledge receivers and play a passive role in the classroom	Learners are owners of their language learning, and play an active role in the process
Classroom teaching methods	Teacher's lectures and students' exercises are essential language classroom teaching methods	Creativity and innovation are necessary in the organization of "in-class" and "after-class" activities

Figure 5.7: Dichotomy in Ying's Educational Ideology

5.3.3.2   Ying's students are aiming for high academic achievement

Ying's students, like many other Chinese students, see that their life's future hinges on their university education, and they regard EFL classroom learning as the gateway for them to pursue further education or to get good job positions. The immediate goal of language learning, in their eyes is to pass the TEM4 and TEM8 tests. Ying, who has a reputation for good teaching in the School, is seen by these students to be a very important way of ensuring that they can fulfil this goal.

One learner from Ying's classroom once said:

> Tingting: It is extremely important for us to pass TEM4 and TEM8 tests in these four years so that we can find good jobs with these certificates. We have heard from students in their senior years that Ying is a very good teacher and we think she will help us to get good scores in the exams (Interview data, 11/2004).

The means to this end, as these students see it, is to "get English language knowledge" from Ying and be disciplined in class. They expect their teacher-Ying to be "authoritarian", to control the class talk and make all major decisions while they comply with her directions and classroom organization.

This is evident in the comments made in interviews by the majority of the students. Some typical responses are as follows:

> Lei: I expect the teacher to do more lecturing (than students' speaking in class). Because we think we come to the classroom to learn, teachers should tell more, and make good preparation.
>
> Yu: I think teachers should tell students everything they know.
>
> Chuan: It is good if the teacher demands us to do many language exercises and asks us to behave well in class. Maybe because I have formed some habit from high school, if the teacher stops to expect something from me and stops demanding me to do something, if she stops checking my progress, I will stop working hard.
>
> Jing: I will try to follow what the teacher has said. I will do what the teacher tells me to do, and if she tells me where I am weak (in language knowledge), I will do more exercises related with that part.
>
> Lili: I think we should follow what the teacher has said (Interview data, 11/2004).

From the above, it can be seen that for these students, it is only natural in a classroom that teacher *is* and *should be* the knowledge provider and authority when they, as students, *should* be the passive knowledge recipients and subordinates to the teacher.

It is not surprising, then, that they have the expectations for a "traditional" classroom, as many language learners expressed in a focus group interview; I here illustrate with Bingchao's statement as it stands for most interviewees' points of views:

> Bingchao: We expect her (Ying) to stand in the front and talk for most of the class time, so that we can sit in our seats, listen to and try to understand what she says. When she asks a question, we answer (Interview data, 12/2004).

Among the students interviewed, only a few expressed their liking for group works and role-plays. On the whole, this group of Chinese students in Ying's classroom are used to being told and taught by their teacher and the classroom routine in a "traditional" classroom- "teacher talks, students listen; teacher asks, students answer". In other words, they prefer low learner control and a structured language learning environment for they perceive this as helping them to achieve high scores in various tests.

5.3.4   Norm of behaviour in Ying's classroom culture

"Interpretation" being the subject taught in Ying's class is considered as an important subject at the School, therefore Ying and her students meet more frequently than many other classes. They meet three times a week, each session lasts two hours, which is divided into two classes with a 10 minutes' break in between. So the contact time between Ying and her students is six hours per week.

149

Many of Ying's lessons can be divided into three parts. The first part of the lesson is "test-related", the middle part of the lesson is "text-related", and the last part "exercise or assignment-related".

It is a routine in Ying's EFL classroom culture that Ying spends the first five or ten minutes of the class time on something relevant to language testing: sometimes she asks her students to do a "translation exercise", which is a component in students' future TEM4 and TEM8 exams; sometimes she summarizes the results of the tests that students have taken in the previous lesson, or comments on the mistakes students have made in these tests. Then she uses a large part of the class time to assiduously explain English grammatical and linguistic knowledge based on the textbook, which is a line-by-line paraphrasing of the text accompanied by students' language drills. The last 10 minutes or so of the lesson is mainly spent on students' exercises or assignments.

The textbook in Ying's classroom is of utmost importance as it is the blueprint for students' final exam in this semester; the two major exams students have to sit-TEM4 and TEM8 are designed to check whether students have grasped the content they are supposed to have learned from their textbooks. Entitled "*College English*", the textbook being used by Ying and her students is co-edited by Chinese and Western EFL educational experts and widely used among tertiary English major students in China. It consists of 16 English articles selected mostly from American literature books and newspapers covering an array of topics such as commentary of current world affairs, excerpts of English drama, and knowledge about American geography and culture. Almost in every class, Ying and her students keep their eyes glued to textbooks with Ying's lectures and instructions revolving around the content of the textbook and the students being preoccupied with textbook-reading and note-taking.

Like in Esther's EFL classroom culture, MOI in Ying's classroom culture is also double-coded. English is the main medium of instruction in this class (roughly around 70% of class talk is in English); Chinese, as the mother tongue shared by Ying and her students, is applied at times for a number of reasons. Sometimes Ying employs Chinese language to assist her instruction and ease students' comprehension; sometimes Ying uses extended lengths of Chinese language in her telling of personal experiences and moral stories. When the students are ignorant of certain target language use, they would occasionally turn to Chinese language in their language output. An inherent reason for the indispensable usage of Chinese language in this classroom culture is because of the subject being taught, for "interpretation" naturally involves the switch of the two codes.

In the aspect of classroom organizations, Ying's classroom is much of the traditional "teacher-fronted" scenario-Ying as the language instructor gives lectures for the majority of class time, her students mostly sit there listening to her lectures except for when they are involved in classroom activities. So for much of the class time, students are seated quietly listening, thinking, and writing.

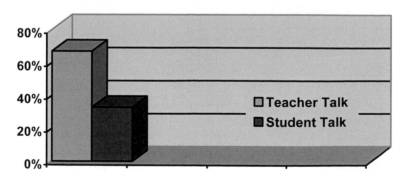

Figure 5.8: Ratio of Teacher Talk to Student Talk in Ying's Classroom

Apart from listening to Ying's lectures and answering her questions, students in Ying's classroom appear to have relatively limited classroom activities. However, when there are times students do participate in certain classroom activities, they show their passion for them and get actively involved. These activities include "classroom drama", "kinestic expression of English words and idioms", "inter-team competitions". In addition, Ying has asked her students to compile portfolios so that they can record their own progress and communicate with their teacher. These classroom activities will be further discussed in the next section.

5.3.5 Interpersonal and textual interactions in Ying's classroom culture

In the three months' life in Ying's classroom culture, the participants have established their interaction patterns. There are two kinds of interactions in Ying's classroom culture-the interpersonal verbal interactions and the textual interactions. Interpersonal verbal interactions are mostly bilateral between the teacher and the students as the two parties involved and as such, they are mainly unidirectional-directed from the teacher to the students. "Textual interactions" is another form of interaction in Ying's classroom culture-there are interactions between the participants and their textbooks or exercise books; there are exchanges of information between the teacher and students via written portfolios.

5.3.5.1 "T-S" bilateral, unidirectional verbal interactions

The dominant pattern of interpersonal verbal interactions in Ying's classroom culture is "T-S" bilateral unidirectional verbal interactions that happen between the teacher and the students, directed from the teacher to the students in teacher's "monologues" and in "T-S" "dialogues".

One characteristic of this EFL classroom culture is the regular occurrence of Ying's long stretches of "monologues" either in English or in Chinese. These monologues can be Ying's instructional speeches, her evaluative feedback and her telling of personal values and life stories.

One occasion for Ying's monologues to occur was when she tried to explain some English language knowledge. Holding the textbook in her hands, Ying read the text sentence by sentence, each sentence was followed by its Chinese translation or English paraphrase. Her verbatim sentence translations were intermittently interrupted by the display questions asked and answered by herself. Apparently, this was a straightforward knowledge transmission process through unidirectional verbal interaction from the teacher to the students. Ying imparted English language knowledge; her students tried to take in what was said by the teacher while they were busily reading their textbooks, hunting for words in their dictionaries, and taking notes. In her delivery of these long talks and the intermittent display questions, Ying means for her students to listen, rather than respond, as shown in her classroom discourse.

Extract 5.2

1	Ying:	(Reading the text): "Don't stare at me!"
2		"Stare at" means "look at somebody because you are,
3		you are surprised, afraid, etc. You are afraid of her,
4		right? So you stare at her. If Lucy Liu gets Oscar
5		Award, what do you say to her? You STARE AT her,
6		and say, "congratulations"! (Ying speaks in Chinese)
7		比如說由於敬佩，吃驚，驚訝，眼睛瞪大了。叫瞪，

8   是嗎？瞪著 (For example, you can "stare at"

9   somebody because you admire him, or you are

10   shocked. You open your eyes wide).

In Line 1, the teacher-Ying first read out loud the line that she was going to address in the text: "Don't stare at me", which was to draw the attention from her language learners. Then she went straight into the explanation of the phrase "stare at". The question "you are afraid of her, right?" in line 3-4 and the question "what do you say to her?" in line 5 were more like "attention attractors" than questions waiting to be answered. Instead of leaving the floor for her students to take the turns and answer the questions she has asked, she answered the questions herself-"you stare at her" in order to exemplify the use of this English idiom. She has further given a Chinese explanation of the phrase to make sure that her students have understood the English idiom completely.

This is an "instructional monologue" that is directed by Ying towards the whole class, and it is a typical example of bilateral, unidirectional "teacher-fronted" verbal interactions.

Ying's monologues can also occur when she gives students evaluative feedback on their assignments or on their exam results. These "evaluative monologues" can be an assessment of the progress and mistakes students have made as well as the bad habits they have formed that need to be got rid of. For example, after the marking of exam papers, Ying initiated an evaluative monologue in which she criticized some students' handwriting and pointed out the importance of calligraphy.

Extract 5.3

Ying: Your English is good, but your writing is not good. That will do you harm someday. When I read your writing, I don't know you, I want your writing to be tidy. As for spelling, I want to check how many of you are exactly familiar with the words...

Sometimes, Ying's monologues are related with her personal values, beliefs and life stories or are the recounting of her language learning experiences, which can arouse the students' interest and attention instantly.

Below is an example of her preaching about "learning social morality" by watching English movies.

Extract 5.4

Ying: I would like you to watch those English classics and some movies in the English original. Those good films can not only help you to improve your English skills, but also teach you how to be a good person in life. As a person, you have to be kind and upright, ready to help other people but criticize those who do harm to our society.

These "instructional monologues", "evaluative monologues" and "preaching monologues" are profuse in Ying's classroom culture and this inevitably yields formal teacher-fronted classroom dynamics.

But establishing and maintaining the patterns of classroom interactions is also a joint venture between the teacher and the students. In Ying's EFL classroom culture, there can also be "dialogues" between her and her students although these dialogues are almost entirely connected with their textbooks and language exercises in "question-and-answer" form. These interactions are still bilateral, but the two parties involved can be the teacher and one student, or between the teacher and the whole class; they are still unidirectional-directed from the teacher to the student(s).

Extract 5.5

(Ying is asking one student some questions prior to the introduction of a new text about American geography)

1 Ying: Where's New England?

2 Lei: In America.

3 Ying: Do you think it is in America?

4 Lei: Yeah.

5 Ying: How many states are there in America?

6 Lei: 50.

These adjacency pairs show that Ying was in complete control of
the topic as she asked information about a region in the United States.
She started the talk and asked to see if the student-Lei had got some
general knowledge of America. When Lei provided the correct answer
in line 2, Ying further challenged Lei to verify if Lei was really certain
about her answer. After Lei showed that she was sure of the information,
Ying shifted the topic from New England's location to the number of
states in America, which Lei answered accordingly.

The procedure for this kind of teacher-student dialogues as demonstrated in Ying's EFL classroom culture is that it's the teacher's task to
interrogate and evaluate; while it is the students' duty to answer. If a
student gives a wrong answer, it's the teacher's duty to supply a correct
one. When there is a communication breakdown and silence appears, the
teacher would fill this void. In strings of utterances between one teacher
and one student like the above, the rest of the class are on-lookers and
listeners. Sometimes, although infrequently, Ying would also invite the
other students to supply an answer to the question she has asked if the
called student can not provide a correct answer.

In these "T-S" bilateral unidirectional verbal interactions, Ying's
students show their preference for "teacher-whole class" interactions

over the "teacher-individual student" interactions; very often they voluntarily provide choral answers to Ying's questions when doing oral exercises. By answering in chorus, those who know the answer to a question teacher has raised can speak up while those who do not know the answer will listen to the others.

> Extract 5.6
>
> (Ying is asking her students questions after their study of a text entitled "Diet"):
>
> 1 Ying: What's the passage about?
> 2 Learners: We should have a healthy diet.
> 3 Ying: Who released the figures?
> 4 Ying &
> 5 Learners: The Health Department.

In these adjacency pairs, it was still the teacher who controlled the topic, asked questions, and initiated interactions. The sequence organization was still teacher's question was followed by students' answer; only this time, the answer was provided by the whole class. In line 4 & 5, the teacher even joined the students to answer her question.

The "T-S" bilateral unidirectional interaction pattern can be illustrated with the figure below:

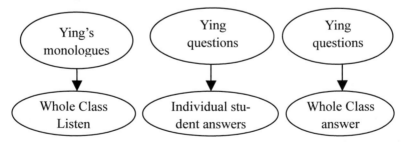

Figure 5.9: Bilateral, Unidirectional Verbal Interactions between Ying and Her Students

It can be seen from the above that in Ying's EFL classroom culture, Ying is the "taken-for-granted" repository of knowledge and appraiser of learners' intellectual performance, and even-the preacher of social morality. The language learners, on the other hand, habitually find comfort in their dependence on Ying, who has got tight control of the content and structure of the EFL classroom education, as some learners expressed in focus group interviews. Below is one learner's comment on how she perceives this kind of classroom dynamics:

> Xinmeng: We are used to accepting what is being taught and obey our teacher's instructions and orders (Interview data, 12/2004).

5.3.5.2 Ying's kinestic approach and learner-learner interactions

An unusual characteristic of Ying's classroom organization is her "kinestic approach" to EFL classroom teaching and this, as it emerges, is much to students' liking. Sometimes although only occasionally, Ying asks her students to "perform the English words and phrases", or divides her students into groups and asks them to "play a drama based on the text". Expressive forms of communication as they are, these kinestic activities have become one constituent of Ying's classroom interactional repertoire and they lead to the occasional learner-learner interactions.

The kinestic activities first include students' bodily "expression" of some English words, phrases or sentences: one or several students are the body language performers, the others are the audience; the performers "act out" words and phrases, the audience "guess out" and "speak out" their meanings. The English words and phrases students perform come from the textbook.

Extract 5.7

(Two students step forward in front of the class, and blink at each other)

1 Ying (toward the class): What are they doing?

2 Learners (laughing and answering in chorus): "Exchanging looks".

In this extract, there were learner-learner nonverbal interactions as the two students performed the words in front of the class while their fellow classmates tried to make sense of what they were doing. "Exchanging looks" was the English phrase the learners wanted to express through their body language and it turned out that the students did get to know what they were trying to express from their body language. Here the teacher was only a mediator to let the language learners make sense of the two performers' actions, it was the language learners who were acting, thinking, speaking, and interacting.

Drama is another form of kinestic activity in Ying's classroom culture. Based on the adapted drama scripts in their textbooks, students improvise and rehearse outside the classroom before they play on stage in the classroom when they interact with exaggerated actions, gestures, and dialogues. After a drama performance, the actors and actresses go back to their seats cheerfully, the audience give them a heated applause, amongst which the teacher shows her appreciation with some positive and encouraging comment.

Extract 5.8 (Drama script is in Appendix 10)

(A group of students change into their drama costumes and go to the front of the class; the "drama" is about how a special agent has managed to cover his true identity and get rid of his killer. "Ausable" is the special agent and "Max" is the killer in the drama played by two female students)

...

"Ausable": I'm angry. This is the second time that somebody broke into my room through the balcony.

"Max": No, I have the door key, I don't know about the balcony. Please sit down.

"Ausable": I wish.. (someone knocks at the door)

"Max": What's that? Who's at the door? I'll shoot. Or I'll take my chances.

"Ausable": Well, if I do not open the door, police will enter. (The door knob turns.)

"Max": Argggggggh!

(The student who plays Max pretends that she "falls from the balcony" by jumping down a chair in front of the class. The door is opened. A "waiter" is holding a tray with bottles of water)(Students burst into laughter)

The improvised dramas like this have fuelled excitement among the classroom participants. At moments like this, the EFL classroom has become a stage for action; language learning is a pedagogical as well as an entertaining event. There are both verbal and nonverbal interactions involved in these drama plays which are chiefly between and among the language learners, while the teacher is at first one in the audience watching the drama and later a commentator on students' performance.

Kinestic activities as such in Ying's classroom culture have helped to bring language learning to life and enhanced participants' interpersonal interactions, especially those between and among learners.

5.3.5.3   Participants' interactions with text

In Ying's EFL classroom culture, "test" has become an omnipresent theme, which leads to the fact that learners are in constant interaction with texts in their textbooks and test papers.

Since the tests including the TEM4, TEM8 and students' finals are without exception based on the textbooks, the textbooks have become the exclusive reference source of almost all of the classroom talks and classroom activities that Ying and her students involve. Not only are classroom activities related with textbooks, students' assignments after class are also associated with textbooks.

The teacher's and students' heavy reliance on textbooks results in a form of interaction-the "textual interaction" that is largely ignored in SLA research literature when the previous researchers mainly investigate the link between participants' verbal interactions and their linguistic development (see Section 3.1).

In the reading of textbooks and in the paraphrasing of certain English expressions and idioms, learners are interacting with the text when they try to comprehend the target language knowledge and incorporate this into their own knowledge system. In addition, in doing exercises and exams, learners are "interacting" with texts when they try to understand the testing items in English and rummage through their English linguistic knowledge in order to find the right knowledge patch to complete the test papers.

The textual interactions in Ying's classroom culture also embrace teacher-learner communication via the portfolios, in which the students are given the chance to act or speak for themselves.

5.3.5.4 Beyond the pedagogical hierarchy of teacher- fronted interactions

With the predominance of bilateral, unidirectional verbal interactions between the teacher and the learners that are directed from the teacher to the learners, Ying's EFL classroom culture may seem to show a pedagogical hierarchy characterized with asymmetric power relationship between the teacher and the learners. However, the portfolio project that Ying has launched makes possible the one-to-one communication between the teacher and the individual language learners on a more or less equal footing, only this teacher-learner's one-to-one communication is realized through participants' interactions via the text. Ying's aim for launching this portfolio project is to develop learner autonomy in her classroom, which she endorses and is also advocated by the School (see Sections 5.1 and 5.3.3.1).

Bearing in mind that certain cultural traits might restrain or assist the development of learner autonomy (Ho & Crookall, 1995), the challenge for educators is to create a learning structure which enables them to do this (Murray, 1999). How can these Chinese students progress from being recipients of language learning to owners of language learning? The teacher has an important role to play in helping learners to realize that they too must take responsibility for their learning. The learning structure to promote learner autonomy and teacher-learner interaction in Ying's EFL classroom culture takes a subtle form in written text through portfolios.

An artist's portfolio may contain a record of the different types of work created –a range of drawings or paintings over time, and provides a comprehensive picture of his or her capabilities, strengths, and weaknesses. In many pedagogical situations, portfolio is part of an alternative assessment programme that documents the students' learning process; others use it as a means of promoting learner reflection (Nunes, 2004).

A portfolio in Ying's classroom culture is a collection of students' written works, students' self-reflexive remarks, and the teacher' comments that are put in loose-leaf binders. These written works include students' assignments, test papers, written exercises, and their informal journal entries. Students' remarks include their reflections on their own progress and achievement, the questions they have about certain linguistic knowledge, their suggestions on class organization and activities. Teachers comments are usually the answers to students remarks or suggestions for the students as to how they can make further progress in their language learning.

The students hand in their portfolios to Ying once a week. After some scrutinized read, Ying would write down her response to students' remarks and give students her suggestions for their further progress. Then after these portfolios are sent back to the students and they have learned what is said by the teacher in their portfolios, Ying would sometimes openly make a synthesis of solutions to students' problems and suggestions for students' progress in class. In this manner the portfolios have served as a bond between Ying and her students, reifying and reinforcing the reciprocity of interaction they would otherwise not achieve in the classroom. In the communications with their teacher via portfolios, students are compelled to be introspective and reflexive on their own work and progress.

The following is a sample of "T-S" bilateral bidirectional interactions via portfolios:

> Sample 1:
> (After the display of a dictation exercise which has been marked by the teacher, the student and the teacher have written down the following remarks and comments)

Chuan   (reflects on his own deficiency in doing dictation exercises): I've got difficulty in getting to know what the title of the passage is, and I can't understand the meaning of the whole passage.

Ying   (makes suggestions accordingly): Then you'll have to analyze the cause of this problem-is it because of the long sentence structure of the title, or is it because of the new vocabulary in it?

Sample 2:
(One student made a suggestion for English drama competition in her portfolio, and Ying has given her response)

Yu: Can we have an English drama competition sometime in this semester? I love drama plays in our class, so I think it will be very interesting if we can organize a competition of our drama plays in English.

Ying: Of course we can, I will discuss with the whole class about this when we have time.

In these portfolio communications, students can have their say on their own progress and sometimes although less frequently on their class organization. Their voices are heard by the teacher and their questions are replied by the teacher. These participants' interactions via the text enable the teacher to get to know the individual student's preferences, merits, deficiencies and progress. The students take the initiative in this two-way communication and their opinions count when they remark on the class content, their favourite form of class activities and dislike to other activities for they can make Ying reflect on and adjust her design of the class.

Ying: I believe this (Portfolio) is a very good communication process between the students and me because
they can write down their thoughts and I write down
mine in the portfolios before we talk about them and
exchange our ideas in the class. When reading their
remarks, I can think about how to make my class better and make them progress faster (Interview data,
12/2004).

Judging from the evidence available so far, the answer to the question
"Is Ying's classroom an authoritarian classroom culture?" should be both
"yes and no". The answer is "yes" because teacher authority remains important for classroom discipline and control of the classroom activities, and
the Chinese teacher has a strong moral responsibility to guide students on
the right path (Watkins & Biggs, 1999). The answer is "no" because the
in-class kinestic activities enhance learner-learner interactions and promote
interactional symmetry; additional teacher-learner communications via
portfolios generate "democratic communications" between the teacher and
the learners which also contribute to the promotion of symmetrical
teacher-learner relationship.

Taken as a whole, in Ying's EFL classroom culture, Ying is under
the influence of educational tradition while keeping an open mind to
innovation; the goal of Ying's classroom culture is to achieve students'
excellence in academic tests. Besides participants' interpersonal interactions in verbal and nonverbal forms, there are "textual interactions" in
Ying's classroom culture. "Teacher-fronted" classroom interactions still
predominate, although learners' peer interactions are enhanced in the
kinestic activities. Moreover, participants' interactions via portfolios
create a learning structure that is for promoting learner autonomy and
democratic teaching and learning.

The juxtaposition of these two EFL classroom cultures in this chapter has revealed two different classroom cultural lives. Situated in the same institution and similar physical settings, these two EFL classroom cultures have different participants with dissimilar demographic and dispositional features and are targeted at different pedagogical goals. The most conspicuous difference between the two is one being highly participatory with overt verbal interpersonal interactions, while the other being distinctly teacher-fronted with less learner-learner verbal interactions but more textual interactions. Given that much research literature posits the positive correlation between verbal interactions in the language classrooms and the production of learning opportunities, one might assume that Esther's communicative classroom is more successful in the construction of language learning opportunities than Ying's teacher-fronted classroom.

However, this is not the case in the current study for both EFL classroom cultures have been found to be favourable for the construction of learning opportunities and both classroom cultures are considered as positive for language learning in learners' views. In the next chapter, I am going to use these two classroom cultures to expound on the relationship between classroom interactions, EFL classroom cultures and the construction of learning opportunities.

Chapter 6

EFL Classroom Cultures and the Construction of Learning Opportunities

So far, I have described the cultural characteristics of the two EFL classrooms under study. In this chapter, I will describe how learning opportunities are constructed in these two EFL classroom cultures. I have found that despite the notable cultural differences in the two EFL classrooms, language learners in either classroom feel settled and genuinely believe they can garner bountiful learning opportunities for language learning. Cultural characteristics that contribute to the construction of learning opportunities in the two EFL classrooms include the congruence of participants' perceptions, the teachers' language learning experiences and the use of learners' native language in MOI in both EFL classrooms. Although these two classroom cultures are very different in their classroom interaction patterns, these interactions are found to be beneficial for the construction of learning opportunities by the learners in both classrooms. In the last part of the chapter, I extend my theoretical framework regarding the construction of learning opportunities and explain the "types" of learning opportunities that I have found.

6.1 Congruence of participants' perceptions and learning opportunity

The two EFL classroom cultures sometimes demonstrate very different features: one is comprised of a British teacher and a group of Chinese students who are oriented towards a participatory language classroom, the other is comprised of a Chinese teacher and a group of Chinese students working for students' academic excellence in exams and their competitiveness in the future job market; one is characterized with high interactivity in interpersonal verbal interactions while the other has both verbal and textual interactions with teacher-fronted interaction as the dominant interaction pattern.

If verbal interaction is an important standard we use to judge whether or not an EFL classroom culture is rich in language learning opportunities, then it should be said that of the two EFL classroom cultures, Esther's EFL classroom culture offers far more learning opportunities than Ying's. But the truth is-participants in either EFL classroom culture are willing to sustain their classroom cultural characteristics because they perceive their classroom culture to be beneficial for the construction of learning opportunities. An important reason for this is that the teachers' and their learners' perceptions regarding classroom language teaching and learning are very much in congruence.

In the two EFL classrooms, the two teachers-a British teacher and a Chinese teacher differ most noticeably in their pedagogical outlook and ideology that lead to different classroom practices. There seems to be a clear contrast between Esther's and Ying's EFL teaching approaches, which is in line with the observation Cortazzi and Jin (1996) made regarding Western and Chinese language teaching approaches: the former tends to emphasize on communication skills in English language, student-centred classrooms and the process of learning, the latter tends to emphasize on the content of English knowledge, teacher-centred class-rooms and exam results.

The two groups of Chinese students, a group of "atypical" Chinese students in Esther's class and a group of freshmen Chinese students in Ying's class also show different attitudes towards language teaching and learning, which correspond with their teachers' perceptions as for how language teaching and learning should be carried out.

Comparatively speaking, Ying's EFL classroom seems to be less interactive than Esther's because Ying appears to be occupying an authoritarian and didactic position in her classroom culture. She tries to deliver knowledge to her students based on the textbook and guide them to learn "how to learn", which reinforces her didactic role in the class-room. Ying believes that what she is doing is in the best interest of her learners for their common goal-to achieve good results in academic tests.

> Ying: Some people think that "communicative" means "interactive", I don't think that is the real meaning for CLT. We should emphasize on the substance taught. I have to try to give them (students) as much information as I can in class, we have a textbook and I have to complete the task of explaining the texts and let them (students) understand the texts, so that they can achieve good scores in exams, so I have do the talking for most of the time (Interview data, 12/2004).

And this is exactly what her learners have expected and hoped for. Below is a summary of learners' perceptions as they expressed in a focus group interview with respect to how they expect their teacher to teach and how they think they can achieve good learning.

Learners: We expect the teacher to do more lecturing (than our talking). Because we think we come here to learn, teachers should tell more, and make good preparation. If we want to get good scores in exams, we have to depend on our teachers' talks (Adapted from interview data, 12/2004).

Ying's pedagogical beliefs and learners' expectations contribute to the construction of an EFL classroom culture that is dominated by teacher-fronted bilateral, unidirectional verbal interactions, as I have presented in Section 5.3.5.1. But learners give these teacher-fronted interactions welcome rather than rejection for they behold that these interactions have advantages over learner-learner interactions for language learning. Learners believe that these teacher-fronted interactions can ensure that a large amount of information or language knowledge is transferred from the teacher to them within the limited class time. In other words, they believe these teacher-fronted interactions in their classroom culture offer learning opportunities for them; some learners even regard expatriate teachers' classes as a waste of time for all their outward interactivity:

Wei: I don't think there is anything wrong with the teacher being authoritarian and doing the talking for much of the class time, I think this way I can get more English language knowledge from her.

Zhen: Our class time is limited; she can give us a lot of information in this time.

Xiaoxue: Actually I think our class is interactive, and I do feel I learn a lot from her class.

Hong: I prefer her class over an expatriate teacher's class, I think an expatriate teacher's class is a waste of

> time, I can't learn anything "practical" (Interview
> data, 12/2004).

The other group of Chinese learners who are under an expatriate teacher's teaching are also happy with the expatriate teacher's instruction for they generally believe what Esther has to offer is what they want out of an expatriate teacher's class. Both parties in Esther's EFL classroom adopt a favourable attitude toward participation in the language classroom.

Esther, with her communication-centred educational ideology, makes every effort to create opportunities for her language learners to communicate.

> Esther: The purpose for them (students) to learn English is to
> communicate in English. They rarely have chances to
> talk with native speakers of English, so I have to ask
> them to speak and practise their oral skills in class,
> and I try to involve everyone of them, even the quiet
> ones (Interview data, 12/2004).

Esther's perceptions find their resonance in the language learners' beliefs as they perceive opportunities for communication and participation in the EFL classroom to be learning opportunities:

> Alice: Because communication opportunity with a native
> speaker is really rare here, I would like to take up
> every chance I can get to talk in Esther's class.
> Cathy: I am wiling to talk a lot in Esther's class so that I can
> practise my English (Interview data, 12/2004).

The congruence of participants' perceptions of what a language classroom should be like, what a learning opportunity is and how language learning is achieved is also shown through their attitude toward error-corrections in the two EFL classroom cultures. Both teachers believe error-corrections are opportunities for the learners to solidify their language knowledge and to avoid further mistakes of the same kind, which coincide with learners' conceptions of error-corrections.

In Ying's classroom, Ying considers it necessary to correct the learners' mistakes immediately after they have made them to achieve accuracy in the learners' future language output.

> Ying: Linguistic mistakes should be corrected immediately after being committed; or else, my students won't notice them and remember the correct expressions, especially this is the starting point of their university life, it is wrong to leave them there (Interview data, 12/2004).

Regardless of their usual fear of "losing face" in the public, when being asked if they mind their mistakes being corrected in front of their classmates, the Chinese language learners in Ying's classroom show a positive attitude toward error-correction and understand well Ying's expectations, some of them even think this is a motivating force for them to progress.

> Tingting: She (Ying) IS strict with us, and she has high expectations towards us. For me, I need some pressure on myself, so that I can make it my motivating force. Maybe because I have formed a habit from high school learning, if the teacher stops demanding me to do the correct thing, or she stops checking my progress, I will stop working hard. I will just relax, and wait and then leave it aside.

Linsong: I hope that she can correct me immediately after I make a mistake, so that I can remember where I am wrong, and do not make the same mistake again (Interview data, 12/2004).

In Esther's class, the teacher and the learners also perceive error-corrections as learning opportunities for the learners.

Esther: I have to correct some mistakes that they are likely to make very often such as the use of gender and tense, so that they can communicate without causing confusion (Interview data, 12/2004).

Below is a summary of learners' points of views regarding error corrections in Esther's class as they expressed in a focus group interview:

Learners: The more mistakes she (Esther) corrects, the better; so that we won't make the same mistakes again. It is an opportunity for us to remember the mistakes and avoid making them again (Adapted from interview data, 12/2004).

Nonetheless, participants' perceptions cannot always be in congruence between the teacher and the language learners. When learners don't perceive a learning opportunity as perceived by their teacher, the "learning opportunity" offered by the teacher may lose its pedagogical value and may not in fact be a learning opportunity because the learners will dismiss it as something non-essential for their language learning.

What is worse, the continuing existence of divergence in participants' perceptions may act as a hindrance for the progress of classroom culture and learners' language learning. Learners can give the impression of experiencing frustration and disinclination to work to their full capacity when their agenda is felt to be in conflict with the one imposed by their teacher's (Graham, 1997). For the smooth progress of learners' learning, the teacher has to negotiate with the learners' classroom performance and make compromises should discrepancies in perceptions occur. This can be illustrated with the different perceptions held by participants regarding the benefits of pair work for language learning in Esther's classroom culture.

Allegedly, pair work provides scaffolding and feedback at precisely the point when it will be most useful (Boyle, 2000) and enables language learners to receive adjusted input and to provide adjusted output when needed (Damhuis, 2000). The British teacher Esther has held the same opinion as the above for she thought that pair work could give her Chinese students learning opportunities in need. At the very beginning of the classroom culture formation, Esther has believed that pair work would be a good classroom activity for learners to practise their oral English and offer practice opportunities for her language learners.

> Esther: Well, I think when they (students) speak in pairs, they can listen to each other, and become more critical. Because obviously when I speak, they assume what I am speaking is accurate. But if they listen to somebody who is speaking English as a foreign language, they have to listen discriminately and critically at the same time so that they could improve (their language abilities) (Interview data, 11/2004).

But her Chinese learners' conception of pair work is very different from hers and they don't consider pair work to be conducive for their language learning because they don't trust the accuracy in their partners' English expressions or because the partners' linguistic capability involved in pair works are unequal.

> Heather: When doing pair work, because she (partner) is better than me (in English), I have to keep silent most of the time while she is talking, and the dialogue can become a monologue. I feel I can't learn anything out of pair work except letting the other person practise all the time (Interview data, 11/2004).
>
> Melinda: There are times when neither of us know how to express in English, and the way she (partner) puts it, I am not sure if that is correct or not (Interview data, 11/2004).
>
> Learners: We don't think we can learn much from pair works, for we (partners in pair works) are both language learners, very often our partners can't point out the mistakes and they often make the same mistakes, too (Adapted from focus group interview data, 12/2004).

This divergence between Esther's perception of pair work and the language learners' resulted in the learners' evasions of such activities when being asked to do so. When assigned pair works, the Chinese language learners would sometimes strike up a chat in Chinese language in the class as Esther found out later, to which Esther has given her attention and she has made adjustments in her classroom organization.

> Esther: When I found that these learners often slip into informal chat in Chinese when asked to do pair

works, I started to give them more individual presentations and group discussions, and that has worked well (Interview with Esther, 12/2004).

Meanwhile in Ying's class, there is no pair work at all, as one language learner remarked:

Yu: Our conversation in English is very restricted because of our insufficiency in English vocabulary, so we can only use very limited English to express our meaning. When neither of us can put what we want to say in English words, it is very frustrating and we are unwilling to continue doing pair works. Our teacher knows this so she won't let us do pair work (Interview data, 12/2004).

When I was doing participant observation in the first couple of weeks of my field work, I have noticed that pair work indeed very often ended up with one student's monologues or students' dialogues in Chinese in Esther's class and there was no pair work in Ying's classroom culture. Under the circumstances in the current study, pair work has been regarded as defective by the language learners for they don't perceive and experience it as providing much learning opportunities.

It can be said then that in an EFL classroom culture, if there is congruence of participants' perceptions regarding classroom language teaching and learning, there is the tendency that the classroom environment is favourable for the construction of learning opportunities. If there is great discrepancy between the teacher's and learners' perceptions, then the language classroom and the activities or interactions that happen in it might not be beneficial for the construction of learning opportunities.

Therefore, to understand the construction of learning opportunities in an EFL classroom culture, an emic knowledge of what a learning opportunity means for the language learners is essential. Learners have their parts to play in the construction of learning opportunities with their teachers; the learners can be said to be the legitimate judges as for whether a classroom interaction pattern or a classroom activity is a learning opportunity for them that is conducive for their language learning.

The figure below illustrates the relationship between the congruence and discrepancy of participants' perceptions, and the construction of learning opportunities (dotted lines indicate uncertain link).

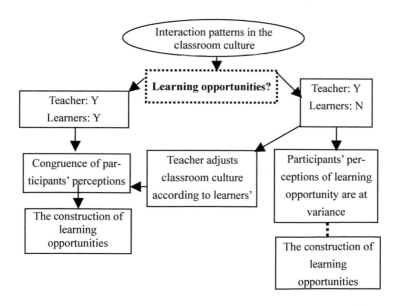

Figure 6.1:   Participants' Perceptions and the Construction of Learning Opportunities

As illustrated above, when there is congruence between teacher's and learners' perceptions of learning opportunities regarding certain classroom interactions, learning opportunities can be constructed; when there is variance between teacher's and learners' perceptions of certain classroom interactions, the construction of learning opportunities is hampered or might not occur.

In the two EFL classroom cultures in the current study, there is congruence between the teachers' and their learners' perceptions regarding language classroom dynamics, goals of language learning, and how language learning should be achieved. The construction of learning opportunities is therefore greatly promoted, which might facilitate learners' language learning process.

6.2 "Language learner" teachers and learners' learning opportunity

As I have revealed in the demographic features of the two EFL classroom cultures, both teachers in these two classrooms have a dual identity- they are foreign language teachers as well as foreign language learners. Esther is a "Chinese-as-a-foreign-language" learner; Ying is an "English-as-a-foreign-language" learner. In this study, it has been found that the teachers' language learning experiences have contributed to the construction of learning opportunities.

Ying's learning strategies that she has gleaned from her years of language learning experiences have made it possible for the construction of a type of learning opportunity that facilitates learners' language learning process-a type of learning opportunity that makes the learners get to know how to learn. Ying's and Esther's language learning experiences have enabled them to sometimes make comparison and contrast of the two language systems in class, which engenders a type of learning opportunity that brings learners' attention to the understanding of the target language. As such, the benefits of these learning opportunities for language learners have gone beyond what a particular lesson or a particular piece of text can offer for them.

In Ying's class, Ying would always convey to her students some of the learning strategies that she has summarized from her language learning experiences. In one episode of her class, Ying recommended to the language learners that listening to tapes and recording their own voices were good ways of learning English.

> Extract 6.1
> Ying: One of the most effective ways of studying English is to listen to tapes, as you listen and repeat, you read the text, listen to your own voice. You can record your own voice. I've seen many students reading outside, but if you record your voice, it will work much better. My point here is through recording yourself, you will become more interested (in learning English), because your voice sounds very different on the tape. Recording is very effective in learning English.

In another episode, Ying recalled her language learning experience when she was a university student and introduced to her students that reading and listening to English in the original could improve their sensitivity to English language use.

> Extract 6.2
> Ying: I still remember when we were at university, we used to read a lot (of English materials in the original) and listen to a lot of English radio programmes, so that we

could develop sensitivity to the genuine usage of English idioms.

Ying's introduction of personal language learning strategies in her students' eyes is beneficial for their language learning as students have expressed in focus group interviews. One of the students in the group said:

> Lei: I think her introduction of learning strategies is very, very useful. She is an excellent teacher, and her English is very good. I believe her strategies are beneficial for our learning, and I have tried some which have worked for me (Interview data, 12/2004).

While Ying's English learning experiences have been helpful in the construction of learning opportunities for language learners to learn "how to learn", Esther's Chinese learning experience is invaluable for her classroom language teaching and her students' language learning as discussed below.

Esther's knowledge of Chinese language has become an aid for her instruction of English language, which I will further discuss in the next section. What her Chinese language learning experience has brought for the language learners is her anticipation for and empathy of their possible errors in English usage; more importantly, her comparison of the two language systems has brought learners' conscious attention to the understanding of the form of English language.

In the following extract, Esther is trying to explain the denotation of relatives in the English language.

Extract 6.3
1 Ether: How do you distinguish your grandparents in English?
2   Which word do you use when you describe your
3   father's father (Students are thinking)?

4　Esther:　You can say PATERNAL.

5　Learners (in chorus): Paternal.

6　Esther:　or MATERNAL. Or you can say "on my mothers

7　　　　　　side", or "on my father's side".

8　　　　　　For example, you can say my maternal aunt or my

9　　　　　　aunt on my mother's side.

10　　　　　When you use Chinese (to speak of a relative), it's

11　　　　　so complicated. I will forget how to address a relative

12　　　　　five minutes after my husband has told me the Chinese

13　　　　　word (Students laugh).

When Esther asked about the English expressions for one's "father's father", she expected the language learners to take the turn and answer her question. But the language learners kept silence simply because they did not know the expression. So Esther provided the answer "paternal", which was an input opportunity for the language learners because she has acquainted her students with an English word that was new to them (Line 4). Then without Esther's invitation, the learners voluntarily advanced a practice opportunity for themselves with mimicry of the word (Line 5). Esther then continued the explanation of "maternal", which was another input opportunity for the learners. Further, she drew learners' attention to the differences between Chinese and English language systems. Unlike the use of "maternal" or "paternal" to denote relatives on one's mother's side or father's side in English, there are different words to denote different relatives in Chinese language. The comparison of the two language systems has drawn language learners' attention to the understanding of the English expression in question.

　　Similar comparison of English and Chinese languages can be found in Esther's explanation of the use of English tenses. Since Chinese is a language that does not have tense differentiations and verb variations, the Chinese language learners tend to overlook or mess up the use of tenses in English. Esther frequently brings this up in her classes with a comparison of the two language systems, so that the learners in her classroom can be aware of the importance of tenses in English and make efforts to grasp their usage.

> Extract 6.4
>
> Esther: You have to be very careful about the tenses. They are a very important part of my language (English). In Chinese, you don't have to change the verbs to tell the time, because you can usually tell from the context. But in English, you have to pay attention to the usage of tenses. When you are speaking Chinese, it doesn't really change, right? There is no tense change, so it means that when you are speaking English, you use the present tense all the time (students laughing). But in English, it's WRONG, you CAN'T. When English speakers learn Chinese, they try to put it into English as well, so we'd like to use tense (teacher smiling). So it's a real problem. A big problem. So while people speak Chinese, I just can't understand. When is it that you are talking about? Is it now, or you know, is it past? Because everything is without tense. There are many differences (between English and Chinese).

What have the language learners made of this constant comparison between Chinese and English systems then? Once a student in Esther's class has made such comment on the benefits of Esther's Chinese knowledge and learning experience for her and her classmates' language learning:

Jane: She (Esther) is very clear as for when we'll get con-
        fused, where we won't understand, she can point out
        very easily, and she can relate this with Chinese so
        that we feel it very beneficial in that way (Interview
        data, 12/2004).

Speaking of why she could have such anticipation, Esther reasoned:

Esther: I think probably because I have the knowledge of
         Chinese customs and Chinese language, and Chinese
         is a foreign language to me, so I've got the learning
         experience and know where students are more in-
         clined to produce the incorrect form of English lan-
         guage under the influence of their mother tongue (In-
         terview data, 12/2004).

With her Chinese learning experience, Esther could have the anticipation for learners' mistakes and make clarification of differences
between the two language systems. The opportunities for learners to pay
attention to and understand the form of English language are hereby
constructed in these comparisons and clarifications.

It can also be seen from the above extracts taken out of Ying's and
Esther's EFL classroom cultures that the concept of "learning opportunity" does not only refer to the essential "input" opportunity and "output" opportunity for language learning; it can also be linked with the
opportunity for learners to develop an understanding of the target language, as well as the opportunity for learners to develop their language
learning skills.

Below I am going to further expand the implications of teachers'
language learning experiences for their classroom culture organization

and the construction of learning opportunities. One of the characteristics of the two EFL classroom cultures is that the MOI is coded in both English and Chinese (see Sections 5.2.4 and 5.3.4), and this has been found to contribute to the construction of learning opportunities.

6.3 Double-coded MOI and learning opportunity

It is a common feature shared by the two EFL classroom cultures that the medium of instruction is double-coded: Chinese language has been used as an ancillary tool for the instruction of English language knowledge. Through the analysis of my observation and interview data, it is found that the proportionate use of Chinese language in these two EFL classroom cultures have helped the construction of learning opportunities for the language learners.

Since many English language learners in China yearn for a "genuine language environment" (take learners in Esther's classroom for example) in which English language is spoken all the time, it may be worth questioning why the combined use of English and Chinese in class is much appreciated and deemed as conductive to the construction of learning opportunities by language learners in the two EFL classroom cultures.

To start with, for EFL learners at certain level, it may be counter-productive to apply English as the medium of instruction for 100% of the class time. For example, language learners at the beginning level may not be able to make much sense of a genuine English learning environment. If English is used throughout the class irrespective of the learners' stock of the target language knowledge, then the side effect of this "pure English environment" might show up-learners may feel overwhelmed and anxiety may result. The input of the target language may not even be reckoned to be learning opportunity per se, as a language learner in Esther's classroom remarked on his frustration experienced in another expatriate teacher's language class:

> John: In Craig's (another expatriate teacher at the School) class, he talks too fast and he seems not concerned about whether we understand or not, but simply keeps on talking all the time. At first, I tried very hard to understand what he says, but after some time, I simply feel very frustrated and would rather read my textbook than listen to his talking (Interview data, 12/2004).

The prerequisite for the spontaneity of target language expression is that learners have to have sufficient knowledge of the target language including grammatical, lexical, and phonological knowledge about the target language. But before the language learners reach spontaneous output of the target language, they have to depend on their mother tongue as a language aid or a reference point.

The native language of foreign language learners has always had a role in the learners' language learning process. It is a highly significant system on which learners rely to predict the target language system and this native language system can exercise both facilitating and interfering (positive and negative transfer) effects on the production and comprehension of the target language (Brown, 2002). The constant comparison and contrast between the forms, meanings and structures of their first language and those of the target language can actually be seen as part of learners' language learning process.

In the two EFL classroom cultures in which learners are at intermediate level and pre-intermediate level, the use of Chinese language as a medium of instruction in the two EFL classroom cultures has been proved to be extremely useful. It helps the construction of opportunities for learners to develop the target language knowledge and skills, and opportunities for learners to develop an understanding of the target language form and structure.

When the teachers in the two EFL classroom cultures use Chinese to clarify the meaning of English word or phrases through verbatim translation, they have generated the "input opportunities" for the learners as shown through the following extracts. In Esther's classroom, sometimes Esther could even use the local Chinese dialect to explain certain English word.

> Extract 6.5
> Esther:　"Chat" means "嘮嗑" ("嘮嗑" is pronounced as Laoke, it is the equivalent of "chat" in local Chinese dialect).
> Learners (Laugh and repeat the word in chorus): Chat.

Here Esther explained the English word "chat" in the local Chinese dialect, which has sparked students' burst of laughter for they found it interesting for their expatriate teacher to teach English using Chinese explanation, especially this Chinese explanation has been in the local Chinese dialect. But Esther's use of the Chinese equivalent for the English word "chat" was precise so that the learners in her classroom have understood its meaning immediately and they were willing to initiate a practice opportunity for themselves-they repeated the word in chorus voluntarily after their laughter.

As the participant observer, I found Esther's use of Chinese to explain English to be a distinctive feature of this EFL classroom culture, and a feature that helps with the construction of learning opportunities.

> I am surprised to find that Esther can even explain English word in the local Chinese dialect. I haven't experienced any

expatriate teacher's language instruction to be assisted with the use of Chinese. As a language learner, I would say this is really helpful for my understanding of the English word. Although "chat" is only a simple word, Esther's Chinese explanation of the word can surely help me to remember and understand this word instantly. Besides, I like her use of the Chinese language in classroom instruction; it is so interesting and exciting to observe this (Researcher's field notes, 12/2004).

In Ying's classroom, very often Ying would give a literal translation of the English word or sentence so that her language learners can get to know its exact meaning.

Extract 6.6
Ying (reading from the text): "Anytime you want me to come, say the word." (In Chinese) 你想我什么時候回來, 吱一聲.
(Students are busy taking notes)

Here she also used the local Chinese dialect to help with her explanation and the language learners' understanding of the English expression "say the word", which might be seen as an input learning opportunity.

Besides, there are examples to show that both teachers have tried to eliminate or diminish the "negative transfer" of mother tongue in these learners' language learning. One good example of this is Esther's illustration of tenses which are used in the English language system but do not exist in the Chinese language system, as I have shown in Extract 6.4. Likewise, Ying constantly makes her learners notice the differences between the two language systems in class:

Extract 6.7

Ying: To address people, you have to put the title before the name (in English); this is opposite to Chinese expressions. For example, you have to say "Mr. President" 總統先生 in English, instead of "President Mr" 先生總統 as in Chinese. The structure of English is very different from that of Chinese, and you have to pay attention to those differences to avoid mistakes.

In this extract, Ying has explicitly created the possibility for language learners to develop their conscious understanding of the structure of the target language through the illustration of different ways of addressing people in the two language systems.

Regarding the usage of Chinese as an ancillary tool for the instruction of English language, the teachers reasoned:

Esther: I think in language teaching, no matter what approach a teacher uses, it will inevitably involve translation from one language into another to some degree.

Ying: I don't think my students can get rid of the influence of their mother tongue-Chinese language at this stage. If I don't give them a clear and accurate explanation in Chinese regarding some English vocabulary and language use, they won't be able to know the English knowledge by themselves (Interview data, 12/2004).

Learners in both EFL classroom cultures have considered the use of Chinese as being beneficial for their English language learning.

In Esther's classroom, learners observed:

Echo: We have been taught by some other expatriate teachers who don't know Chinese, so sometimes we are

　　　　　　　　not clear what they are talking about. Esther can tell
　　　　　　　　us the exact meaning in Chinese for some phrases,
　　　　　　　　almost everything is crystal clear.

Vivien:　　We really hope the other expatriate teachers can learn
　　　　　　　　some Chinese. It will be very good for us in lessons
　　　　　　　　(Interview data, 12/2004).

In Ying's classroom, a language learner-Jing expressed:

Jing:　　　If she (Ying) uses Chinese to explain some English
　　　　　　　　words that we find it hard to understand, it saves a lot
　　　　　　　　of our time and we can remember the new English
　　　　　　　　words easily (Interview data, 12/2004).

　　The combined use of the target language and the native language as media of language instructions in the two EFL classrooms has become a classroom cultural characteristic that is advantageous for the construction of learning opportunities for language learners in this study. But a word of caution would be that when native language is used as an aid to English language instruction, it has to be ancillary and cannot overshadow the instruction of English language in class for too much turning back to the native language system might also cause language learners to be reliant on their native language and deprive them of the exposure to the target language knowledge.

　　In addition, although we can't expect all expatriate teachers to have the knowledge of Chinese language like Esther does, it can be concluded that the knowledge of the language learners' native language, if used appropriately, can surely be valuable in one's EFL language instruction and contribute to the construction of learning opportunities in the language classroom.

The two EFL classroom cultures share some commonalities that are conducive to the construction of learning opportunities as I have discussed above. But interaction, as a key component of the classroom culture, is expressed in different forms and various patterns in the two classroom cultures. Whereas in Esther's EFL classroom culture, interactions are mainly "verbal" between and among the participants; in Ying's EFL classroom culture, there are "verbal" as well as "textual" interactions. The forms of interactions in these two EFL classroom cultures vary. But one thing is definite for the two classroom cultures: both groups of learners are satisfied with the interactions they are involved in and find learning opportunities are constructed in them.

Below I am going to discuss the interrelationship between interactions and the construction of learning opportunities in Esther's classroom culture followed by the discussion of that in Ying's classroom culture.

6.4 Interaction in Esther's classroom culture and learning opportunity

As I have revealed in Chapter 5, Esther's EFL classroom culture is characterised with high interactivity in interpersonal verbal interactions. A large part of the class time is devoted to learner-centred verbal interactions in learners' individual presentations and group works; these interpersonal verbal interactions in class are complemented with extracurricular communications after class between Esther and her learners and among the learners themselves. Through these interactions, extended input and output learning opportunities are constructed and uti- lized. Learning opportunities are also found to be constructed in the significantly less teacher-fronted interactions in Esther's talks.

6.4.1 Esther's talk and learning opportunity

Esther sometimes talks at length about her personal life experiences and tells stories about British people and culture.

> Extract 6.8
>
> Esther: In my country, there were two very popular TV series. They were called *Absolutely Fabulous*. They were very very popular in my country. There were two women who were main actresses. Absolutely Fabulous was about two middle-aged women who wanted to be very fashionable and they wanted to relate to young people. They wanted to bridge the generation gap. They were very very fashionable. They were so fashionable that they were "mutton dressed as lamb".
>
> "Mutton-dressed as lamb" (Esther writes on the blackboard) - "mutton" means old people; "mutton dressed as lamb" means, often it means the way you wear clothes. You are an older woman, but dressed like a teenager. They were mutton dressed as lamb. And one of the women, she was so fashionable, so funny, that her daughter was very embarrassed. Her mother was too fashionable, and too cool, too trendy, so her classmates were laughing at her, saying her mother was "mutton dressed as lamb".

Here Esther was doing the talking while the learners were listening to her talk. In this talk, Esther introduced something about two popular TV series in Britain. It is noticeable that she intentionally used short sentences for the ease of learners' comprehension, providing input that was slightly above the learners' language ability in the interests of their language improvement (Krashen, 1985). When she introduced the English idiom- "mutton dressed as lamb", she wrote it down on the blackboard and explained to her learners the meaning of this English expression with exemplification. Learners were thus provided with the opportunity to develop their knowledge about British culture and knowledge of English language. In other words, input opportunities have been provided by Esther to her language learners.

But do the language learners believe they are learning opportunities? The learners, as they expressed in interviews, find talks like this to be most intriguing and beneficial for their language learning.

> Vivien: I like to listen to her talks, they are so interesting.
>
> Tracy: I can learn a lot of things from her talks. I can learn new words and idioms, and I can learn something about British culture.
>
> Wendy: I enjoy listening to her talks; I can get to know about the general way of living in Britain while listening to a native speaker's talk in English. After all, that is what I have hoped to learn from an expatriate teacher's class (Interview data, 12/2004).

Essentially, these learners believe "learning opportunities" are constructed in Esther's talks like this in their classroom culture. With these learning opportunities, they think they could learn new words and idioms, practise their listening skills and learn about British culture.

6.4.2 Individual presentation in Esther's classroom and learning opportunity

An individual presentation in Esther's class can be subdivided into three phases, in each phase, there are learning opportunities initiated and taken up. I will illustrate with Crystal's presentation entitled *How Will I Meet My Husband.*

Extract 6.9 (Abridged from transcript data):

Phase 1: Crystal's presentation

1 Esther: Who would like to make a presentation today?
        (Crystal holds up her hand)

2 Esther: O.K. Crystal.

3 Crystal (goes to the front of the class): The title of my speech

4   is "How Will I Meet My Husband?" (Students laugh)

5   I'll wear skirt to meet my husband, we must love at

6   first sight. (bursts of laughter) (Students are listening

7   very attentively, smiling.) I'll love my dog more than

8   my husband (students' laughter).

9   We'll live in the South of China. (laughter) We'll

10   try to work together... So that's all.

11 Esther (sitting at the back of the classroom): Oh, wow.

12   Thank you very much for your speech.

13 Crystal: One last sentence-We'll live happily thereafter.

14 Esther: Well done!(students' laughter and applause)

In Phase One, Esther presented the learners an opportunity to practise the target language by inviting one of them to do an individual presentation. She left the learners to decide who would like to take up the opportunity (Line 1). Then Crystal took it up and started the presentation. The topic of her presentation was self-chosen because Crystal thought that was of interest to her and might also attract her audience. The presentation was a continuous natural flow of talk directed from Crystal the presenter to the audience including the teacher and the other learners. Therefore, practice opportunity has been constructed in the individual presentation for the presenter.

For learners in the audience, this meant an input opportunity as well as a practice opportunity when they were exposed to the target language. But the input opportunity might be somewhat problematic because the presenter, who was also a language learner, may not always give the right input as I will explain later. The presenter's talk was also a practice opportunity for the learners in the audience as they needed to put their language knowledge into test when they attempted to comprehend the talk and discern the linguistic mistakes in the talk. It was characteristic of Esther not to make interruptions in the middle of the presenter's talk; instead, she made some positive comment on the presenter's talk at the end and left error corrections until later, which helped to form a meaning-and-fluency context.

In Esther's classroom, every learner is ensured a chance of making an individual presentation in the front at the beginning of classes during a semester. By being given the opportunity of making oral presentation at least once in a semester, even the most timid can have practice opportunities and have to make use of them. Ho and Crookall (1995) claim that to develop learners' communicative competence, it is important for them to have opportunities to use stretches of discourse. With or without vocabulary and grammatical mistakes, input and output opportunities are constructed in Phase One in these verbal interactions in individual presentations.

Esther's final comment "well done" was a reward for the presenter's performance and a hint for the learners to know that it is perfectly safe to take up these practice opportunities in oral presentations. It was also a closing remark for Phase One and a transition to Phase Two. Directly after Crystal's presentation came the "Question and Answer" session, which was an occasion for the audience to ask the presenter any questions that they would like to ask.

Extract 6.10

Phase 2: Q & A

1　Esther:　Any questions?

　　　　　　(A boy student stands up)

2　John:　　What's your standard of choosing a husband?

　　　　　　(students' laughter)

　　　　　　(Crystal waits till the laughter has ceased):

3　Crystal:　We must love each other no matter who he is.

4　John:　　Can I take part in your (the other students are

5　　　　　　laughing), in your wedding ceremony?

　　　　　　(students' laughter)

6　Crystal:　Of course you can-or I will ask my husband.
　　　　　　(Laughter)

7　Rachel:　If you get married, where do you… Which city will

8　　　　　　you choose to live in?

9　Esther (whispers): Good question.

10 Crystal:　Beijing.

11 Lucy:　　You said you'll love your dogs more than your

12　　　　　　husband, will your husband be jealous?

　　　　　　(laughter)

　　　　　　(Crystal is thinking)

13 Emma:　Do you mind if your husband loves dogs more than

14　　　　　　you?

　　　　　　(bursts of laughter)

　　　　　　(Crystal falls into silence, looking aside)

　　　　　　(students' laughter)

15 Esther:　O.K. Thank you. Today's presentation is very good.
　　　　　　(Esther goes to the front of the classroom and
　　　　　　writes something down on the blackboard before
　　　　　　she turns back to ask the students)

Out of genuine interest in the topic, the learners demonstrated that they were eager to listen to Crystal's presentation and ask her related questions. The above scene exhibited a social communicative event, which was a de facto pedagogical event in this EFL classroom culture. Language learning here has been turned into a communicative event for a real purpose-to talk about Crystal's "future meeting with her husband".

Phase Two was a time for all the learners in the language classroom to construct and utilize learning opportunities. When Esther asked if the learners have got any questions, she gave the floor to the learners and the learners were quick to take the floor and produce learning opportunities for themselves. As the questioners and the answerer produced and utilized these practice opportunities in the target language, they had to summon up their limited language resource to improvise and get their messages across in the target language, as shown in Lines 2-7, 9-12. The learners were able to locally manage the interaction to some extent in that they were able to nominate themselves for turns rather than having the teacher to allocate turns for them. The focus was still on meaning rather than form, on fluency rather than accuracy of the output in the target language. In this kind of communication for communicative purposes, extended learning opportunities are produced and utilized, with which learners' communicative competence is developed.

To help language learners to maintain the uninterrupted flow of talk, Esther usually leaves error-correction until Phase Three before she moves on to the next class procedure. In Phase One and Two, Esther would write down the linguistic mistakes the presenter learner and learners in the audience have made. Then in Phase Three, Esther would write down these linguistic mistakes on the blackboard and ask students to do error-corrections, as shown through the following extract from Crystal's presentation.

Extract 6.11

Phase 3: Error detection and error-correction

1   Esther: I want you to think of some mistakes you have
2   made.
                 (pointing at the blackboard)
3   This one, Kathryn.
4   Kathryn: Northerner.
5   Esther: Thank you. Crystal said, "…he is Northern…" We
6   say "a Northern Chinese"or "a Northerner". In my
7   country, even though my country is so small, but
8   there are also differences between Northerners and
9   Southerners. Northerners are motivated, and more
10   critical; Southerners are friendly, cool, very patient.

In Phase Three, Esther wrote down on the blackboard some of the sentences Crystal has used in her presentation and learners have asked in Phase Two. These sentences contained hidden errors, and Esther left the error-detection and error-correction to the learners before she explained about the English language knowledge. The repair or error-correction was initiated by Esther (Line 1-3), but made by the learner (Line 4). The learners, including the presenter herself, then had to search through their limited linguistic knowledge to find out how to correct the error. For those who have detected the error and known how to correct it, this became an output opportunity in that it put their hypothesis about language knowledge into test before Esther confirmed it, as shown in lines 5-6. For those learners who did not know how to do error-correction in this case, this became an input opportunity for them to get to know a correct English expression. In lines 6-10, Esther described "Northerners" and "Southerners" in Britain, although this might be her own generalization of the characteristics of British Northerners and Southerners, learners could at least get some knowledge about British culture and people from her explanation-the input opportunity has been thus generated in such talks.

Hence, a well exploited individual presentation in Esther's EFL classroom culture has got its many benefits for learners' language learning:

1). Phase One of the individual presentation provides the presenter-who is a language learner with practice opportunities to produce extended stretches of discourse in the target language; it provides the audience-who are also EFL learners with input and output opportunities when listening to the target language;

2). A topic of real interest in the individual presentation enables the language learners to make use of their limited linguistic resources and converse in the target language in Phase Two, thereby engendering practice opportunities in the extended learner-directed classroom verbal interactions. Learners are encouraged to make use of the target language to achieve its communicative value of language, which is the pedagogical goal in pursuit in Esther's classroom culture;

3). Both input opportunity and output opportunity can be constructed in Phase Three when learners test and extend their EFL knowledge;

4). The individual presentation at the beginning of a class can serve as a helpful prelude for later class organization. As shown through the above extracts, it effectively attracts the attention of the whole class so as to facilitate further language instruction and classroom participation.

Generally speaking, many Chinese learners dread oral presentations in front of their class, especially if their presentation is to be formally assessed. But in this particular class, the learners' performance in the three phases of individual presentations has proved that when they have the ownership of the subject matter in classroom talks, learners have the power to make contributions to the construction of classroom culture and learning opportunities.

6.4.3 Group work in Esther's classroom and learning opportunity

In Esther's EFL classroom culture, group work is a major class-room activity that prompts verbal interactions between and among almost all of the classroom participants. It takes a variety of forms. There are group discussions on topics assigned by the teacher or chosen by the learners; there are group interviews in which group members play the roles of interviewer and interviewee in turns; there are role-plays to express English idioms; there are group competitions on general knowledge in English; there are group story-telling activities in which a group of learners tell a story together in English to the rest of the class; and there are even group puzzle solving activities to test learners' English vocabulary and logical thinking. There can be intragroup interactions in which group members work collectively to complete a task; there can be intergroup interactions in which the members of one group compete against the members of another group.

Without the constraint of a textbook, the topics for group discussions and the content for group activities that Esther and her learners have chosen are closely related with learners' daily life, which they are well familiar with and are excited to talk about. Here the pedagogic emphasis shifts from the verbalizing of de-contextualized language items to the purposes language serves in the interpretation and expression of meaning in social contexts (Widdowson, 1978).

Take, for instance, the topics for group discussions include: *"China's Female Suicide Rate"*, *"Generation Gap"*, *"Your Grandparents"*, *"Today's Pop Stars"*, *"Martial Arts"*, etc. This has made learners have a real purpose in classroom talk and sparked heated group discussions. There is an attempt on both sides-the teacher and the learners, to connect the real world with the classroom community.

It is through these different forms of group work that classroom interactions involve as many classroom cultural members as they possibly can involve. No matter in what forms these group works show up in Esther's EFL classroom culture, they excite the learners to engage in them and to construct and make use of learning opportunities. These multilateral multidirectional verbal interactions help to develop a classroom culture in which cooperation and participation are valued; this classroom culture then acts in favour of additional group work and further learning opportunity construction.

I will illustrate the construction of learning opportunities in group work with an extract of participants' talk in an intergroup quiz competition in Esther's classroom culture. The 33 learners were divided into five groups competing against each other; the group members worked as a team in each group. Each group took turns to ask the other groups questions; any member from the team could speak on behalf of his or her team. If a group answered a question correctly, it could win three points; if a group answered a question wrongly, it had to lose three points. The one group who answered the most questions correctly could win the most points and would therefore be the winning group. Esther drew a "leader board" on the blackboard to show the points each team has got or been marked off.

Extract 6.12

1   Esther: Listen carefully. Let's start with Team One, the rest
2   of you listen carefully.

3　　　　Team Two will have ten seconds (to answer). If they
4　　　　cannot answer, you may have the chance to answer
5　　　　the question. (Esther explains in Chinese) 如果他們
6　　　　答錯了其他人還可以回答. Let's start. Team One.
7　　　　The rest of you listen carefully, you may have the
8　　　　chance to answer the question.
9　Team 1: What's the relationship between Queen Mary and
10　　　　Elizabeth I?
11 Esther:　What's the relationship between Queen Mary and
12　　　　Elizabeth I?
13 Team 2:　Daughter and mother.
14 Esther:　Is that the right answer?
15 Team 1:　No.
16 Team 4:　Sisters.
17 Esther:　Sisters, is that right?
18 Team 1:　Half-sisters.
19 Esther:　They were born by Henry VIII, but they have different
20　　　　mothers.
21　　　　Now the next question?
22 Team 2:　The capital of Ethiopia?
23 Esther:　The capital of Ethiopia? (Esther counts down, 10,
24　　　　9, …)
25 Team 3:　Give up.
26 Esther:　Give up. O.K. Any other team?
27 Team 1:　Addis Ababa.
28 Team 3:　How does a worm go through a river without a
29　　　　bridge?
30 Esther:　How does a worm go through a river without a
31　　　　bridge?
32 Team 4:　Worm?

33 Esther: Worm.

34 Team 3: How does a worm go through a river without a

35   bridge?

36 Team 2: When it changes into a butterfly.

37   (students' applause)

38 Esther: Wow.

39 Team 5: What is the No. one cause of death in Britain?

40 Esther: "Cause of death", (Esther explains in Chinese) 死因.

41 Team 1: Diabetes?

42 Team 5: No.

43 Esther: What is the answer?

44 Team 5: The answer is "cancer".

...

In the introduction to quiz rules, Esther made it clear that if the team who were supposed to answer the question could not provide a correct answer to the question asked, then the chance would be left open to the other teams. The interactions in the process of the quiz made it possible for the learners to create and utilize practice opportunities for themselves because they had to ask and answer in English language. Throughout the quiz, Esther has been playing the role of a judge. The Chinese language Esther used in lines 5-6 served for administrative purpose as she tried to clarify the instruction of the quiz rules.

The first question asked by Team One was about British history. For Team One, this was a practice opportunity as they put what they wanted to ask into English (Lines 9-10); for Team Two and the rest of the class, this was also a practice opportunity-they had to rummage through their language knowledge base and find the right answer to the question before they provided the answer in the correct English expression. Although Team Two uttered an answer in English (Line 13), that answer was not the correct one. This left the opportunity to the other teams and Team Four took up the opportunity and provided the correct answer (Line 16). Esther further provided a more exact answer to the question, the answer being "half-sister". The answer provided by Team One (Line 18) and Esther (Lines 19-20) could be input opportunities for language learners in respect of knowledge about English language and in respect of knowledge about British history.

When Esther asked "the next question" in Line 15, she gave the floor to Team Two, which was a practice opportunity for them to ask a question in English. Team Two took the turn to ask a question about geography in English (Line 22). Again, the answer "Addis Ababa" was an input opportunity for those who did not know the answer.

The third question asked by Team Three was a brainteaser (Lines 28-29). This time, the learners had to think hard to find out the right answer to this brainteaser question before they could translate it into English. This has drawn learners' attention from the output of the linguistic form to the meaning of the language.

In the question asked by Team Five (Line 39), there was an English expression "cause of death", which was clarified by Esther in both English and Chinese (Line 40). This was a practice opportunity for Team Five as they put the English expression into use and an input opportunity for others as they were exposed to an idiomatic use of English language. When Team One answered "diabetes", actually they have initiated a practice opportunity to use the English word, which might be an input opportunity for the others who did not know the word. When nobody could answer the question, Esther gave Team Five the turn and let them disclose the correct answer-"cancer" (Lines 43-44), which was another practice opportunity for Team Five and another input opportunity for the other learners for them to develop both English language knowledge and common knowledge about Britain.

It can thus be seen that the input and output opportunities were profuse during this group work. There are plenty of similar examples in Esther's classroom culture. As learners explore an issue or solve a problem, they are improving their linguistic competence as well as their overall communicative language competence (Fang, 2005). In the sharing of opinions, debating on a topic, describing of a story, groping for the solution to a puzzle, learners apply and develop their language knowledge and skills simultaneously.

In this classroom environment, participants have forged cooperation and cohesion; and these interpersonal connections developed in verbal interactions in group works nurture student engagement in them. They provide multiple opportunities for language learners to use and extend their knowledge of the target language (Hall, 2000). The learners in these group works mutually construct, promulgate, and utilize language learning opportunities in the production of improvised, non-planned classroom discourse (Savignon, 2001). Essentially, EFL learners in Esther's classroom culture are positively interdependent on each other. They do not only cooperate with each other for the purpose of fulfilling a group task, they also learn from each other in the process. When learners feel they are being part of a cohesive group as they do in Esther's classroom culture, they are inclined to stand up and speak for they know their speech behaviours will be met with support and encouragement instead of humiliation and mockery. Language learning thus becomes a collective effort in which the learners are co-workers for a common goal-to develop their communicative competence.

As Esther comments:

> Esther: Chinese students are used to cooperating with one another, sometimes this works in a beneficial way in language learning. It's a kind of team work, team ef-

fort. I mean, I mean, generally speaking, they (this group of Chinese students) are different from the other Chinese students. They enjoy speaking out in front of the class doing presentations, they enjoy doing group work with each other, and they enjoy one speaking while the rest are listening. But the attitude of "the rest" is essential and it makes a great difference (Interview data, 11/2004).

Esther: They've got good rapport among them, and that makes a lot of difference, because obviously, in language learning, a lot of it is listening to another person. These students are willing to listen to each other, and learn from each other's mistakes. They are very good. In this particular class, each minute, each minute is valuable (Interview data, 12/2004).

When group works are successfully completed, learners feel that they have had the desire to communicate in English for a real purpose. It can be seen that in this supportive language learning environment, these language learners have cast away their vulnerability and become courageous "intellectual risk-takers". In this EFL classroom culture, there are pronounced mutual encouragement and interdependence among the participants which not only help to establish their pro-social interpersonal relationships, but also help to construct extended learning opportunities among them.

6.4.4   Repair in Esther's classroom and learning opportunity

Esther's classroom culture as shown in many cases is a meaning-and-fluency context. Esther shows much leniency towards learners' mistakes for as she expressed in her communication-centred educational ideology, she aims at creating a language learning context to maximize the opportunities for learners' output of the target language. Many linguistic mistakes that have been made in individual presentations and group works would go completely unnoticed without repair. Esther puts more weight on "fluency of expression" than on "accuracy of linguistic forms".

> Esther: About the error-correcting, you have to balance between what you expect the students to achieve-speaking fluently, or speaking accurately. (Since I hope they can develop conversation skills,) I do rather try to listen than interrupt them. I mean, for part of my class, I expect them to speak to make a presentation or get involved in a discussion, and I would try not to interrupt (Interview data, 12/2004).

The repairs are mostly done in Phase Three of individual presentations in "error-detection and error-correction". One such example is error correction made as shown in extract 6.11. Usually, Esther would leave the opportunity for repair to the learners, which can mean both input and output opportunities for the language learners. If the learners don't know the correct form to replace the mistaken one, she would provide the correct use of the language and give some explanation; if the learners know the correct answer, she would expand on the language knowledge.

It is mainly the "global errors"-errors that interfere with communication or impede the intelligibility of a message (Krashen, 1982) that have attracted most of Esther's attention. These "global errors" include mistakes in tenses and genders in English which occur most frequently in Chinese learners' output.

Extract 6.13

(After two individual presentations)

1	Esther:	Now, I enjoyed the speeches. But most of them
2		had serious problems. What are they?
3	Learners	(answer in chorus): Tense.
4	Esther:	Yes, what tense should be used today?
5	Learners	(answer in chorus): Past tense.
6	Esther:	Did you notice this? They kept using present
7		tense. (students laugh) I did not interrupt you (the
8		presenters) because your speeches are receiving
9		most of your attention. So I didn't interrupt you.
10		But it is a SERIOUS problem.
11		We rely on singular or plural, masculine or feminine
12		and tenses. These are maybe the most important
13		bits of English.

Here Esther has initiated an opportunity for learners to make repairs. She first tried to elicit learners' "error-detection" by asking them to find out the problems with the speeches made. When asked, learners answered in chorus saying that the problem was with the tense used. Esther then further initiated the opportunity for learners to do "error-correction", which they did by saying that the tense used should have been past tense. This has completed a "teacher-initiated learner-repair". The teacher made available a practice learning opportunity to put learners' language knowledge into test, and the learners took it up (Lines 1-5). But the repair didn't stop at this stage; Esther further expanded on the language knowledge about tenses, and explained the importance of the use of tense, gender and numeric expression in English, which has created input opportunities for these EFL learners.

In Esther's classroom culture, learners can also initiate repair after they have become aware of the importance of the correct use of tense and gender in English.

> Extract 6.14
> Rose :   ...My mother usually stays at home and work, he...
> Learners (in chorus): SHE.

When Rose made a "global error" in gender, the learners automatically corrected her; this is an example of learner-initiated learner repair, which can also been as an output opportunity for the learners who have done the error correction and an input opportunity for the speaker who has made the error.

Besides the learner-repairs, there are teacher-repairs when Esther directly replaces learners' mistaken English expressions with correct ones, although these happen much less frequently than learner-repairs. In these teacher-repairs and learner-repairs, the input and output learning opportunities have been initiated and utilized.

6.4.5 Extracurricular communication and learning opportunity

One characteristic of Esther's classroom culture is that the construction of learning opportunities has been extended to extracurricular communication. There are times that Esther and the students converse in English after class; there are also times when the language learners try to communicate in English with each other after class.

During the break time, for example, Esther would talk with the students about weather, transport, news of the day, food, etc. Sometimes she invites her students to be her home guests when they would talk about anything they are interested in such as Esther's family or the learners' family. In these casual exchanges of information, the learners' knowledge base is enlarged as these exchanges can enable the learners to improve their oral skills and get to know those English expressions related with daily life.

Esther would also give students advice on "creating an English speaking environment" for themselves outside the EFL classroom. Below is only one such example when Esther tried to urge her students to talk with each other in English so as to improve their conversation skills.

> Extract 6.15
>
> Esther: It is really something beneficial for you to speak English after class. You grow as you listen and talk to each other. There are very few foreigners, you have very limited chance to speak with native speakers (of English) while you have many opportunities to speak Chinese. And you have opportunities to speak with other foreigners who use English as a foreign language-Koreans and Ukrainians (on campus). So it is important English language can be used as a medium for conversation. There aren't many native speakers speaking English to you at all.

In this extract, Esther has brought the learners' attention to their own language learning process-they need to create opportunities for speaking English themselves. In doing this, Esther has created an opportunity which is neither input opportunity nor output opportunity, but an opportunity that develops learners' consciousness of managing their own learning which might eventually lead to the development of their language knowledge and skills.

The learners agree with Esther's idea of "speaking English after class with each other". For example, as a participant observer, I have overheard the learners talking in English in their dormitories and on their way to the cafeteria. When I asked them why they would like to talk in English after class and how they felt about this in focus group interviews, many of them thought this was a good way of language learning. As Tracy said:

> Tracy: Sometimes we do talk in English in our dormitory when all the roommates stay together. We can learn something new about English language in our conversation. For example, when none of us is sure about a language usage, we can look it up in the dictionary, so that we can learn something (Interview data, 12/2004).

The "conversation class" then can also take place in these language learners' cafeteria, in their dormitory and practically anywhere the learners would feel like talking in English. When these learners realize the importance of producing learning opportunities for themselves and start to consciously produce and utilize learning opportunities whenever and wherever they can, the EFL classroom culture's productivity of learning opportunity is greatly enhanced.

In Ying's EFL classroom culture, interaction patterns and forms are very dissimilar to those in Esther's EFL classroom culture; nonetheless, participants in Ying's classroom have found that plenty of learning opportunities are constructed in their classroom as well which I will show below.

6.5 Interactions in Ying's classroom culture and learning opportunity

Based on their textbooks and revolving around the central theme of exams, the majority of verbal interactions in Ying's classroom culture

are teacher-fronted that frame a form-and-accuracy context. But participants found that these teacher-fronted verbal interactions plus their textual interactions are conducive to their language learning. Ying's kinestic approach to language teaching and launch of portfolios in her language classroom has added some innovative features to this EFL classroom culture, which enhances the construction of learning opportunities.

6.5.1 Participants' interaction with text and learning op-
portunity

"Text and test" is like a major theme that governs almost all of the
interactions in Ying's classroom culture. Ying once accounted for the
omnipresence of text and test in interactions in her classroom:

> Ying: I think so much of the university examination system
> here requires them (students) to memorize the text-
> book. There is a need (for the students) to memorize
> the material in the textbook because the test is based
> on what is in the book. So we are teaching in com-
> plete accordance to the requirement of the examina-
> tion system here when the exams reward the students
> for remembering all the information from the text-
> book (Interview data, 11/2004).

The textbooks are used both inside and outside classroom so that
participants' interaction with text has become a major form of interaction in Ying's classroom culture besides teacher-fronted verbal interaction. The texts are used as a source of authentic English knowledge as
they are abridged or adapted from the English articles in the original
(see Section 5.3.4). The language learners are asked to do previews and

reviews of the texts; sometimes learners are asked to paraphrase sentences from a text, or retell and write a summary based on its content. These "interactions with text", as they emerge, are accepted by the teacher and the learners as making available input and output learning opportunities for learners to develop their knowledge and reading and writing skills.

Below is an example of participants' interactions with text based on a text entitled "*Diet and Health*" (see Appendix 9). Learners answered the questions posed by the teacher in chorus.

Extract 6.16

Ying:	So what's the passage mainly about?
Learners:	Health and diet.
Ying:	What do you know from the passage?
Learners:	You should eat more fruit and vegetables.
Ying:	There are some figures. Who released the figures?
Learners:	The Health Department.

In order to answer these questions in teacher-learner verbal interactions, the language learners had to interact with their texts for they had to go back to the text and search for the needed information from the whole passage. In this information-searching process, they had to undergo a complex mental process: first of all they had to understand the passage; secondly, they had to find the information needed; thirdly, they had to produce the answer in the English language. In reading the passage, when there were words that they did not recognize in the passage, there were input opportunities for them to enlarge English vocabulary as they looked up the words in their dictionaries; when they tried to make sense of the passage, there were practice opportunities for them to develop reading comprehension skills. In addition, there were also oral output opportunities when the learners answered their questions based on a text.

As I have noted in my research field notes:

> When the teacher asks a question from the text, the learners are looking at their textbooks. Some of them use their pencils to underline some words or sentences, some of them look up some words in their dictionaries, and almost all of them are reading and writing notes (Researcher's field notes, 11/2004).

Sometimes, Ying asked the learners to write a summary of the text they have just learned.

Extract 6.17

Ying: This is today's homework. Turn to page 59, please write a summary of the text in 150 words. When you go home, think about it carefully. Hand in your homework at the beginning of our next lesson.

In writing a summary of the text, learners have to identify the most important ideas in a text before they put those ideas into their own words and organize them into a coherent piece in English. The teacher believes output opportunities have been produced when learners are asked to write a summary based on a text, only this time the output is not "verbal" output, but "written" output.

Ying: I think there are two kinds of output opportunities, one is for them (the learners) to produce "oral" output, and the other is for them to produce "written" output. I think after they have learned a text and got to know those new words and vocabulary, they can put them into use in writing a summary of a text-to produce "written" output (Interview data, 12/2004).

The learners concede that these interactions with text are beneficial for their language learning.

> Bingchao: I have to remember those new words in the text, so I think I can get more new words from the text.
>
> Weiqing: Reading and paraphrasing the text can develop my reading skills (Interview data, 12/2004).

Participants' interactions with text then have the potential for the construction of input learning opportunities for these language learners to develop their EFL knowledge, practice opportunities for them to develop reading comprehension skills; oral output opportunities for them to answer teacher's questions based on a text, or written output opportunities for them to write a summary based on a text.

6.5.2 Teacher-fronted verbal interaction and learning opportunity

Teacher-fronted verbal interactions far outweigh learner-learner verbal interactions in Ying's classroom culture. These are realized through teacher's monologues and language drills between the teacher and the learners (see Section 5.3.5.1). Contrary to the presumption that teacher-fronted interactions deprive the learners of learning opportunities, it is found that substantial learning opportunities are constructed in these interactions in Ying's classroom culture in the current study.

Teacher-learner interactions happen when the teacher asks the learners to do some language drills. Below is an example when the teacher asked the whole class certain linguistic knowledge, the learners answered in chorus together with the teacher.

Extract 6.18

Ying:　　　To get all straightened out? What does it mean?

Ying &
Learners:　弄明白，弄清楚.

Ying:　　　How to change "light" into a verb?

Ying &
Learners:　Lighten.

Ying:　　　What else?

Learners:　Wide-widen, and fast-fasten.

When the teacher asked about the meaning of an English phrase, the learners immediately spoke out its Chinese meaning as they were supposed to; Ying joined them in answering the question. When Ying asked the learners to change an English noun-"light" into its corresponding verb form, the learners provided the answer-"lighten", and Ying spoke out the correct answer along with the learners' utterance. Then Ying asked "what else" as she intended for the learners to take the next turn and produce similar linguistic examples from their knowledge base, which the learners did accordingly.

In the above extract, participants-the teacher and the learners spoke in a fashion that showed they were aiming to simultaneously co-produce a turn-constructional unit more or less in unison by recognizably attempting to match the words, voicing, and tempo of the other party. Choral co-production here is a powerful means of displaying teacher's empathy with the learners (Lerner, 2002). These interactions usually appear after the learners' study of a text when the teacher would like them to practise and review what they have learned. Opportunities for the learners to practise their linguistic knowledge have been constructed in these choral co-productions.

Teacher-fronted interactions also occur when Ying singles out one learner to answer certain questions. When asked how they feel about this situation and whether this only makes learning opportunity available for the one learner involved, the learners answer:

> Rongrong: When my classmate is asked to answer the question, I can listen and practise in my own mind.
>
> Xiaoyun: I can learn in this situation. I can speak in my mind. If my classmate makes mistakes and our teacher corrects them, I can learn from the mistakes (Interview data, 12/2004).

So here learning opportunities are not only constructed and utilized by the participants who are directly involved in verbal interactions in language drills, they are also utilized by learners who are observers and listeners. In Ying's classroom culture, for those who haven't got actively involved in verbal interactions, many of them are actually engaged in active thinking and making use of these learning opportunities.

As I have described previously, many times the teacher-fronted interactions happen in Ying's monologues. Part of Ying's monologues is her explanation and verbatim translation of the text, which both the teacher and the learners perceive to be the most efficient way of "knowledge delivery" and providing input opportunity (see Section 6.1). Apart from that, Ying's monologues are felt by the learners to offer instructions on the understanding of the English language and the development of their language learning skills.

Learners in Ying's EFL classroom culture are all freshmen students who have just become university students and are virtually undergoing the "transition phase" from being high school students who were heavily dependent on teachers' instructions to university students who might not need to have so much reliance on the teacher. At this stage, many learners feel that they are somewhat at a loss and don't know how they should go about their language learning, as Jianming reflected:

> Jianming: I want to learn, but don't know how to. When I was in high school, I knew where my weak point was and I would try to improve that; but now, I don't know how to start. I feel that there is too much for me to learn, and I don't know where to start (Interview data, 11/2004).

This is echoed by many other learners who expressed in interviews their loss of direction in language learning. One learner said:

> Hong: Now we haven't got a real idea of how to go about our studying yet. When we were at high school, we simply listened to our teachers; but since we are now enrolled in university, we need to know how to go about English studying (Interview data, 11/2004).

Ying has observed this acute problem. In response to this urgent need for "knowing how to go about English learning", she gives the language learners instructions on the understanding of English language and on developing their learning skills apart from giving them instructions on the English language knowledge.

In Ying's monologues, she frequently brings the learners' attention to the understanding of the structure and rules of English language, sometimes this is achieved with the differentiation between the English language system and the Chinese language system (see Extract 6.7). In the following extract, Ying gave an explanation of the organization of English paragraphs.

Extract 6.19

Ying: Many English paragraphs are organized in this way: topic sentence-further explanation-further exemplification-small summary-conclusion. If you can grasp this rule, your listening comprehension and English writing will both be improved.

When Ying explained to the learners how English paragraphs are usually organized, a type of learning opportunity-the opportunity for learners to pay conscious attention to the form and structure of the target language system is produced, which may facilitate their future language learning.

One of the most important reasons for learners in Ying's classroom culture to find teacher-fronted interactions to be constructive for their language learning is that Ying tries to provide guidance for her learners on "how to learn" as shown in her monologues.

Extract 6.20

Ying: You have to make your language learning "effective"; do not isolate any aspect of language learning from the others (other aspects). You have to make connections between listening, speaking, reading and writing. Try to improve your comprehensive English skills. Try to find out the right language learning methods. This is different from your high school English learning.

Not only does Ying try to let her learners know the importance of "effective learning" and find the right language learning methods for themselves, she also makes efforts to persuade the learners into believing the importance of "active learning", or "autonomous learning".

Extract 6.21

Ying: When in class, you should take every chance to practise, if the teacher hasn't called your names, you
should try to practise in your mind how to answer the
question being asked, and then listen attentively to
what others have to say. Those who raised their hands,
they have got their chances. If you don't, you lose
your chances. After class, you should try to practise
with the teacher or take part in English Language Society to practise. Try to make yourselves actively
learn the English language.

What she has expressed in the above extract can be heard frequently in a single lesson and in fact in many lessons. She has very often
stressed the importance of learner autonomy, that is, learners should assume the responsibilities for their own learning. They should, as she has
said above, actively learn the English language.

Ying explained the rationale for her advocacy of learner autonomy
in an interview:

Ying: I want to teach them how to learn, I want to cultivate
their language learning attitude and habit (Interview
data, 12/2004).

On many occasions in her classroom, she has tried to ask the learners to:

* understand the importance of English language learning;
* understand the importance of being responsible for one's own
learning;
* take actions and be committed to produce and utilize learning
opportunities whenever and wherever they possibly can.

Bit by bit, learners start to understand the significance of developing learner autonomy and the significance of developing an awareness of learning opportunities.

> Lili: This is very different from high school when I simply did what teachers told me to do; she (Ying) keeps telling us that we should be responsible for our own language learning. Now I have to reflect on my own learning, and think where I need to improve.
>
> Xiaoyu: I now realize that I should be responsible for my own learning, and I am willing to listen to what the teacher says and what the others say and learn from them (Interview data, 12/2004).

As illustrated with the above extracts of classroom discourse and interview data, teacher-fronted verbal interactions in this study are found to be conducive to learners' language learning. Learning opportunities are constructed in verbal interactions between the teacher and an individual learner or between the teacher and the whole class; learning opportunities are constructed in participants' verbal interactions and learners' introspections. Moreover, in teacher's monologues, there constructed opportunities for learners to develop an understanding of the target language; and opportunities for them to learn "how to learn", for example, Ying has made the learners be aware of learning opportunity and realize the importance of being responsible for their own learning.

6.5.3 Repair in Ying's classroom and learning opportunity

In this classroom culture, Ying exercises a more immediate influence on learners' output of the target language than Esther does and the repairs in Ying's classroom culture have manifested the fact that this is a "form and accuracy" language learning context.

A main reason for this academic rigor is that both the teacher and learners strive for learners' good academic performance in exams, which requires accuracy in learners' output of linguistic forms. Besides, the pedagogical goal of Ying's class is to train "professional interpreters" who are supposed to produce language forms correctly on formal occasions. Another reason lies in Ying's perceptions of error-correction for she believes it is better to point out the mistakes sooner rather than later so that the learners won't be misled or make similar mistakes in the future (see Section 6.1). This academic rigor leads to the fact that repairs in Ying's classroom culture are enacted more by the teacher than by the learners although sometimes Ying does invite learner-repair.

The following extracts show how repairs are achieved in Ying's classroom culture.

> Extract 6.22
> (The teacher asks the learners to practise the usage of "be conscious of somebody doing something")
> Yu: She left suddenly, conscious of someone chase her.
> Ying: Chasing her. Be conscious of someone chasing her.

In this extract, the language learner was practising the idiomatic usage of "conscious of somebody doing something". Here the learner Yu produced an output of the target language containing a linguistic error, which was immediately corrected by teacher Ying. This might also be seen as an input opportunity-an opportunity for the learners to incorporate this new grammatical knowledge into their knowledge system. This was a teacher-initiated teacher-repair.

Extract 6.23

Tingting: This "shoup" is nice.

Ying: "Soup" or "shoup"?

Tingting: Soup.

Ying: The soup tastes good. Good.

In this extract, following the learner's error in pronunciation, Ying put forward two possible pronunciations for the word "soup" as this was not a new word to the learners. She framed this error correction as a question and offered an alternative which in effect gave the learner the opportunity to do self-repair in the next turn. It was an affiliative action in that it portrayed the second speaker as orienting to and attempting to help the first speaker (Seedhosue, 2004). When the learner corrected her own pronunciation mistake in the next turn, Ying repeated the sentence as a confirmation of the right answer and gave the learner a positive comment. This was a teacher-initiated learner's self-repair in which the learner was given the opportunity to correct herself.

Extract 6.24

1 Xinmeng: I go to school when I was 7 years old.

2 Ying   (facing the students): There is a mistake in her

3   sentence. Anybody knows?

4 Learners (in chorus): I WENT to school.

5 Ying: Yes, I WENT to school.

This is an instance of teacher-initiated learner's other-repair in which Ying invited the other learners to make correction for Xinmeng's linguistic error. Xinmeng's output contained a linguistic mistake in its tense. Ying pointed out that there was an error but she left the floor to the other learners when she asked "anybody knows" in Line 3. In the next turn in Line 4, the learners took the opportunity and made the repair by producing the correct utterance. Ying's repetition of the sentence was then a confirmation of the right form of English expression.

These error-corrections or repairs have enabled learners to notice problems in their output and pushed them to conduct an analysis leading to "modified output" (Swain & Lapkin, 1995). The teacher-repairs let learners get to know the correct language use instantly, which may be very effective in introducing and practising new language knowledge; the self-repairs and other-repairs made by the learner(s) impel the learner(s) to re-evaluate the linguistic output in question and correct the errors made. The learners are pushed by the teacher in these repairs to achieve accuracy in the target language output.

All the above have shown that Ying's classroom culture is pretty much in consistency with the traditional image of Chinese classrooms in which the teacher takes the lead. But the other side of Ying's classroom culture is that it is in line with the School's mission of innovation (see School Mission Statement, Section 5.1) and there is teacher-learner communication through a more or less symmetrical power relationship.

6.5.4 Innovation in the "traditional classroom" and learning opportunity

One break from tradition is Ying's kinestic approach to EFL teaching. Learners are asked to act out the English words and expressions, such as "lean on the wall", "shake one's head", etc.. Sometimes they are engaged in drama plays such as the "stage show" they perform about a special agent named Ausable (see Extract 5.8). A bonus of these kinestic activities is that the learners have the chance of practising their expressive skills and they have found these activities to be highly entertaining.

The chief merit for the learners though is that they find these kinestic activities to be conducive to their learning, as expressed by Yue:

> Yue: I enjoy drama plays and performing English words. I can understand clearly the meanings of those English idioms and remember them firmly after the performances. They (performances) also help me to understand the the text better (Interview data, 12/2004).

Thus the opportunities for learners to further develop their language knowledge are constructed in these highly entertaining kinestic performances.

Another innovative teaching strategy that Ying has exercised in her classroom is the use of portfolios as I have described in Section 5.3.5.4. Below are examples of "portfolio talks" between Ying and her learners in written form in learners' portfolios. These "portfolio talks" are mostly in English written below the display of learners' written work such as their dictation exercises, assignments, or exam papers.

> Portfolio talk 1:
>
> Wei: I feel that I have made progress, but only too slowly, and I think I need to improve my listening skills.
>
> Ying: Please focus on the difficulty. When you practise listening, try to make out the context of the passage. Put the difficult words into context. If you can't understand a word or a sentence when you listen to the tape, put it into the context of the whole passage.
>
> Portfolio talk 2:
>
> Jinjin: I can notice the difference between singular and plural, but I often ignore the use of past tense when I need to.

Ying: It's very good that you have realized this. But "practice makes perfect", the more you use it, the better you will become good at it. You need to cultivate your "language sense", take it easy, you will improve gradually.

Portfolio talk 3:
Chuan: When listening to a passage, very often I miss the title or can't understand what the title means.

Ying: You've got to analyze the reason for this problem-is it because the title is too long? Or is it because you haven't worked hard at it? Sometimes you can come back to the title after you have understood the whole passage. Or is the problem to do with your vocabulary? If it is, then you need to work on building your vocabulary.

Ying also explained to her students how to use the portfolios in class:

Extract 6.25
Ying: ...Don't fool yourself, you have to make everything clear when you go back and compile your portfolios, make clear what your weaknesses are, why is this, how to solve the problem.

The learners in Ying's classroom culture are undoubtedly thirsty for guidance on language learning strategies and learning management skills. They keep these portfolios to record the teacher's advice on language learning for later recall in their language learning process. Writing in portfolios in English itself can be seen as an opportunity for learners to produce written output of the target language.

When asked about their perceptions of portfolios, learners on the whole acknowledge and value their benefits, for they regard them as providing a unique chance for them to have confidential communication with their teacher. Seeing the progress they have made over a period of time as displayed in their portfolios would yield them a sense of achievement, which motivates them and leads to further goal-setting.

Lei: I am a shy girl. I dare not to speak my ideas in class. But in the portfolio, I can write down my questions and ask for her (Ying's) advice.

Weiqing: I have had this portfolio for three months now. When I look at the first page of my portfolio, I can't believe that my English language is so much better now. I will still work harder and make my English language better (Interview data, 12/2004).

The use of portfolios is beneficial for both the learners' learning process and the teacher's teaching process in Ying's EFL classroom culture for the following reasons.

In the first place, portfolio construction is also a negotiation process between the learners and their learning processes for actually it offers the opportunity for learners to plan and organize their own language learning. Learners' compilation of portfolios is also learners' self-monitoring process: learners constantly review their own progress through the collection of their own work, which leads to chances for self-reflection, self-assessment and further goal-setting. The portfolios increase the chances for learners to critically examine their own work and get feedback from the teacher so that they become aware of their weaknesses and strengths.

Moreover, the teacher's reviews of learners' portfolios allow the teacher to weave evaluation of and suggestion on learners' language learning into her in-class language instruction. Learners' suggestions as disclosed in their portfolios may lead to the teacher's self-reflection and adjustment of her EFL classroom teaching approaches. All these can directly and indirectly lead to the construction of learning opportunities for language learners.

There are only a few of the learners interviewed in Ying's EFL classroom culture who think that portfolio compilation is adding to their workload and when they don't see progress being made, they can experience a sense of frustration. Overall in learners' portfolio compilations and in teacher-learner's "portfolio talks", learning opportunities are constructed for learners to develop their planning, organizing and managing skills in language learning.

6.6 Extending the understanding of learning opportunity

What I have found in this ethnographic study regarding the characteristics of the two EFL classroom cultures and the construction of learning opportunities have provoked my further thoughts on learning opportunity as a key concept in classroom research.

The value of "learning opportunity" as a unit of analysis in classroom research has been demonstrated by the current study for it has yielded new insights into the benefits of certain classroom cultural characteristics for learners' language learning. What is more, I have found certain characteristics of the learning opportunity construction process in classrooms and developed a three-way distinction of learning opportunities which is different from what is exhibited in Allwright and Bailey's (1991) two-way distinction and Crabbe's (2003) coverage of learning opportunity categories (see Section 3.2.3.1).

The construction process of learning opportunities, as found in my study, possesses the following characteristics:

The construction of learning opportunities is contingent upon the context where language learning occurs. The construction of learning opportunities is not determined solely by the observable oral classroom interactions; instead, the construction of learning opportunities is under the influence of various classroom cultural components. For example, the congruence of participants' perceptions, language teachers' language learning experiences, double-coded media of instruction have all been found to be related with the construction of learning opportunities in the two EFL classroom cultures in this study (see Section 6.1, 6.2, 6.3).

The construction of learning opportunities is contingent upon the perception of the person who is doing the learning. When learners perceive certain classroom activities, classroom interaction patterns or certain language teaching resources to be helpful for their language learning, then the construction of learning opportunities can be promoted; otherwise, the construction of learning opportunities might be reduced or inhibited (see Section 6.1).

The congruence of participants' perceptions, as one of the characteristics of classroom cultures found in this study, can greatly enhance the construction of learning opportunities. When there is congruence of participants' perceptions, the construction of learning opportunities is enhanced; otherwise, the construction of learning opportunities is reduced or inhibited (see Section 6.1).

It can thus be said that learning opportunity is a variable concept. It may mean different things in each different individual learner's mind. What is counted as a learning opportunity may vary from one individual to another; and may also vary from one learning site to another. Take for instance, learning opportunities may mean the access to activities that lead to the development of communicative competence for learners in

Esther's classroom culture; whilst they may mean the access to activities that help learners to produce good exam results for learners in Ying's classroom culture.

Besides, learning opportunities as I have observed in this research mean more than just the opportunities for learners to develop their language knowledge and skills, and I have arrived at a three-way distinction of learning opportunities.

The two-way distinction ("input" and "output") of learning opportunities (Allwright & Bailey, 1991) is not adequate and there seem to be some overlappings in Crabbe's (2003) coverage of learning opportunity categories (see Table 3.2) as I have explained in my theoretical framework in Chapter 3. Through this study, I have found that learning opportunities in language learning can be best describable with a "three-way distinction":

"Type A" learning opportunities refer to access to activities that develop learners' language knowledge and skills;

"Type B" learning opportunities refer to access to activities that develop learners' understanding of the target language;

"Type C" learning opportunities refer to access to activities that develop learners' language learning skills.

Opportunities such as "input", "output", "interaction", "feedback", and "rehearsal" opportunities as shown in Crabbe's table all straightforwardly lead to the production and accumulation of language knowledge and skills, which belong to "Type A" learning opportunities. One thing I have noticed from this study is that besides the "oral" output opportunities, there can also be "written" output opportunities, as constructed in Ying's classroom culture when learners are asked to write a summary of based on a piece of text.

"Type B" learning opportunities refer to access to activities that can develop learners' mental consciousness of the form of the target language so that they can quickly notice and grasp language knowledge. For example, in the comparison and contrast between the two language systems, Esther and Ying have offered "Type B" learning opportunities for learners to develop their understanding of the target language.

In Extract 6.4, Esther has mentioned a major difference between English and Chinese language systems. That is, in Chinese, there are no tenses while in English there are. In Extract 6.19 when Ying explained to the language learners the organization of English paragraphs, she has also created the learning opportunities for the learners to understand the form of the target language. These opportunities, when created and utilized, will help to diminish the negative transfer of the native language and facilitate learners' grasp of the target language. Different from "Type A" learning opportunities which offer learners access to activities that lead directly to the increase in their language knowledge and skills, "Type B" learning opportunities offer learners access to activities that enhance their "language sense", an ability that allows learners quickly notice, understand and grasp the rules in the English language and think in English before their oral or written output.

"Type C" learning opportunities are learners' access to activities that develop learners' language learning strategies and learning management skills. For example, Ying has provided the learners with a "Type C" learning opportunity when she introduced the use of tape recorder in language learning. In portfolio compilation in Ying's classroom culture, "Type C" learning opportunities have been constructed when learners have to monitor, plan, organize and reorganize their language learning process. These opportunities are learners' access to activities that get them to learn "how to learn" the language.

While "Type A" learning opportunities palpably contribute to the enlargement of the learner's knowledge base and the development of their language skills, "Type B" and "Type C" learning opportunities can ease and speed up language learning process, potentially multiply "Type A" learning opportunities and induce the eventual knowledge increase and language skills development. For example, in Ying's classroom culture, with "Type C" learning opportunities, learners are enabled to realize the importance of learner autonomy. Once they start to manage their own learning and are aware of the existence of learning opportunities, they are consciously creating and making use of learning opportunities for themselves, they are constantly looking for and making use of the opportunities for them to develop language knowledge and skills, or "Type A" learning opportunities (see Xiaoyu's comment in the interview, p. 220 of this book). In this sense, "Type C" learning opportunities have contributed to the multiplication of "Type A" learning opportunities.

My three-way distinction of learning opportunities and their relationship are illustrated in the figure below on the next page (dark arrow stands for direct link, dashed arrow stands for indirect link, "LO" stands for "Learning Opportunity"):

Extended learning opportunities are without doubt of crucial importance for learning. As it is the verbal form of interaction that has been studied most often in research (see Section 3.1), it is the construction of "Type A" learning opportunity that has drawn most researchers' attention concerning language learning. This doesn't mean that "Type B" and "Type C" learning opportunities are nonexistent or unimportant. Rather, they are latent in the language classrooms and can be converted into "Type A" learning opportunities which directly lead to knowledge augmentation and language skills development as I have shown in figure 6.2.

In this chapter, I associate the classroom cultural realities that I have unfolded in Chapter 5 with the construction of learning opportunities in them. With the support of empirical evidence, I have found that both EFL classroom cultures are nurturing learning environments for the construction of learning opportunities. In the next chapter, I am going to highlight the findings of this research project, and expound on my contributions to knowledge before I suggest the implications of the current study and put forward questions for further investigation.

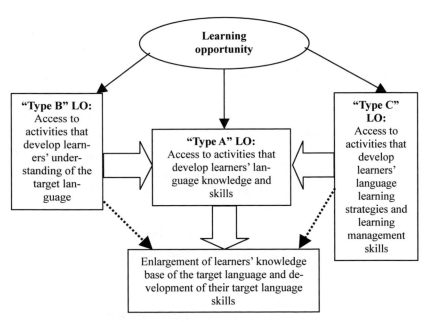

Figure 6.2: Three-way Distinction of Learning Opportunities

Chapter 7

New Horizons for Learning: Developing a Positive Classroom Culture

This chapter is intended to summarize the findings of my study and draw out their implications for pedagogical theory and practice. I revisit my research questions and recapitulate the characteristics of the two EFL classroom cultures as well as the construction process of learning opportunities in them. Then I describe my contribution to knowledge at pragmatic and theoretical levels. On the one hand, I believe this study provides some important insights into the "cultural lives" of two EFL classrooms in a modern China, which is potentially informative for language teaching practitioners in China and in the international community; on the other hand, this study helps illuminate and lead to a deeper understanding of the concept of "interaction", "learning opportunity" and the interface between them. In particular, my study highlights the significant role learners play in the construction process of learning opportunity. The positive traits I synthesize from the two EFL classroom cultures which I will describe in this chapter may be of value for educationalists in general to develop positive classroom cultures towards good quality of classroom life (Wright, 2006) and ultimately towards efficient learning.

My study implies that a sophisticated view of the language class-room and its interactions need to be adopted to replace those stereotypi-cal perceptions of classroom practices in this postmethod era (Kumara-vadivelu, 2006). At the end of the chapter, I point out further lines of investigations that might deepen an understanding of the classroom cul-ture and the construction of learning opportunities.

7.1 A summary of my research findings

I started this research project with the aim of gaining a better un-derstanding of classroom teaching and learning; specifically, the objec-tive of this study has been to interpret the varied effects of patterned classroom events on the construction of learning opportunities within their specific contexts in search of solutions to optimize classroom teaching and learning.

Towards this end, I have chosen two EFL classrooms led respec-tively by a British teacher and a Chinese teacher at the School of For-eign Languages in a provincial Normal University in China as the tar-gets of investigation. The two EFL classrooms have been approached as two cultural entities and I have addressed the following research ques-tions:

1). What are the characteristics of the two EFL classroom cul-tures?

2). How are learning opportunities constructed in these two EFL classroom cultures?

With the assistance of empirical evidence that I collected in the re-search field, I have revealed two EFL classroom cultures, two scenarios, and two modes of classroom teaching and learning. The commonality they share is that learners in both of them consider they live in a classroom environment that is favourable for the construction of learning opportunities, and learners genuinely believe they can achieve good learning in either classroom culture. The two EFL classroom cultures have exhibited some common positive cultural traits for the construction of learning opportunities, which I am going to discuss later in the chapter.

The EFL classroom culture led by the British teacher Esther is characterised by its high interactivity in verbal interpersonal interactions among the classroom participants. Esther has approximately seven years of language teaching experience in China and a good grasp of knowledge about Chinese language and culture; the language learners are sophomore students whose English is at intermediate level. The pedagogical goal of Esther's EFL classroom culture is to cultivate learners' communicative competence because the subject being taught is "conversation" and also because Esther has a communication-centred educational ideology. The medium of instruction is mostly English although Esther occasionally would use Chinese language to make explanations and clarifications. Esther's communication-centred educational ideology directs her to maximize her learners' opportunities to speak in class in individual presentations and various group works. The language learners in Esther's classroom culture are predisposed towards classroom participation and they are actively engaged in classroom activities. All of these lead to a participatory classroom culture which is in line with the democratic classroom model.

Conversely, the Chinese teacher Ying's classroom culture exhibits an image of a traditional language classroom which is suffused with teacher-fronted interactions. The subject being taught in Ying's classroom is "interpretation"; the pedagogical goal of the classroom is to train professional interpreters, secondary school language teachers and administrators. The language learners in Ying's class have just started their university life and their English is at pre-intermediate level. Like Esther, Ying has also got years of language teaching experience. Both Ying and her learners strive for learners' good performance in academic tests. But unlike Esther's classroom culture which is oriented towards classroom participation, Ying's classroom culture is test driven. With the textbook as the blueprint for exams, "test" has become a predominant theme which permeates almost all kinds of classroom activities. The classroom culture is imbued with teacher-fronted verbal interactions with learner-learner verbal interactions that happen much less frequently. Textual interaction is another form of interaction in Ying's classroom culture which is realized in participants' interactions with text and teacher-learner extracurricular communication via written portfolios. Ying's classroom culture may to some extent represent reconciliation between tradition and innovation; an asymmetrical power relationship between Ying and her students is demonstrated through the teacher-fronted classroom dynamics while a more or less symmetrical relationship is exhibited through teacher-learner "portfolio talk".

The two EFL classroom cultures are thus two different systems, but both have been found to be conducive for the construction of learning opportunities. Considering the commonly held assumption that verbally interactive classrooms are better environments for learning to occur (Van Lier, 1998), the fact that one EFL classroom culture in my study is perceptibly more "interactive" than the other may lead to the conclusion that the former is a better environment for language learning than the latter. However, my study of the two EFL classroom cultures has manifested that both classroom cultures are considered to be good learning environments which help the construction of learning opportunities.

On the one hand, there are certain commonalities they share that contribute to the construction of learning opportunities. For example, in both EFL classroom cultures, participants' perceptions concerning classroom language teaching and learning are very much in congruence, both of the two language teachers have got years of language learning experiences, the media of instruction in both EFL classrooms are double-coded. These have been found to contribute to the construction of learning opportunities for the language learners. On the other hand, the two EFL classroom cultures demonstrate very different classroom interaction patterns as Esther's classroom culture is characterized by high interactivity in interpersonal verbal interactions and Ying's classroom culture is characterized by teacher-fronted verbal interactions and textual interactions. But it is found that learning opportunities have been constructed through these interactions in the two EFL classroom cultures.

The findings of this study have provided insights into the nature of the learning opportunity construction process and have led me to distinguish different types of learning opportunities as shown in figure 6.2. I have found that the construction of learning opportunities is contingent upon context, it is contingent upon the perception of the person who is doing the learning, and the congruence of participants' perceptions can greatly enhance the construction of learning opportunities. Moreover, I have given learning opportunity a three-way distinction. Learning opportunities, I have found, are more than input and output opportunities that can develop learners' language knowledge and skills; there are also opportunities for learners to get access to activities that can develop their understanding of the target language and develop their language learning skills.

My conclusion from the study is that we can not make hasty or stereotypical judgement on the value of a language classroom based on its observable verbal interaction patterns. Notwithstanding the benefits of verbal interactions for language learning, it might be oversimplistic to say that an apparently less interactive (in the sense of verbal interaction) classroom culture would deprive the learners of learning opportunities and therefore is detrimental to language learning. To understand if a classroom is a good environment for language learning, we will need to have an emic knowledge and a holistic understanding of the classroom culture in which language learning takes place.

7.2 The contribution of my study to knowledge

7.2.1 A revelation of life in the two Chinese EFL classroom cultures

My display of life in the two Chinese EFL classroom cultures is informative for language teaching professionals. Considering that China is a language teaching market of huge potential because of its dramatic economic growth, it informs language educationalists of EFL teaching and learning situations in modern day China. My study, having attracted great interest and received positive feedback at IATEFL 2006 conference presentation in Harrogate, U.K., is explicitly pertinent to EFL teaching practitioners. In particular, what I have revealed in this study may help to yield insights into EFL classrooms for Western language teachers who are teaching or are going to teach in China.

My study demonstrates the necessity for a context-sensitive language teaching approach (Bax, 2003) and illustrates the importance of knowledge about the indigenous language and culture for language teaching practitioners. When a native speaker of English teaches language in an environment other than their home country, he or she may not always lead a successful classroom. Some Western teachers may experience classroom culture shock when they first come to teach in China's EFL classrooms as I have reviewed in Chapter 3.

In my study, Esther's classroom culture has been thought of as being conducive to language learning by her Chinese language learners. One underlying reason for this might be the congruence of perceptions between Esther and her learners, which is one of the positive classroom cultural traits that I am going to explain later. Another important reason might be attributed to her exceptional knowledge about Chinese language and culture. To a great extent, she can remove the linguistic and cultural barrier in her language instruction, which has largely enhanced her classroom teaching and the construction of learning opportunities for the language learners in her classroom. My study shows that for expatriate teachers, some knowledge of the local custom, classroom etiquette and even the native language of their learners would be genuinely advantageous to the construction of learning opportunities in their language classrooms.

On a larger scale, this study and the future dissemination of its research findings will contribute to the current language classroom research literature. Rarely if there is any has research been conducted on the relationship between "classroom culture" and "learning opportunity" although much classroom research has been carried out in language classrooms to study the relationship between verbal interactions and the construction of learning opportunities. There is also little research that has been carried out to study EFL classroom cultures in a Chinese setting. Being an ethnographic case study, this research has produced findings that reveal the intricate relationship between classroom interaction, classroom culture and the construction of learning opportunities.

7.2.2   A recognition of learners' significant role

Teaching, as Allwright (2006) holds it, is thought of as sowing seeds: only some, not all, of which will turn into fruits. The prerequisite for us to have a good harvest of fruits is that we have to have the seeds to be sowed in the first place. Seeing from this angle, a learning opportunity can be said to be a seed that might be cultivated into the fruit of learning outcome and as such it is crucial for learning to occur.

My study has tried to investigate how we can have the seeds that can potentially be turned into fruits in the language classrooms, that is, how learning opportunities are constructed in the two EFL classrooms. In doing so, I have found that learners have a significant role to play in the production of these seeds because learning opportunity is subject to learners' perceptions and interpretations. What I have revealed in this investigation of "classroom culture and the construction of learning opportunities" is that learners have their own understandings as for what a learning opportunity is and what this means to them that may or may not be in line with the teacher's recognition of a learning opportunity.

As I have shown, in Ying's EFL classroom culture, actually the Chinese learners expect and demand the teacher to act a leading role in the classroom. Both parties in the EFL classroom culture are used to and accept the knowledge transmission model as being the most effective mode of instruction and the language learners perceive these teacher-fronted interactions to generate learning opportunities that will bring the desired language learning outcome. In Esther's EFL classroom culture, pair work was first applied because Esther regarded it as providing good practice opportunities for the learners, but the learners held different opinions from Esther which eventually led to the dismissal of pair work in their classroom culture.

This shows that apart from teacher expectations, learners also bring with them their whole experience of learning and life into classrooms, their own reasons for being there, and their own particular needs that they hope to see satisfied (Allwright & Bailey, 1991). Learners work selectively within their environment of learning and upon the linguistic and communicative data made available to them in that environment. This selectivity derives from the learners' conceptualization of the conditions that they see as facilitating or hindering their learning (Breen, 2001).

Learning opportunities might be seen to be inscribed into curriculum (Crabbe, 2003) or to be constructed in interactions (Allwright, 1993; Van Lier, 1991; 2001), but ultimately they are subject to the idiosyncratic perceptions and interpretations of learners as for what can be counted as learning opportunities. "These understandings are of greater intrinsic importance to them than how productive or efficient classroom outcomes are by external standards" (Gieve & Miller, 2006, p.23). Irrespective of a language teacher's efforts and good intentions, if the learners have perceptions of learning opportunities that are at variance with his or hers, then it is likely that the "teacher-perceived" learning opportunities might not be seen as learning opportunities by the learners.

In this sense, the condition for a classroom activity or a classroom interaction pattern to be a learning opportunity or to be a seed that can bear fruits is that it is accepted to be one by the person who is doing the learning in the language classroom. The classroom implication for this is that we will have to get to know learners' needs in the language classroom, which I will discuss later in this chapter.

7.2.3 A synthesis of positive classroom cultural traits

"Classroom culture" as a notion has been used to approach classroom phenomena (Breen, 2001; Holliday, 2002); in my research project, I have studied two EFL classroom cultures for the purpose of analysing and describing the construction of learning opportunities under the influence of various classroom cultural components. Through this study, I

Box 7.1: Positive Traits of the Two EFL Classroom Cultures

Positive Traits of the Two EFL Classroom Cultures

- The learners have a strong motive to achieve a clear goal of language learning;
- Most of the time, there is congruence between teacher's perceptions and learners' perceptions regarding how language learning is best achieved and what constitutes a learning opportunity;
- The teacher is sensitive to learners' needs and is willing to adjust the classroom culture when there is discrepancy between the teacher's and the learners' perceptions of learning opportunities;
- The teacher has foreign language learning experience so that he or she has the empathy for the language learners;
- The expatriate teacher has good knowledge of the learners' native language and the local culture;
- Both the target language and the native language of the learners are used as media of instruction, and they are used appropriately;
- There is the construction of "Type B" and "Type C" learning opportunities for learners to develop their understanding of the target language and language learning skills;
- Learning opportunities are constructed both inside the classroom and outside the classroom.

have identified certain "positive cultural traits" as shown above that contribute to the construction of learning opportunities. I propose that teachers should be conscious of the existence of EFL classroom culture, and further, aspire to develop a positive classroom culture that is configured optimally for the construction of learning opportunities that learners need.

In reality, not many teachers and learners are aware of such a "classroom culture", and in many classrooms neither teachers nor learners are aware that such a "classroom culture" may be influencing the processes of teaching and learning (Coleman, 1996). Amid the ebb and flow of educational fashions, many teachers pay attention to how to make their classroom teaching methodology more effective. What I propose from my study is that rather than concentrating on the comparison of the "goods" and "bads" of certain classroom teaching methodologies, we should put more emphasis on the improvement of "quality of life" (Wright, 2006) in the classrooms. We should develop a "positive classroom culture" in which learning opportunities are constructed to meet learners' needs, so that both the teacher and the learners can have a fulfilling educational experience.

7.3 Implications and recommendations

7.3.1 Implications for classroom methodology

Methodologically, my study has implied that language teaching in EFL situations has to be carried out under the constraint of local conditions; to update English teaching methods, EFL countries like China need to modernize, not westernize, English teaching (Rao, 2002).

The educational traditions of the society in which learners have been brought up deserve particular attention from the language instructors and educational policy makers. Previously in Chapter 2, I have stated that CLT was "imported" from the West in the wake of growing dissatisfaction with the traditional EFL classroom practices in China, but in many places across the country, CLT has been met with resistance, which has been the direct result of a superimposed approach instead of a contextualized approach to EFL classroom methodology. CLT, originated in the West and preserved in the Western educational setting, may

243

well suit the needs of language learners who are used to dialogic thinking or who are keen to pursue a communicative language classroom as
learners in Esther's EFL classroom culture are. But in the Chinese context where learners have long been used to the "knowledge transmission
model" at school and face the overwhelming pressure of language tests
of all kinds and at all levels, the abrupt swerve of classroom language
teaching methodology might produce results that depart far from the
intended goal.

All problems are reducible, ultimately, and in practice, to "local"
ones, and so require "local" solutions, solutions that respect the unique-
ness of all human situations, and of all humans (Allwright, 2003). The
cultural and educational experience of Chinese teachers and learners
position them to expect knowledge including language knowledge to be
taught using a carefully controlled, structured, memory-oriented approach (Cortazzi & Jin, 1996). The benefits and advantages of the traditional approach in EFL teaching and learning in China may not be relevant in a Western situation of second language teaching and may not
seem to be obvious to a Western language teacher (Tang & Absalom,
n.d.). But classrooms are social constructions where teachers, learners,
dimensions of the local educational philosophy, and the more general
sociocultural values, beliefs, and expectations all meet (Locastro, 2001).
The cultural and social situation of China and its linguistic environment
have determined that EFL education in China must be based on China's
reality; the adoption of certain EFL pedagogical methodologies must be
associated with this reality to achieve the intended effect.

What is more, my study has implied that local sociolcultural context and its pedagogical traditions determine that the implementation of
pedagogical innovations is a gradual process. At the beginning of this
book, I have posed the question: "Is 'pedagogical democracy' viable in
China's EFL classrooms?" (cf. Chapter 2). In the two EFL classroom

cultures in this study, Esther's EFL classroom culture is ostensibly more "democratic" than Ying's in the sense that learners' voices are more often heard and learners share the responsibility of classroom decision-making. However, learners in Ying's classroom culture don't feel the constraint of an "authoritarian" classroom culture; instead, they take it as something normal and perfectly acceptable; the EFL classroom culture they are located within has, in their eyes, made possible "good learning". This may bring about further thoughts on "pedagogical democracy" and classroom learning.

In my view, the findings from this study suggest a need to move away from simplistic connotation of the concept "pedagogical democracy". Of the two EFL classroom cultures, Esther's might seem to be more "democratic" than Ying's, but can we say there is no pedagogical democracy in Ying's classroom culture? Western teachers may play down their authority over students for fear of stifling their freedom of expression and threatening a warm teacher-student relationship (Freire & Macedo, 1995) in the language classroom as shown in Esther's classroom culture. But the teacher still has to contrive the required enabling conditions for learning, has still to monitor and guide the progress of learning. All this presupposes teacher's control in Esther's language classroom, applied perhaps with more subtlety and consideration and discretion, but applied none the less (Widdowson, 1987). Besides, outside Ying's "authoritarian" classroom which is dominated with teacher's one-sided control and asymmetrical relationship, there is a more or less symmetrical relationship achieved through teacher-learner "portfolio talks".

My view is that given the fact that classroom learning is situated in the local institutional and sociocultural context, teacher-fronted classroom dynamics might still be dominant in EFL classroom cultures in China. The "knowledge transmission model" in China only sustains the asymmetry between teachers and learners in the language classrooms. Speaking of "pedagogical democracy", it will be fair to say that we cannot expect any radical changes in the language classrooms at the present moment unless there are larger social transformations in China (Yu, n.d.). But on the other hand, the subtle and gradual innovations starting from the classrooms (e.g. "portfolio talks" in Ying's classroom) to the institutions (e.g. the School's commitment to innovation) may help to bring about social changes in the long run.

Therefore, in enriching the repertoire of language teaching methodology, the local conditions should be exploited rather than disregarded; the educational traditions should be advanced rather than discarded. Put it briefly, there can be a marriage of pedagogical tradition and pedagogical innovation.

7.3.2 Implications for classroom research

My study implies that "learning opportunity" can be a valuable unit of analysis in classroom research. A classroom culture with less verbal interactions may not necessarily be less conducive to language learning because learning opportunity can also be constructed within a traditional classroom context of acknowledged and sanctioned teacher power and authority. We cannot see the cognitive process in which learners transform these learning opportunities into language knowledge and integrate the knowledge into their mental realities; what we can see from the classroom is the construction and utilization of learning opportunities. In the end to educators and above all to learners, how classrooms provide opportunities for learning is of more importance than how classroom life can be controlled and directed (Wright, 2006). Thereby, the employment of learning opportunity as a unit of analysis enables us to adopt an "open-ended approach" rather than to wear "stereotypical lenses" in the examination of classroom realities and the evaluation of certain classroom practices.

In Chapter 6, I have developed a new framework to understand and analyze learning opportunities which I draw from my research findings. I have discussed the characteristics of the learning opportunity construction process and provided a three-way distinction of learning opportunity. This three-way distinction of learning opportunities, if used in future research, may make it possible for the understanding of "what forms of learning are made available and what forms of learning are made difficult or impossible" (Hodkinson, Biesta, & James, 2007, p.31) in different classroom cultures. What I have discovered in my study, for example, is that "Type A" and "Type B" learning opportunities are constructed in Esther's classroom culture, while "Type A", "Type B" and "Type C" learning opportunities are constructed in Ying's classroom culture. Despite their differences in cultural characteristics, both language classrooms afford learning opportunities but only of different types.

In the research on the relationship between learning opportunities and classroom interaction patterns, if we do not use "learning opportunity" as a generic concept, instead, we attempt to investigate the types of learning opportunities that certain classroom interactions generate and the significance of these learning opportunities have for learners' language learning, then we may crystallize the potential benefits some classroom activities or interactions bring for learners' language learning. For example, a language classroom in which there is no observable verbal interaction may not always be negative, if the language learners are engrossed in reading activities when they create and utilize "Type A" learning opportunities for the development of reading skills. Likewise, a teacher-fronted language classroom may have deeper meanings for the learners if "Type B" and "Type C" learning opportunities are constructed for the learners to develop their language sense and language learning management skills.

Therefore, it is not enough to comment on the quantity and quality of learning opportunities constructed in a language classroom based on its interactivity in verbal interactions in language classroom research; we need to have a deeper understanding of classroom language teaching and learning-to understand what types of learning opportunities are nurtured through what kinds of classroom interactions, and to understand the significance these have from the learners' standpoints. "Learning opportunity" as a unit of analysis, if used in future language classroom research, may bring about more revealing results in the understanding of classroom realities and their significance for the construction of learning opportunities.

Another implication of my study for classroom research is that to understand whether a language classroom is beneficial for language learning, we need to develop a holistic and emic understanding of the classroom reality.

A holistic understanding of participants' EFL classroom performances is needed to better translate the relationship between classroom interactions, classroom culture, and language learning opportunities. Any single classroom cultural component cannot be isolated from the other components in an EFL classroom culture for there exist the innate connections between and among classroom cultural components. These elements constantly interact with each other, and it is the chemistry among these elements that determines the progress of the lesson, the kind of learning opportunities that are made available and finally the learning that takes place (Tsui, 1995). It is time for us to take a holistic approach and develop an emic perspective to examine the classroom cultural life and its relationship with language learning on the basis of empirical evidence.

7.3.3 Recommendations for future research

Given the restraints of time and resources and given I am a novice researcher, this study is not without limitation. For example, the two cases in this study may not be very representative for the other language classroom realities in China.

One recommendation for future research is that there can be further research conducted in more EFL classrooms to interrogate the intricate relationship between classroom realities and the construction of language learning opportunities. Another recommendation is that if time and money allowed, a longitudinal study of a single classroom culture or multiple classroom cultures and their relationships with the construction of learning opportunities may yield more revealing research results.

In addition, more studies of the institutional and sociocultural impacts on the development of classroom culture and the construction of learning opportunities will also shed more light on the understanding of classroom language teaching and learning.

7.4 Concluding remarks

In Introduction, I have mentioned that it was my personal reflexive experience that has compelled me to conduct this research project. To actually carry out this research, as it turned out, has also been a personal reflexive experience for me.

As I have elucidated in the implications of my study for classroom research (see Section 7.3.2), what I found in my study has shown me that in understanding the impact of certain classroom practices on language learning, I need to have a holistic approach and avoid making presumptions; in understanding the benefits of certain classroom for language learning, I need to gain the native experience and avoid making external judgments. What is more, classroom language learning is a complex process. Rather than constantly assess the merits and demerits of certain classroom teaching practices and compare the benefits of language classrooms for learning based on their perceivable verbal interactions, I, as a teacher, need to put emphasis on the development of a positive classroom culture so as to make classroom teaching and learning an enjoyable and fulfilling experience under the constraint of local situations.

Appendix

Appendix 1: Background information about the university in the study (as in the School document, 2004)

SYNU is one of the first two accredited teaching universities in China's Northeast region. Both teachers and students of the university are held to have high standards and work creatively for the advancement of the university. They take it upon themselves to rejuvenate China. They have always deemed it their duty to educate others and have nurtured several generations of talented individuals. In the process, they have created a prestigious reputation for the university.

With over fifty years of diligent work, many generations of both the staff and students of SYNU have refined the spirit of bettering oneself through education. They have done so with high aspirations, courage, and intelligence. This kind of spirit has taken root in their character, and has changed into a spiritual motivating force to address the realities of today's world.

At the beginning of this new millennium, we said farewell to our downtown campus in order to welcome our new campus in the suburbs of Shenyang. We have built an imposing campus with beautiful landscaping in the north of downtown Shenyang, expanding and encompassing learning, arts, ecology, and modernity. Walking leisurely alongside the green grass and enjoying the modern environment for living, studying, and working will make your body, mind, and imagination free and at ease. It will give you new inspiration, and provide you with broader space for your wisdom and intelligence to take you to new heights.

"The competition of the twenty-first century is the competition for talent." More than sixty thousand graduates of the university have dispersed to all corners of the country, and various parts of the world, to contribute their heart and soul for the development, prosperity, and prestige of their motherland. Not only does SYNU offer multi-disciplinary education, it also undertakes the task of directing the pedagogical research at the primary and secondary school level, as well as supervises the teacher and cadre training for Liaoning Province. The university also combines instruction with teaching research, and has created the first, and only, new pedagogical model in the whole country for cultivating and raising the standards of adult education, for those already working in society. The training of pedagogical-category students of the University and the educational practice done by them under the new model have already earned unanimous admiration of the broad student body and the leadership and teachers of the schools where our students are currently teaching. The scientific nature and effectiveness of the new model have already gained preliminary theoretical and practical confirmation by wide circles of the society.

An ancient Chinese saying goes that "the rocks of other mountains can be used to polish the jade here." Searching for the cooperation of the excellent domestic and overseas educational resources to run our university has been an audacious attempt of reformation of SYNU during the recent years. The university has continuously broadened its train of thought for conducting education. The university has successively signed agreements of international academic exchange and scientific cooperation with the higher educational organizations and scientific research institutes of more than thirty countries of the world, such as the United States of America , Great Britain , Canada , Japan , Russia , Belgium , Denmark , Australia , and the Republic of Korea .

The "independent, tireless, innovative, and creative" people of SYNU are rejuvenating Shenyang, the old industrial base of China's Northeast Region, and developing extensive and high standard education as their turning point for pursuing greater progress with one heart and one mind in exploring new fields for creation and accelerating development. They are striding forward on the expressway of reformation and development to write new magnificent chapters of success for building a first-rate well-renowned teaching and research institution.

Appendix 2: The three types of courses for English majors at tertiary level (National Curriculum for English Majors at tertiary level, 2000)

Three types of courses for English majors at tertiary level are as follows:

(1) Courses for English language skills: Basic English, listening, speaking, reading, writing, interpretation and translation.

(2) Courses for English language knowledge: English linguistics, English vocabulary learning, English grammar, English stylistics, British and American literature, British and American culture.

(3) Courses for English majors associated with the professional expertise: namely the diplomatic, economic, legal, management, journalism, education, science and technology, culture, military, and other aspects of professional knowledge courses.

The total hours of English learning for English majors in class in 4 years of university life amount to 2,000-2,200 hours.

Appendix 3: Sample Test for English Majors Band Eight (TEM8)

2005 年 03 月 06 日
TEST FOR ENGLISH MAJORS (2005)
-GRADE EIGHT-

PART I LISTENING COMPREHENSION (30 MIN)
SECTION A MINI-LECTURE

In this section you will hear a mini-lecture. You will hear the lecture ONCE ONLY. While listening, take notes on the important points. Your notes will not be marked, but you will need them to complete a gap-filling task after the mini-lecture. When the lecture is over, you will be given two minutes to check your notes, and another ten minutes to complete the gap-filling task on ANSWER SHEET ONE. Use the blank sheet for note-taking.

Writing a Research Paper
I. Research Papers and Ordinary Essay
A. Similarity in (1) _____ :
e.g. -choosing a topic
-asking questions
-identifying the audience
B. Difference mainly in terms of (2) _____
1. research papers: printed sources
2. ordinary essay: ideas in one's (3) _____
II. Types and Characteristics of Research Papers
A. Number of basic types: two
B. Characteristics:

1. survey-type paper:

-to gather (4) _____

-to quote

-to (5) _____

The writer should be (6) _____.

2. argumentative (research) paper:

a. The writer should do more, e.g.

-to interpret

-to question, etc.

b. (7) _____varies with the topic, e.g.

-to recommend an action, etc.

III. How to Choose a Topic for a Research Paper

In choosing a topic, it is important to (8) _____.

Question No. 1: your familiarity with the topic

Question No. 2: Availability of relevant information on the chosen topic

Question No. 3: Narrowing the topic down to (9) _____

Question No. 4: Asking questions about (10) _____

The questions help us to work out way into the topic and discover its possibilities.

SECTION B INTERVIEW

In this section you will hear everything ONCE ONLY. Listen carefully and then answer the questions that follow. Mark the correct answer to each question on your coloured answer sheet.

Questions 1 to 5 are based on an interview. At the end of the interview you will be given 10 seconds to answer each of the following five questions. Now listen to the interview.

1. What is the purpose of Professor McKay's report?

A. To look into the mental health of old people.

B. To explain why people have negative views on old age.

C. To help correct some false beliefs about old age.

D. To identify the various problems of old age

2. Which of the following is NOT Professor McKay's view?

A. People change in old age a lot more than at the age of 21.

B. There are as many sick people in old age as in middle age.

C. We should not expect more physical illness among old people.

D. We should not expect to find old people unattractive as a group.

3. According to Professor McKay's report,

A. family love is gradually disappearing.

B. it is hard to comment on family feeling.

C. more children are indifferent to their parents.

D. family love remains as strong as ever.

4. Professor McKay is _____ towards the tendency of more parents living apart from their children.

A. negative

B. positive

C. ambiguous

D. neutral

5. The only popular belief that Professor McKay is unable to provide evidence against is

A. old-age sickness.

B. loose family ties.

C. poor mental abilities.

D. difficulties in maths.

SECTION C NEWS BROADCAST

In this section you will hear everything ONCE ONLY. Listen carefully and then answer the questions that follow. Mark the correct answer to each question on your coloured answer sheet.

Question 6 is based on the following news. At the end of the news item, you will be given 10 seconds to answer the question. Now listen to the news.

6. Scientists in Brazil have used frog skin to

A. eliminate bacteria.

B. treat burns.

C. Speed up recovery.

D. reduce treatment cost.

Question 7 is based on the following news. At the end of the news item, you will be given 10 seconds to answer the question. Now listen to the news.

7. What is NOT a feature of the new karaoke machine?

A. It is featured by high technology.

B. It allows you to imitate famous singers.

C. It can automatically alter the tempo and tone of a song.

D. It can be placed in specially designed theme rooms.

Question 8 is based on the following news. At the end of the news item, you will be given 10 seconds to answer the question. Now listen to the news.

8. China's Internet users had reached _____ by the end of June.

A. 68 million

B. 8.9 million

C. 10 million

D. 1.5 million

Question 9 and 10 are based on the following news. At the end of the news item, you will be given 20 seconds to answer the question. Now listen to the news.

9. According to the WTO, Chinese exports rose _____ last year.
A. 21%
B. 10%
C. 22%
D. 4.73

10. According to the news, which trading nation in the top 10 has reported a 5 per cent fall in exports?
A. The UK.
B. The US.
C. Japan.
D. Germany.

PART II READING COMPREHENSION (30 MIN)

TEXT A

I remember meeting him one evening with his pushcart. I had managed to sell all my papers and was coming home in the snow. It was that strange hour in downtown New York when the workers were pouring homeward in the twilight. I marched among thousands of tired men and women whom the factory whistles had unyoked. They flowed in rivers through the clothing factory districts, then down along the avenues to the East Side.

I met my father near Cooper Union. I recognized him, a hunched, frozen figure in an old overcoat standing by a banana cart. He looked so lonely, the tears came to my eyes. Then he saw me, and his face lit with his sad, beautiful smile -Charlie Chaplin's smile.

"Arch, it's Mikey," he said. "So you have sold your papers! Come and eat a banana."

He offered me one. I refused it. I felt it crucial that my father sell his bananas, not give them away. He thought I was shy, and coaxed and joked with me, and made me eat the banana. It smelled of wet straw and snow.

"You haven't sold many bananas today, pop," I said anxiously.

He shrugged his shoulders.

"What can I do? No one seems to want them."

It was true. The work crowds pushed home morosely over the pavements. The rusty sky darkened over New York building, the tall street lamps were lit, innumerable trucks, street cars and elevated trains clattered by. Nobody and nothing in the great city stopped for my father's bananas.

"I ought to yell," said my father dolefully. "I ought to make a big noise like other peddlers, but it makes my throat sore. Anyway, I'm ashamed of yelling, it makes me feel like a fool. "

I had eaten one of his bananas. My sick conscience told me that I ought to pay for it somehow. I must remain here and help my father.

"I'll yell for you, pop," I volunteered.

"Arch, no," he said, "go home; you have worked enough today. Just tell momma I'll be late."

But I yelled and yelled. My father, standing by, spoke occasional words of praise, and said I was a wonderful yeller. Nobody else paid attention. The workers drifted past us wearily, endlessly; a defeated army wrapped in dreams of home. Elevated trains crashed; the Cooper Union clock burned above us; the sky grew black, the wind poured, the slush burned through our shoes. There were thousands of strange, silent figures pouring over the sidewalks in snow. None of them stopped to buy bananas. I yelled and yelled, nobody listened.

My father tried to stop me at last. "Nu," he said smiling to console me, "that was wonderful yelling. Mikey. But it's plain we are unlucky today! Let's go home."

I was frantic, and almost in tears. I insisted on keeping up my desperate yells. But at last my father persuaded me to leave with him.

11. "unyoked" in the first paragraph is closest in meaning to
A. sent out
B. released
C. dispatched
D. removed

12. Which of the following in the first paragraph does NOT indicated crowds of people?
A. Thousands of
B. Flowed
C. Pouring
D. Unyoked

13. Which of the following is intended to be a pair of contrast in the passage?
A. Huge crowds and lonely individuals.
B. Weather conditions and street lamps.
C. Clattering trains and peddlers' yells.
D. Moving crowds and street traffic.

14. Which of the following words is NOT suitable to describe the character of the son?

A. Compassionate

B. Responsible

C. Shy

D. Determined

15. What is the theme of the story?

A. The misery of the factory workers.

B. How to survive in a harsh environment.

C. Generation gap between the father and the son.

D. Love between the father and the son.

16. What is the author's attitude towards the father and the son?

A. Indifferent

B. Sympathetic

C. Appreciative

D. Difficult to tell

TEXT B

When former President Ronald Reagan fell and broke his hip two weeks ago, he joined a group of more than 350,000 elderly Americans who fracture their hips each year. At 89 and suffering from advanced Alzheimer's disease, Reagan is in one of the highest-risk groups for this type of accident. The incidence of hip fractures not only increases after age 50 but doubles every five to six years as the risk of falling increases. Slipping and tumbling are not the only causes of hip fractures; weakened bones sometimes break spontaneously. But falling is the major cause, representing 90% of all hip fractures. These... ...

17. The following are all specific measures to guard against injuries with the EXCEPTION of

A. removal of throw rugs.

B. easy access to devices

C. installation of grab bars

D. re-arrangement of furniture

18. In which paragraph does the author state his purpose of writing?

A. The third paragraph

B. The first paragraph

C. The last paragraph

D. The last but one paragraph

19. The main purpose of the passage is to

A. offer advice on how to prevent hip fractures

B. emphasize the importance of health precautions

C. discuss the seriousness of hip fractures.

D. identify the causes of hip fractures.

TEXT C

In his classic novel, "The Pioneers", James Fenimore Cooper has his hero, a land developer, take his cousin on a tour of the city he is building. He describes the broad streets, rows of houses, a teeming metropolis. But his cousin looks around bewildered. All she sees is a forest. "Where are the beauties and improvements which you were to show me?" she asks. He's astonished she can't see them. "Where! Everywhere," he replies. For though they are not yet built on earth, he has built them in his mind, and they as concrete to him as if they were already constructed and finished.

Cooper was illustrating a distinctly American trait, future-mindedness: the ability to see the present from the vantage point of the future; the freedom to feel unencumbered by the past and more emotionally attached to things to come. As Albert Einstein once said, "Life for the American is always becoming, never being." ... ...

20. The third paragraph examines America's future-mindedness from the _____ perspective.

A. future

B. realistic

C. historical

D. present

21. According to the passage, which of the following is NOT brought about by future-mindedness?

A. Economic stagnation

B. Environmental destruction

C. High divorce rates

D. Neglect of history

22. The word "pooh-pooh" in the sixth paragraph means

A. appreciate

B. praise

C. shun

D. ridicule

23. According to the passage, people at present can forecast _____ of a new round of future-mindedness.

A. the nature

B. the location

C. the variety

D. the features

24. The author predicts in the last paragraph that the study of future-mindedness will focus on

A. how it comes into being

B. how it functions

C. what it brings about

D. what it is related to.

TEXT D

25. The phrase "men's sureness of their sex role" in the first paragraph suggests that they

A. are confident in their ability to charm women.

B. take the initiative in courtship.

C. have a clear idea of what is considered "manly".

D. tend to be more immoral than women are.

26. The third paragraph does NOT claim that men

A. prevent women from taking up certain professions.

B. secretly admire women's intellect and resolution.

C. doubt whether women really mean to succeed in business.

D. forbid women to join certain clubs and societies.

27. The third paragraph

A. generally agrees with the first paragraph

B. has no connection with the first paragraph

C. repeats the argument of the second paragraph

D. contradicts the last paragraph

28. At the end of the last paragraph the author uses humorous exaggeration in order to

A. show that men are stronger than women

B. carry further the ideas of the earliest paragraphs

C. support the first sentence of the same paragraph

D. disown the ideas he is expressing

29. The usual idea of the cave man in the last paragraph

A. is based on the study of archaeology

B. illustrates how people expect men to behave

C. is dismissed by the author as an irrelevant joke

D. proves that the man, not woman, should be the wooer

30. The opening quotation from Margaret Mead sums up a relationship between man and woman which the author

A. approves of

B. argues is natural

C. completely rejects

D. expects to go on changing

PART III GENERAL KNOWLEDGE (10 MIN)

31. _____ is the capital city of Canada.

A. Vancouver

B. Ottawa √

C. Montreal

D. York

32. U.S. presidents normally serves a (an) _____ term.

A. two-year

B. four-year √

C. six-year

D. eight-year

33. Which of the following cities is NOT located in the Northeast, U.S.?

A. Huston. √

B. Boston.

C. Baltimore.

D. Philadelphia.

34. _____ is the state church in England.

A. The Roman Catholic Church.

B. The Baptist Church

C. The Protestant Church

D. The Church of England √

注：The Church of England is the officially established Christian church in England and acts as the mother and senior branch of the worldwide Anglican Communion as well as a founding member of the Porvoo Communion.

35. The novel Emma is written by

A. Mary Shelley.

B. Charlotte Bront?.

C. Elizabeth C. Gaskell.

D. Jane Austen. √

36. Which of following is NOT a romantic poet?

A. William Wordsworth.

B. George Elliot. √

C. George G. Byron.

D. Percy B. Shelley.

37. William Sidney Porter, known as O. Henry, is most famous for

A. his poems.

B. his plays.

C. his short stories. √

D. his novels

注：O. Henry was the pen name of William Sydney Porter (September 11, 1862 - June 5, 1910), He was famous for his short stories and a master of the surprise ending, O. Henry is remembered best for such enduring favorites as "The Gift of the Magi" and "The Ransom of Red Chief." The combination of humor and sentiment found in his stories is the basis of their universal appeal.

38. Syntax is the study of

A. language functions.

B. sentence structures. √

C. textual organization.

D. word formation.

注：Definition of Syntax:

a. The study of the rules whereby words or other elements of sentence structure are combined to form grammatical sentences.

b. A publication, such as a book, that presents such rules.

c. The pattern of formation of sentences or phrases in a language.

d. Such a pattern in a particular sentence or discourse.

39. Which of the following is NOT a distinctive feature of human language?

A. Arbitrariness.

B. Productivity.

C. Cultural transmission.

D. Finiteness.

Design feature: features that define our human languages, such as arbitrariness, duality, creativity, displacement, cultural transmission, etc.

40. The speech act theory was first put forward by

A. John Searle.

B. John Austin. √

C. Noam Chomsky.

D. M.A.K. Halliday.

注 : John Langshaw Austin (March 28, 1911 - February 8, 1960) was a philosopher of language, who developed much of the current theory of speech acts. He was born in Lancaster and educated at Balliol College, Oxford. After serving in MI6 during World War II, Austin became White's Professor of Moral Philosophy at Oxford. He occupies a place in the British philosophy of language alongside Wittgenstein in staunchly advocating the examination of the way words are used in order to elucidate meaning.

PART V TRANSLATION （60 MIN）

SECTION A CHINESE TO ENGLISH

Translate the following text into English. Write your translation on ANSWER SHEET THREE.

提示：本文節選自文章《生命的三分之一》作者：馬南邨該文原始出處爲《燕山夜話》（北京出版社 1980 年版）。

一個人的生命究竟有多大意義，這有什麼標準可以衡量嗎？提出一個絕對的標準當然很困難；但是，大體上看一個人對待生命的態度是否嚴肅認真，看他對待勞動、工作等等的態度如何，也就不難對這個人的存在意義做出適當的估計了。

古來一切有成就的人，都很嚴肅地對待自己的生命，當他活著一天，總要盡量多勞動、多工作、多學習，不肯虛度年華，不讓時間白白地浪費掉。我國歷代的勞動人民及大政治家、大思想家等等都莫不如此。

部分譯文：Accomplished men of all ages treat their lives very seriously. As long as they are living, they always labor, work, and study as hard as possible, unwilling to spend time in vain, let alone waste even a single moment of their lives.

SECTION B ENGLISH TO CHINESE

Translate the following underlined part of the text into Chinese. Write your translation on ANSWER SHEET THREE.

提示：本文原文標題 About Reading Books 作者：Virginia Woolf

It is simple enough to say that since books have classes fiction, biography, poetry-we should separate them and take from each what it is right that each should give us. Yet few people ask from books what books can give us. Most commonly we come to books with blurred and divided minds, asking of fiction that it shall be true, of poetry that it shall be false, of biography that it shall be flattering, of history that it shall enforce our own prejudices. If we could banish all such preconception when we read, that would be an admirable beginning. Do not dictate to your author; try to become him. Be his fellow worker and accomplice. If you hang back, and reserve and criticize at first, you are preventing yourself from getting the fullest possible value from what you read. But if you open your mind as widely as possible, then signs and hints of almost imperceptible finesse, from the twist and turn of the first sentences, will bring you into the presence of a human being unlike any other. Steep yourself in this, acquaint yourself with this, and soon you will find that your author is giving you, or attempting to give you, something far more definite.

PART VI WRITING (45 MIN)

Interview is frequently used by employers as a means to recruit prospective employees. As a result, there have been many arguments for or against the interview as a selection procedure. What is your opinion? Write an essay of about 400 words to state your view.

In the first part of your writing you should state your main argument, and in the second part you should support your argument with appropriate details. In the last part you should bring what you have written to a natural conclusion or make a summary. You should supply an appropriate title for your essay.

Marks will be awarded for content, organization, grammar and appropriateness. Failure to follow the above instructions may result in a loss of marks. Write your composition on ANSWER SHEET FOUR.

Appendix 4: Sample transcript of episode in Esther's classroom

Esther: I am not going to interrupt you, now listen carefully, what I want you to do is to be critical, look at this, this is a piece of downloaded information from the internet, you do not know this before, so listen critically. It is revealed that China has the biggest mental health problem in the world.

Particularly about rural women and urban school children. Suicide rate in China is three in every 100, 000; more than 50 % higher than the overall average. Researchers estimated that household depression rate is the highest in the world after the US. The study was undertaken by the Chinese health official, now China finally faces up to suicide crisis.

Esther: Did you understand what has been said?

Learners (in chorus): Yes.

Esther: Who committed suicide?

Learners (in chorus): urban children and rural women.

Esther: Yes, rural, living in the rural area. Suicide rate?

(one of the learners speaks up)

Echo: 10%.

Esther: Can't be that bad.

(students' laughter)

Christina:Three in every 100, 000.

Esther: Good.

Appendix 5: The use of children's literature in Esther's classroom

Esther: This is a children's poem, quite funny. It's about a cat playing with a hat.

(Teacher reads a book)

The children are very bored. Their mother and father have gone out.
I'll not let you get bored,
I'll knock up you high,
And I stand on the ball.
With a book on one hand,
And a hat on my head.
But that's not all I can do,
I am a cat in the hat.

Look at me, look at me,
I am out of the hat.
I can catch 3 books, I can catch fish.
And look I can walk up and down
And that is not all I can do.
Look at me, look at me.
Now upon my tail,
I can stand.
(Students are laughing.)

Appendix 6: Sample transcript of individual presentation in Esther's classroom

Heather: My topic is my part-time job. During the last term summer holiday, I went to hunt job. At first, I went to a bar, and they say we only need a waiter who must have worked over three months, and then I want to send milk, they say only man can do it, (teacher and students laugh,) at last, I went to foreign language school, and want to be-be a teacher, and they say you haven't graduated from the university,

(students are laughing)

but they ask me if I want to be a re-receptionist. And they say o.k. so I started my first job there. At first, I was in the main building, somebody asked about the teaching programme, and asked me if this is a foreign language school, I said yes. Mm, she asked about her son.

(Researcher's note: students are listening attentively, Esther is looking at Heather, smiling)

The woman's voice is very very crazy. (students laughing) I said I don't know because I just a reception. I don't know where you   son is. She said you are the reception, why don't you know this? She's voice is very crazy.

Then two men came, I am afraid if the two men are bad men, I'll be very dangerous. So I left there, I started at 8:30 am, and left at 7:30 pm. The school headmaster told me I should stay later, I should stay a few minutes

more. I go home. And told my mother and father about this job. Next day, I didn't go there.

Esther: Good. Thank you. (Applause)

Appendix 7: Topics for simulated interview in Esther's classroom

1.Departmental Meeting

(hint for group work)

Time:	Friday 1330
Place:	Senior Common Room
Length:	1 Hour.
Chair person:	Prof. Wilkins
Attendance:	Non compulsory/ advisory
Subject:	Funding crisis of project
Outcome:	Suggestions and meetings

2.University Library

(hint for group work)

Procedure:	Application form, sign card.
Number of books:	Postgraduates 10
Period:	Short loan 3 hours
Normal loan:	To the end of the term.
Opening hours:	

Monday-Friday. 9am -2pm;

Sunday: 2pm-7pm

Saturday: 9am – 6pm

Finding books and articles, author and catalogue

Subject guide

Classified catalogue

Type author's name into the computer, ask the librarian

Layout, plan on the wall 6 floors, Penalties

3.University information office

(hint for group work)

Registration: 5 October 7 photos. At the university

Registration with the police within 7 days.

2 passport sized photos

English language test: Not clear.

Health provision: Open to all students. 4 doctors.

Public free, stay over 6 months

Private expensive but better, Prescriptions

Emergencies: 999

Appendix 8: Sample group work in Esther's classroom

(Students were divided into groups, each group were given slips of paper with sentences on them; students were asked to organize these sentences into a coherent story before they went to the front of the classroom to retell the story.)

年   月   日 星 期   第   页

Tomorrow will be wonderful

I'll drive my little car
I'll watch the ships sail by
The next day will be better

I'll take you to the zoo
I'll show you bears and monkeys
And a great gorilla too

We'll have a house with windows
That look out on the sea
So happy, bright and free
With chocolate cake and tea
We'll entertain our neighbours
They'll see us in our little house
As happy as can be

With single beds and tabby cats

We won't need to work all day
We'll just pass the time away
We won't catch those busy trains
The sun will always shine

That whistle down the line
I'll walk along the riverbank
We won't live in basement flats
We won't have to worry

02.3   50340

277

Appendix 9: Sample texts used in Ying's Classroom

Passage 52 Nuclear Power

The big advantage of nuclear power is a large of amount of energy released from a relatively small amount of material. Nuclear power has become an energy in some countries especially in Germany and Japan, the United States and Canada. And most Europeans use nuclear energy. In fact, more abandoned coal reserves. Five problems severely restrict the use of nuclear power instead of coal to generate electricity. The first problem is the danger of an accident. The second is the need to store release of the waste finally into the ocean. No country has devised an appropriate ... to waste products. The third problem is the ...from some material. Nuclear power has the ...in blood twice, the final problem is its high cost. The future of nuclear power has been seriously affected by time, waste and cost.

Passage 53 Diet and Health

Even though we have more choice of what we eat than 40 years ago. The diet of the average American is less healthy. In fact, according to recent study, many a pet... eating specially, tin food, have a healthier diet than most of their owners. The health department was alarmed that the recent figures which show that American has the 3rd highest record in the world for heart disease. Cancer is also a growing cause of death. This has led the government to try to launch a campaign to encourage a healthier eating habit. The campaign will urge people to eat less salt, sugar and animal fat than they do today. It will show the advantages of eating more fresh fruits and vegetables. The health department is going to issue a booklet that will give guidance on which food to eat and which to avoid.

Passage 54 New Year's Celebration

New Year's Day is the world's oldest celebration. In fact, ancient people celebrate New Year even before they have exact ways of measuring time. New Year's Day is also the one holiday that is observed by people of all national and religious groups. More …celebrate New Year at the same time. The Chinese celebrate at different times each year. Sometimes between January 21, and February 19. But the majority of people today celebrate it on January 1st. in some countries, the New Year's holiday is the most important celebration of the year. But this is not true in the United States. Even though it is a celebration that many people enjoy. One reason may be because Christmas comes just one week before the New Year. Christmas is another biggest holiday. American people give it importance that people in other countries give to the start of the New Year.

Appendix 10: The text for a drama play in Ying's classroom (Extract 5.7)

2. Did the writer's response differ from Brando's? In what way?

_____
_____
_____

3. Explain the title "Martin Luther King — They Shot Him?"

_____
_____
_____

V. Go over the text again to find the technique used. Then, complete the statement below by ticking the suitable alternatives, and give examples for what you have chosen if asked.

Some of the technique that can be found in the text are

a. metaphor.

b. repetition.

c. irony.

d. humour.

e. exaggeration.

f. parallelism.

g. personification.

Unit 3 Text C

The Midnight Visitor

Robert Arthur

1. Read the text once without using a dictionary to get a general idea of the content. Then complete each of the statements that follow by ticking the best alternative or filling in the space.

The Midnight Visitor

1 Ausable did not fit the description of any secret agent Fowler had ever read about. Following him down the musty corridor of the gloomy French hotel where Ausable had a room, Fowler felt disappointed. It was a small room, on the sixth floor and scarcely setting for a romantic figure.

2 Ausable was, for one thing, fat. Very fat. And then there was his accent. Though he spoke French and German passably, he had never altogether lost the New England accent he had brought to Paris from Boston twenty years ago.

3 "You are disappointed," Ausable said wheezily over his shoulder. "You were told that I was a secret agent, a spy, dealing in espionage and danger. You wished to meet me because you are a writer, young and romantic. You envisioned mysterious figures in the night, the crank of pistols, drugs in the wine."

4 "Instead, you have spent a dull evening in a French music hall with a sloppy fat man who, instead of having messages slipped into his hand by dark-eyed beauties, gets only an ordinary telephone call making an appointment in his room. You have been bored!" The fat man chuckled to himself as he unlocked the door of his room and stood aside to let his frustrated guest enter.

5 "You are disillusioned," Ausable told him. "But take cheer, my young friend. Presently you will see a paper, a quite important paper for which several men and women have risked their lives, come to me in the next-to-last step of its journey into official hands. Some day soon that paper may well affect the course of history. In that thought is drama, is there not?" As he spoke, Ausable closed the door behind him. Then he switched on the light.

6 And as the light came on, Fowler had his first authentic thrill of the day. For halfway across the room a small automatic pistol in his hand, stood a man.

7 Ausable blinked a few times.

8 "Max," he wheezed, "you gave me quite a start. I thought you were in Berlin. What are you doing in my room?"

9 Max was slender, not tall, and with a face that suggested the look of a fox. Except for the gun, he did not look very dangerous.

10 "The report," he murmured. "The report that is being brought to you tonight concerning some new missiles. I thought I would take it from you. It will be safer in my hands than in yours"

11 Ausable moved to an armchair and sat down heavily. "I'm going to raise the devil with the management this time; I am angry," he said grimly. "This is the second time in a month that somebody has gotten into my room off that confounded balcony!" Fowler's eyes went to the single window of the room. It was an ordinary window, against which now the night was pressing blackly.

12 "Balcony?" Max asked curiously. "No, I had a passkey. I did not know about the balcony. It might have saved me some trouble had I known about it."

13 "It's not my balcony," explained Ausable angrily. "It belongs to the next apartment." He glanced explanatorily at

- 418 -

Fowler. "You see," he said, "this room used to be part of a large unit, and the next room through that door there used to be the living room. It had the balcony, which extends under my window now. You can get onto it from the empty room next door, and somebody did, last month. The management promised to block it off. But they haven't."

14 Max glanced at Fowler, who was standing stiffly a few feet from Ausable, and waved the gun with a commanding gesture. "Please sit down," he said. "We have a wait of a half an hour, I think."

15 "Thirty-one minutes," Ausable said moodily. "The appointment was for twelve-thirty. I wish I knew how you learned about the report, Max."

16 The little spy smiled evilly. "And we wish we knew how your people get the report. But, no harm has been done. I will get it back tonight. What is that? Who is at the door?"

17 Fowler jumped at the sudden knocking at the door. Ausable just smiled. "That will be the police," he said. "I thought that such an important paper as the one we are waiting for should have a little extra protection. I told them to check on me to make sure everything was all right."

18 Max bit his lip nervously. The knocking was repeated.

19 "What will you do now, Max?" Ausable asked. "If I do not answer the door, they will enter anyway. The door is unlocked. And they will not hesitate to shoot."

20 Max's face was black with anger as he backed swiftly toward the window, with his hand behind him, he opened the window and put his leg out into the night. "Send them away!" he warned. "I will wait on the balcony. Send them away or I'll shoot and take my chances!"

21 The knocking at the door became louder and a voice was raised. "Mr. Ausable! Mr. Ausable!"

- 419 -

281

22. Keeping his body twisted so that his gun still covered the fat man and his guest, the man at the window grasped the frame with his free hand to support himself as he rested his weight on one thing. Then he swung his other leg up and over the window sill.

23. The doorknob turned. Swiftly Max pushed with his left hand to free himself and drop to the balcony. And then as he dropped, he screamed once, shrilly.

24. The door opened and a waiter stood there with a tray, a bottle and two glasses. "Here is the drink you ordered, sir." He set the tray on the table, deftly uncorked the bottle, and left the room.

25. White faced and shaking, Fowler stared after him. "But... what about... the police?" he stammered.

26. "There never were any police." Ausable sighed. "Only Henry, whom I was expecting."

27. "But what about the man on the balcony...?" Fowler began.

28. "No," said Ausable, "he won't return."

1. The story is about
a. the struggle between the two secret agents over an important paper.
b. Max and what happened to him in the end.
c. Fowler and what he found one night.
d. Ausable and how he succeeded in keeping the paper for his own men.

2. "The Midnight Visitor" refers to
a. Fowler.
b. Max.
c. the man who would bring Ausable the paper.
d. the waiter who brought Ausable drinks.

· 420 ·

3. Some of the adjectives that can be used to describe Ausable are
_____
_____
_____

II. *Work out the meaning of each of the following words from the context in which it appears, and then tick the best alternative.*

1. FIT in para. 1 probably means
a. like.
b. is suitable for.
c. give.
d. is interested in.

2. FIGURE in para. 1 probably means
a. person.
b. number.
c. writer.
d. novel.

3. ENVISIONED in para. 3 probably means
a. envied.
b. saw.
c. imagined.
d. loved.

4. FRUSTRATED in para. 4 probably means
a. enthusiastic.
b. feeling disappointed.
c. romantic.
d. feeling unlucky.

5. PRESENTLY in para. 5 probably means
a. at present.
b. soon.
c. likely.
d. hopely.

· 421 ·

Appendix 11: Sample transcript of episode in Ying's classroom

1　Ying:　　　　O.k, that's it. 他找到... 意識到情況不妙.

2　Ying & Learners (translate the sentence): He is conscious of the serious situation.

3　Ying: Be conscious of something, very good, very idiomatic. Try.

4　Lei (stands up): He's conscious of his mother watching him.

5　Ying: Mmm, conscious of his mother watching him. Right, o.k, he is conscious

6　of his mother staring at him, that's o.k.

(Ying stands in front of her desk, writes down the idiom on the blackboard)

7　I want you to stand up to do more sentences.

8　Anybody, try.

9　Tingting: He looks at his brother, conscious of danger coming.

10　Ying: The coming danger. Conscious of the coming danger. Anybody else?

11　Yu: She left suddenly, conscious of someone chase her.

12　Ying: Chasing her. Be conscious of someone chasing her. Anything else? O.K.

13　Xiaoyun: She dashed off, conscious of

14　Ying: She dashed off, conscious of-

15　Xiaoyun: Conscious of scarcity of time.

16　Ying: The scarcity of time. O.K. Good. Very good.

17　Ying (opens the book) on page 158, find a sentence in line 58. Find it?

18　Learners (in chorus) Yeah.

Appendix 12: The data collection schedule for my field work

Week	Day	Time	Place	Classroom	Descriptions
1	01/11/04 Monday	10:00-12:00	Room 401 Huiwen Building	Ying's EFL classroom	Participant observation; Audio-recording;
		13:00-15:00	Room 111 Software Building	Esther's EFL classroom	Pre- and post-class interviews with individual language
	03/11/04 Wednesday	8:00-10:00	Room 111 Software Building	Esther's EFL classroom	learners (Semi-structured);
		13:00-15:00	Room 401 Software Building	Ying's EFL classroom	Collection of documents
2	08/11/04 Monday	10:00-12:00	Room 401 Huiwen Building	Ying's EFL classroom	Participant observation; Audio-recording;
		13:00-15:00	Room 111 Software Building	Esther's EFL classroom	Field notes;
	10/11/04 Wednesday	8:00-10:00	Room 111 Software Building	Esther's EFL classroom	Pre- and post- class interviews with individual language learners and
		13:00-15:00	Room 401 Huiwen Building	Ying's EFL classroom	language teachers
3	15/11/04 Monday	10:00-12:00	Room 401 Huiwen Building	Ying's EFL classroom	Participant observation; Audio-recording; Field notes;
		13:00-15:00	Room 111 Software Building	Esther's EFL classroom	Semi-structured interviews and informal interviews with individual
	17/11/04 Wednesday	8:00-10:00	Room 111 Software Building	Esther's EFL classroom	teachers and learners Collection of the textbooks and test papers
		13:00-15:00	Room 401 Software Building	Ying's EFL classroom	

4	22/11/04 Monday	10:00-12:00	Room 401 Huiwen Building	Ying's EFL classroom	Participant observation;
		13:00-15:00	Room 111 Software Building	Esther's EFL classroom	Audio-recording; Field notes;
	24/11/04 Wednesday	8:00-10:00	Room 111 Software Building	Esther's EFL classroom	Semi-structured interviews and informal interviews with individual teachers and learners
		13:00-15:00	Room 401 Huiwen Building	Ying's EFL classroom	
5	29/11/04 Monday	10:00-12:00	Room 401 Huiwen Building	Ying's EFL classroom	Participant observation;
		13:00-15:00	Room 111 Software Building	Esther's EFL classroom	Audio-recording; Field notes;
	01/12/04 Wednesday	8:00-10:00	Language Lab Huiwen Building	Esther's EFL classroom	Collection of students' portfolios in Ying's classroom
		13:00-15:00	Room 401 Huiwen Building	Ying's EFL classroom	
6	06/12/04 Monday	10:00-12:00	Room 401 Huiwen Building	Ying's EFL classroom	Participant Observation;
		13:00-15:00	Room 111 Software Building	Esther's EFL classroom	Audio-recording; Field notes;
	08/12/04 Wednesday	8:00-10:00	Room 111 Software Building	Esther's EFL classroom	Semi-structured and informal interviews with the teachers and student groups
		13:00-15:00	Room 401 Huiwen Building	Ying's EFL classroom	

7	13/12/04 Monday	10:00-12:00	Room 401 Huiwen Building	Ying's EFL classroom	Participant Observation;
		13:00-15:00	Room 111 Software Building	Esther's EFL classroom	Audio-recording; Field notes;
	15/12/04 Wednesday	8:00-10:00	Room 111 Software Building	Esther's EFL classroom	Informal interviews with the teachers and student groups
		13:00-15:00	Room 401 Software Building	Ying's EFL classroom	
8	20/12/04 Monday	10:00-12:00	Room 401 Huiwen Building	Ying's EFL classroom	Participant Observation;
		13:00-15:00	Room 111 Software Building	Esther's EFL classroom	Audio-recording; Field notes;
	22/12/04 Wednesday	8:00-10:00	Room 111 Software Building	Esther's EFL classroom	Semi-structured and informal interviews with individual teachers and learners and student groups
		13:00-15:00	Room 401 Huiwen Building	Ying's EFL classroom	Collection of students' exercise books and written works; Exchange of e-mail addresses

Appendix 13: Sample interview guide for an informal interview

Time	9pm November 17th, 2004
Place	Esther's home
Interview Type	Informal interview with individual teacher
Purpose of Interview	To find out Esther's demographic and dispositional features
Participants	Esther and Yingchun

Interview topics:

Language teaching experience in China;

Goal of classroom language teaching;

Expectations of students;

Preferred classroom language teaching methods;

Preferred classroom activities.

Appendix 14: Sample transcript of a semi-structured interview

Time	9:40am (before Ying's class) November 8th, 2004
Place	Ying's classroom
Interview Type	Semi-structured interview
Purpose of Interview	To find out learners' demographic and dispositional features
Participants	Lei (a language learner in Ying's class) and Yingchun ("Y" stands for Yingchun, "L" stands for Lei)

Y: How long have you been studying at the university so far?

L: Three months.

Y: What did you expect from the teachers?

L: I'm glad to study in this class because Ying is a good teacher.   We have heard this from senior students. She is different from my teacher at high school.

Y: How different?

L: She asked us to learn actively by ourselves. It is very different from our middle school life because back then our teachers used to give us very close inspections; they always told us to do test papers.

Y: What should be the basic classroom interaction pattern, do you think?

L: Well, the basic pattern is teachers stand in the front teaching, and we as students listen.

Y: How do you feel towards teacher's error-correction?

L: It's all right.

Y: Do you feel ashamed when Ying corrects you in front of your classmates?

L: At first, yes. But later I think it is all right because I should do active learning.

Y: Why do you think some students appear to be passive? What about you?

L: I think that must be because they are not well prepared. If they are well prepared, they will answer. I think it is mainly due to the preparation work. If we have all well prepared, then we will all put up our hands.

Appendix 15: Certificate of Ethical Approval from SELL, UK

UNIVERSITY OF EXETER

School of Education and Lifelong Learning

Fieldwork Research by Students

CERTIFICATE OF ETHICAL APPROVAL

To become a Certificate of Approval, you need to fill out this form and have it signed by both your supervisor/tutor and the Chair of the School Research Ethics Committee (see below).

Title of Project: An Ethnographic Investigation of Communication in EFL
Classrooms in a Higher Education Setting in China

Student Name   Yingchun Li   **Student Number**   520024108

Names(s)/Title(s) of Project Research Team Member(s):

Course of Study: PhD in Education
Name of project supervisor/tutor: Prof. Gert Biesta & Ms Sarah Rich
Project Contact Point (incl. Email/telephone no.)
yingchunli2003@yahoo.co.uk
y.li@ex.ac.uk

Brief Description of Project:
including aims/questions and methods

Operated from a perspective that acknowledges the situated nature of learning, this ethnographic study seeks to gain an in-depth understanding of the current EFL teaching and learning situation in higher education in China, and further to get insights into how learning opportunities are constructed. It is proposed to focus on 2 EFL classrooms (one led by a Chinese TEFL teacher, the other led by a foreign TEFL teacher) in one higher education setting in China. The researcher aims to capture the relationship between interaction patterns; the participants' dispositions; and the impact of wider socio-cultural context on the construction of learning opportunities. This study specifically put the following research questions under focus:

*   What are teachers' and students' expectations and perceptions of Chinese EFL classrooms?
*   In what ways are teachers' and students' expectations and perceptions of Chinese EFL classrooms influencing classroom interactions?
*   What are the identifiable patterns of classroom interaction?
*   In what ways can these interactional patterns be seen to impact on the creation and construction of learning opportunities?
*   How can these interactional patterns be seen to both reproduce and impact on the construction of the classroom culture?

The research will be comprised of both classroom observations and interviews with students and their teachers. Audio-taping and possible video-taping will be involved in the research, later-on e-mail interviews will be a complementary element for the fieldwork. Field-notes will act as a major source for the thick description as well as thick explanation in the data analysis process. Before fieldwork starts, informed consent of participation in the project from the participants has been sought; with anonymity and confidentiality assured to the participants during the whole research process.

Note: you should not commence the fieldwork part of the project until you have the signature of your supervisor/tutor.

This project has been approved for the period

from: 10/2003   *to:* 10/2006

by (name of supervisor/tutor /mentor):...... *Sarah Rich* ....

Signature ...... *Sarah Rich* ......   Date ...... *26th May 2005* ......
(research supervisor/tutor/mentor)

Note: This form should now be sent to William Richardson, Chair of Ethics Committee, for countersignature. Once returned, it becomes your Certificate of Ethical Approval and should be kept in your project/course file.

School Ethics Committee approval reference:........... *D/0435/19* ....
(minute number/date reference, etc)

Signature ....   Date ...... *26.7.05* ......
(Chair of School Ethics Committee)

Bibliography

Ackers, J. & Hardman, F. (2001). Classroom interaction in Kenyan primary schools. *Compare, 31*(2), 245-261.

Agar, M. H. (1985). *Speaking of ethnography.* Thousand Oaks: Sage.

Aitken, J. L. & Mildon, D. A. (1992). Teacher education and the developing teacher: The role of personal knowledge. In M. Fullon and A. Hargreaves (Eds.), *Teacher development and educational change* (pp. 10-35). London: Falmer.

Allwright, D. (1993). Integrating research and pedagogy: Appropriate criteria and practical possibilities. In J. Edge & K. Richards (Eds.), *Teachers develop teachers research* (pp. 125-135). Oxford: Heinemann.

Allwright, D. (n.d.). *Interaction and negotiation in the language classroom: Their role in learner development.* Retrieved on October 12, 2006, from http://www.ling.lancs.ac.uk/groups/crile/docs/crile50 allrigh.pdf.

Allwright, D. (2006). Six promising directions in applied linguistics. In S. Gieve & I. Miller (Eds.), *Understanding the language classroom* (pp. 11-18). Basingstoke: Palgrave Macmillan.

Allwright, D. (1988). *Observation in the language classroom.* London: Longman.

Allwright, D. & Bailey, K. M. (1991). *Focus on the language classroom: An introduction to classroom research for language teachers.* Cambridge: Cambridge University Press.

Allwright, D. (1996). Social and pedagogic pressures in the language classroom: The role of socialization. In H. Coleman (Ed.), *Society and the language classroom* (pp. 209-228). Melbourne: Cambridge University Press.

Allwright, R. L. (1983). The importance of interaction in classroom language teaching. *Applied Linguistics, 5*(2), 156-171.

Amidon, E. J. & Hough, J. B. (1967). *Interaction analysis: Theory, research, and application.* Reading: Addison-Wesley Publishing Company.

Angrosino, M.V. & de Perez, K. A. (2000). Rethinking observation: From method to context. In N. K. Denzin & Y. S. Lincoln (Eds.), *Handbook of qualitative research* (2nd ed.) (pp. 673-702). Thousand Oaks: Sage.

Anton, M. (1999). The discourse of a learner-centred classroom: Sociocultural perspectives on teacher-learner interaction in the second language classroom. *The Modern Language Journal, 83*(3), 303-318.

Aarsund, K., Johansen, U., Larsen, S., Pettersen, E.H. (n.d.). *From language teacher to teacher of languages.* Retrieved on October 11, 2006, from http://www.fag.hiof.no/~bu/ilte/introduction.html.

Atkinson, J. M. & Heritage, J. (Eds.). (1984). *Structures of social action: Studies in conversation analysis.* Cambridge: Cambridge University Press.

Baker, C. (1992). *Attitudes and language.* Clevedon: Multilingual Matters.

Ball, S. J. (1990). *Education, politics and policy-making: Explorations in policy sociology.* London: Routledge.

Barbara, L. & Scott, M. (1994). *Reflections on language learning.* Clevedon: Multilingual Matters Ltd.

Barbour, R. S. (2001). Checklists for improving rigor in qualitative research: A case of the tail wagging of the dog? *BMJ, 322,* 1115-1117.

Barnes, D. (1992). The role of talk in learning. In K. Norman (Ed.), *Thinking voices: The work of the national oracy project* (pp. 63-67). London: Hodder and Stoughton.

Bassey, M. (1999). *Case study research in educational settings.* Buckingham: Open University Press.

Bax, S. (2003). The end of CLT: A context sensitive approach to language teaching. *ELT Journal, 57*, 278-287.

Beales, A. R., Spindler, G. and Spindler, L. (1967). *Culture in Process.* New York: Holt, Rinehart and Winston.

Benson, P. & Voller, P. (1997). *Autonomy and independence in language learning.* London: Longman.

BERA revised ethical guidelines for educational research. (2004). BERA: British Educational Research Association.

Biesta, G. J. J. & Burbules, N. C. (2003). *Pragmatism and educational research.* Lanham: Rowman & Littlefield Publishers.

Biesta, G. (2007). Education and the democratic person: Towards a political conception of democratic education. *Teachers College Record, 109*(3), 740-769.

Biggs, J. B. (1987). *Student approaches to learning and studying.* Melbourne: Australian Council for Educational Research.

Black, T. R. (1999). *Doing quantitative research in the social sciences: An integrated approach to research design, measurement and statistics.* London: Sage.

Blake, R. (2000). Computer mediated communication: A window on L2 Spanish interlanguage. *Language Learning & Technology, 4*, 120 - 136.

Block, D. (1996). Not so fast: Some thoughts on theory culling, relativism, accepted findings and the heart and soul of SLA. *Applied Linguistics, 17*, 63-83.

Block, D. & Cameron, D. (Eds). (2002). *Globalization and language teaching.* London: Routledge.

Bloome, D. & Egan-Robertson, A. (1993). The social construction of intertextuality in classroom reading and writing lessons. *Reading Research Quarterly, 28,* 305-333.

Boekaerts, M. (2002). Bringing about change in the classroom: Strengths and weaknesses of the self-regulated learning approach-EARLI presidential address, 2001. *Learning and Instruction, 12,* 589-604.

Bohn, H. (2003). The educational role and status of English in Brazil. *World Englishes, 22,* 159-172.

Bond, M. H. (Ed.). (1986). The psychology of the Chinese people. Oxford: Oxford University Press.

Boyd, M. and Maloof, V. (2000). How teachers build upon student-proposal intertextual links to facilitate student talk in the ESL classroom. In J. Hall and L. Verplaetse (Eds.), *The development of second and foreign language learning through classroom interaction* (pp. 163-182). N.J.: Lawrence Erlbaum Associates.

Boyle, J. (2000). Education for teachers of English in China. *Journal of Education for Teaching, 26*(2), 147-155.

Bourdieu, P. (1977). Cultural reproduction and social reproduction. In J. Karabel & A. H. Haley (Eds.), *Power and ideology in education* (pp. 487-511). New York: Oxford.

Breen, (1985). The social context for language learning-a neglected situation? *Studies in Second Language Acquisition (7),* 135-58.

Breen, M. (1989). The evaluation cycle for language learning tasks. In R. Johnson (Ed.), The second language curriculum. Cambridge: Cambridge University Press.

Breen, M. P. & Littlejohn, A. (2000). *Classroom decision-making: Negotiation and   process syllabuses in practice.* Cambridge: Cambridge University Press.

Breen, M. (Ed.). (2001a). *Learner contributions to language learning: New directions in research.* Harlow: Pearson Education.

Breen, M. (2001b). Language for teaching a language. In C. N. Candlin & N. Mercer (Eds.), *English language teaching in its social context: A reader.* London: Routledge.

Brick, J. (1991). *China: A handbook in intercultural communication.* Sydney: The National Center for English Language Teaching and Research.

Briggs, J. & Monaco, R. (1990). *Metaphor: The logic of poetry.* New York: Pace University Press.

Broadfoot, P. (2001). Culture, learning and comparative education. *Comparative Education 37* (3), 261-66.

Brock, C. A. (1986). The effects of referential questions on ESL classroom discourse. *TESOL Quarterly, 20,* 47-59.

Brown, A. L. (1987). Metacognition, executive control, self-regulation, and other more mysterious mechanisms. In F. E. Weinert & R. H. Kluwe (Eds.), *Metacognition, motivation, and understanding* (pp. 65-116). Hillsdale, New Jersey: Lawrence Erlbaum Associates.

Brown, D. (2001). *Teaching by principle–an interactive approach to language pedagogy.* New York: Addison Wesley Longman.

Brown, H. D. (1994). Teaching by principles: An interactive approach to language pedagogy. N.J.: Prentice Hall Regents.

Brown, H. D. (2000). *Principles of language learning and teaching.* (4th ed.). N.Y.: Pearson.

Brown, H. D. (2002). English language teaching in the "post-method" era: Toward better diagnosis, treatment, and assessment. In J. Richards & W. Renandya (Eds.), *Methodology in language teaching: An anthology of current practice.* (pp. 9-19). Cambridge: Cambridge University Press.

Brown, J. S., Collins. A. & Duguid, P. (1989). Situated cognition and the culture of learning. *Educational Researcher; 18,* 32-42.

Brown, M. (1999). *Action research.* Retrieved on October 7, 2003, from http://www.southernct.edu/.

Bryam, M. & Morgan, C. (1994). *Teaching-and-learning, language-and-culture.* Clevedon: Multilingual Matters.

Bryman, A. & Cramer, D. (1999). *Quantitative data analysis with SPSS release 8 for windows: A guide for social scientists.* London: Routledge.

Burbules, N. C. (2000). The limits of dialogue as a critical pedagogy. In Trifonas, P. P. (Ed.), *Revolutionary pedagogies: Cultural politics, instituting education, and the discourse of theory.* New York: Routledgefalmer.

Burgess, B. (2005). *The educational theory of Socrates.* Retrieved on October 20, 2005, from http://www.newfoundations.com/GALERY/Socrates.html.

Burgess, R.G. (1989). *The ethics of educational research.* New York: Falmer.

Burr, V. (1995). *An introduction to social constructionism.* London: Routledge.

Burton, D. (1981). The sociolinguistic analysis of spoken discourse. In P. French & M. Maclure (Eds.), *Adult-child conversation.* (pp. 21-46.) New York: St Martins.

Candela, A. (1999). Students' power in classroom discourse. *Linguistics and Education, 10,* 139-163.

Candlin, C. N. & Mercer, N. (Eds.). (2001). *English language teaching in its social context: A reader.* London: The Open University.

Carr, D. (1992). Practical enquiry, values, and the problem of educational theory. *Oxford Review of Education, 18* (3), 241-251.

Carr, W. (1987). What is an educational practice. *Journal of Philosophy of Education, 21* (2), 163-175.

Carr, W. (1995). *For education, towards critical educational inquiry.* Buckingham: Open University Press.

Carr, W. & Kemmis, S. (1986). *Becoming critical: Education knowledge and action research.* London: Falmer.

Cazden, C. B. (1988). *Classroom discourse: The language of teaching and learning.* Portsmouth: Heinemann.

Celce-Murcia, M. & Olshtain, E. (2000). *Discourse and context in language teaching: A guide for language teachers.* Cambridge: Cambridge University Press.

Chaudron, C. (1988). *Second language classrooms.* Cambridge: Cambridge University Press.

Chen, T. (2003). Reticence in class and on-line: Two ESL students' experiences with communicative language teaching. *System, 31,* 259-281.

Chen, J. F., Warden, C. A. & Chang, H. (2005). Motivators that do not motivate: The case of Chinese EFL learners and the influence of culture on motivation. *TESOL Quarterly, 39*(4), 609-633.

Chen, Y. (2006). EFL instruction and assessment with portfolios: A case study in Taiwan. *The Asian EFL Journal Quarterly, 8*(1), 69-96.

Cobb, P., Confrey, J., Disessa, A., Lehrer, R., and Schauble, L. (2003). Design experiments in educational research. *Educational researcher, 32*(1), 9-13.

Coffey, A & Atkinson, P. (1996). *Making sense of qualitative data: Complementary strategies.* Thousand Oaks: Sage.

Cohen, L. & Holliday, M. (1982). *Statistics for social scientists: An introductory text with computer programmes in basic.* London: Harper & Row, Publishers.

Cohen, L. & Manion, L. (1981). *Perspectives on classrooms and schools.* London: Holt, Pinehart and Winston.

Cohen, A. (2003). Ethnography and case study: A comparative analysis. Academic Exchange Quarterly, September issue.

Coleman, H. (1996). *Society and the language classroom.* Cambridge: Cambridge University Press.

Conteh, J. (2003). *Succeeding in diversity: Culture, language and learning in primary classrooms.* Trentham Books: Stoke on Trent.

Cook, V. (2001). *Second language learning and language teaching.* New York: Oxford University Press.

Cooper, H. M. (1989). *Integrating research: A guide for literature reviews.* Newbury Park: Sage.

Cortazzi, M. (1990). Cultural and educational expectations in the language classroom. In H. Brian (Ed.), *Culture and the language classroom.* Modern English Publications in association with the British council.

Cortazzi, M., Jin, L. (1996). Cultures of learning: language classrooms in China. In H. Coleman (Ed.), *Society and the language classroom.* Cambridge University Press, Cambridge.

Cotterall, S. (1999). Key variables in language learning: What do learners believe about them? *System, 27,* 493-513.

Confucius, (500 B.C.). *The Analects.* Retrieved on October 17, 2005, from http://classics.mit.edu/Confucius/analects.html.

Crabbe, D. (2003). The Quality of language learning opportunities. *TESOL Quarterly, 37,* 9-34.

Cray, E. N. (1999). *Grammar, text, context and discourse.* Unpublished doctoral dissertation. Department of linguistics and modern English language. Lancaster: Lancaster University.

Creswell, J. W. (1998). *Qualitative inquiry and research design: Choosing among five traditions.* Thousand Oaks: Sage.

Crookes, G. & Chaudron, C. (2001). Guidelines for language classroom instruction. In M. Celce-Murcia (Ed.), *Teaching English as a second or foreign language* (3rd ed., pp. 29-42). Boston: Heinle & Heinle.

Crotty, M. (1998). *The foundations of social research: Meaning and perspectives in the research process.* London: Sage.

Cumming, A. H. (1994). Alternatives in TESOL research: Descriptive, interpretive, and ideological orientations. *TESOL Quarterly, 28* (4), 673-703.

Dai, H. (2004). *Changes in China.* DGSCIC Universities conference speech.

Damhuis, R. A (2000). A different teacher role in language arts education: Interaction in a small circle with teacher. In J. K. Hall & L. S. Verplaetse (Eds.), *Second and foreign language learning through classroom interaction.* (pp. 243-265). New Jersey: Lawrence Earlbaum Associates.

Damen, L. (1987). *Culture learning: The fifth dimension in the language classroom.* Reading, MA: Addison-Wesley.

Davies, A. (1975). *Problems of language and learning.* London: Heinemann.

Degen, T. & Absalom, D. (n.d.). *Teaching across cultures: Considerations for Western EFL teachers in China.* Retrieved on April 23, 2006, from http://sunzi1.lib.hku.hk/hkjo/view/5/500050.pdf.

Denzin, K. (1989). *Interpretive interactionism.* Newbury Park: Sage.

Denzin, K. N. & Lincoln, Y. S. (1994). *Handbook of Qualitative Research.* Thousand Oaks: Sage.

Dewey, J. (1975). *Educational theory.* Illinois: Illinois University.

Denzin, K. N. & Lincoln, Y. S. (2000). *Handbook of qualitative research.* Thousand Oaks: Sage.

Dicks, et al. (2006). Multimodal ethnography. *Qualitative Research. 6,* 77-96.

Dickson, W. P. (1982). Creating communication-rich classrooms: Insights form the sociolinguistic and referential tradition. In Wilkinson, L. C. (Ed.), *Communicating in the classroom* (pp. 131-50). New York: Academic Press.

Dickinson, L. (1987). *Self-instruction in language learning.* Avon: Cambridge University Press.

Donato, R. & Mccormick, D. (1994). A sociocultural perspective on language learning strategies: The role of mediation. *The Modern Language Journal, 78* (4), 453-464.

Dooley, K. (2001). Re-envisioning teacher preparation: Lessons from China. *Journal of Education for Teaching, 27* (3), 241-251.

Douglas, B. H. (1993). *Teaching by principles : An interactive approach to language pedagogy.* N. J.: Prentice Hall Regents.

Duff, P. & Uchida, Y. (1997). The negotiation of teachers' sociocultural identities and practices in postsecondary EFL classrooms. *TESOL Quarterly 31*(3), 451-486.

Duff, P.A. (2000). Repetition in foreign language classroom interaction. In J. K. Hall and L.S. Verplaetse (Eds.), *Second and Foreign Language Learning through Classroom Interaction* (pp. 109-139). New Jersey: Lawrence Erlbaum Associates.

Duff, A. S. (2003). Higher education teaching: A communication perspective. *Active Learning in Higher Education, 4*(3), 256-289.

Duranti, A. (1997). *Linguistic anthropology.* Cambridge: Cambridge University press.

Eder, D. (1982). Differences in communicative styles across ability groups. In L. C. Wilkinson (Ed.), *Communicating in the Classroom.* New York: Academic Press.

Edwards, J. A. & Lampert, M. D. (1993). *Talking data: Transcription and coding in discourse research.* N.J.: Lawrence Erlbaum Associates.

Edwards, A. D. & Westgate D. P. G. (1994). *Investigating classroom talk.* London: Falmer.

Ehrman, M. E. & Dornyei, Z. (1998). *Interpersonal dynamics in second language education: The visible and invisible classroom.* Thousand Oaks: Sage.

Ellen, R. F. (1984). *Ethnographic research: A guide to general conduct.* New York: Academic Press.

Elliot, J. (1991). *Action research for educational change.* Milton Keynes: Open University Press.

Ellis, Rod. (1990). *Instructed second language acquisition: Learning in the classroom.* Oxford: Basil Blackwell.

Ellison, C. M., Boykin, A. W., Towns, D. P. and Stokes, A. (2000). *Classroom cultural ecology.* CRESPAR.

Ely, M. (1991). *Doing qualitative research: Circles within circles.* London: Falmer.

Ely, M., Vinz, R., Downing, M., Anzul, M. (1997). *On writing qualitative research: Living by words,* London: Falmer.

Entwistle, N. J. & Ramsden, P. (1983). *Understanding student learning.* London: Croom Helm.

Ernest, P. (1994). *Educational research, its philosophy and purpose: An introduction to research methodology and paradigms.* Exeter: The Research Support Unit.

Faltis, C. (1997). Case study methods in researching language and education. In N. Hornberger & D. Corson (Eds.), *Research methods in language and education* (pp. 145-152). Dordrecht: Kluwer.

Fang, X. (2005). Sustaining CLT through group work in the Chinese EFL classroom. *CELEA Journal. 28* (2), 39-43.

Ferguson, G. A. (1976). *Statistical analysis in psychology and education.* New York: McGraw-Hill Book Company.

Field, A. (2000). *Discovering statistics: Using SPSS for windows.* London: Sage.

Fink, A. (1998). *Conducting research literature reviews: From paper to the Internet.* London: Sage.

Finkelstein, D. & McCleery, A. (2002). *The book history reader.* London: Routeledge.

Firth, L. A. & Wagner, J. (1997). On discourse, communication, and (some) fundamental concepts in SLA research. *The Modern Language Journal, 81,* 285-300.

Fiske, D. W. & Shweder, R. A. (1986). *Metatheory in social science: Pluralisms and subjectivities.* Chicago: The University of Chicago Press.

Flick, U. (1998). *An introduction to qualitative research,* London: Sage.

Foster, P. & Ohta, A. S. (2005). Negotiation and peer assistance in second language classrooms. *Applied Linguistics, 26*(3), 402-430.

Framke, C. (1969). Notes on queries in anthropology. In Stephan T, (Ed.), *Cognitive anthropology.* New York: Holt, Rinehart and Winston.

Freeman, D. (1992). Language teacher education, emerging discourse, and change in classroom practice. In J. Flowerdew, M. Brock, and S. Hsia (Eds.), *Perspectives on second language teacher education* (pp. 1-21). Hong Kong: City Polytechnic of Hong Kong.

Freeman, D. (1996). Redefining research and what teachers know. In K. M. Bailey & D. Nunan (Eds.), *Voices from the language classroom: Qualitative research in second language education* (pp. 88-115). Cambridge: Cambridge University Press.

Freeman, D. & Johnson, K. E. (1998). Reconceptualizing the knowledge-base of language teacher education. *TESOL Quarterly 32*(3), 397-417.

Freeman, D. (2006). Teaching and learning in "the age of reform": The problem of the verb. In S. Gieve & I. K. Miller (Eds.), *Understanding the language classroom* (pp. 239-262). Basingstoke: Palgrave Macmillan.

Freire, P., and Macedo, D. (1995). A dialogue: Culture, language and race. *Harvard Educational Review, 65*(3), 377-402.

Galloway, A. (1993). *Communicative language teaching: An introduction and sample activities*. Center for Applied Linguistics. Retrieved on September, 6, 2007, from http://www.cal.org/resources/digest/gallow01.html.

Gao, L. & Watkins, D. A. (2002). Conceptions of teaching held by school science teachers in P. R. China. *Identification and cross-cultural comparisons, 24*(1), 61-79.

Garrett, P. & Shortall, T. (2002). Learners' evaluations of teacher-fronted and student-centred classroom activities. *Language Teaching Research, 6,* 25-57.

Garton, S. (2002). Learner initiative in the language classroom. *ELT Journal, 56*(1), 47-56.

Gass, S. M., Mackey, A. & Pica, T. (1998). The role of input and interaction in second language acquisition: Introduction to the special issue. *The Modern Language Journal, 82,* 338-356.

Gass, S., & Varonis, E. (1994). Input, interaction, and second language production. *Studies in Second Language Acquisition, 16*(3), 283-302.

Gass, S. M., Mackey, A. and Pica, T. (1998). The role of input and interaction in second language acquisition: Introduction to the special issue. *Modern Language Journal, 82*(3), 299-307.

Geekie & Raban, B. (1993). *Learning to read and write through classroom talk.* Stoke-on-trent: Trentham Books.

Gibbons, P. (1998). Classroom talk and the learning of new registers in a second language. *Language and Education 12*(2), 99-118.

Gibbons, P. (2003). Mediating language learning: Teacher interactions with ESL students in a content-based classroom. *TESOL Quarterly, 37*(2), 247-273.

Gieve, S. & Miller, I. (Eds.). (2006). *Understanding the language classroom.* Basingstoke: Palgrave Macmillan.

Glew, P. J. (1998). Verbal interaction and English second language acquisition in classroom contexts. *Issues in Educational Research, 8*(2), 83-94.

Goetz, J. & LeCompte, M. (1984). *Ethnography and qualitative design in educational research.* San Diego: Academic Press.

Goffman, E. (1667). Interactional ritual: Essays on face-to-face behavior. New York: Pantheon Books.

Goodwin, C. & Duranti, A. (Eds.). (1991). *Rethinking context.* Cambridge: Cambridge University Press.

Graham, S. (1997). *Effective Language Learning.* Avon: Multilingual Matters.

Green, J. & Harker, J. (1982). Gaining access to learning: Conversational, social and cognitive demands of group participation. In L. C. Wilkinson (Ed.), *Communicating in the classroom.* London: Academic Press.

Greeno, J. G., Collins A. M. & Resnick, L. B. (1996). Cognition and learning. In D.C. Berlinger & R.C. Calfee (Eds.), *Handbook of educational psychology.* New York: Simon & Schuster Macmillan.

Gubrium, J. F. & Silverman, D. (1989). *The politics of field research: Sociology beyond enlightenment.* London: Sage.

Guo, N. & Li, D. (n.d.). *An ongoing teaching experimental project of EFL in a Chinese tertiary education context.* Retrieved on April 24, 2006, from http://www.aare.edu.au/04pap/nai04371.pdf.

Guskey, T. & Huberman, M. (1995). *Professional development in education: New paradigms and practices.* New York: Teachers College Press.

Gutting, G. (1980). *Paradigms and revolutions: Appraisals and applications of Thomas Kuhn's philosophy of science.* Notre Dame: University of Notre Dame Press.

Hadley, G. (1996). *The culture of learning and the good teacher in Japan: An analysis of student views.* Niigata: Japan.

Hardy, I. M. & Moore, J. (2004). Foreign language students' conversational negotiations in different task environments. *Applied Linguistics, 25*(3), 340-370.

Hatfield (1994). *Classroom Dynamics.* Oxford: Oxford University Press.

Hall, J. K. (1998). Differential teacher attention to student utterances: The construction of different opportunities for learning in the IRF. *Linguistics and Education, 9,* 287-311.

Hall, J.K. (2000). Classroom interaction and additional language learning: implications for teaching and research. In J.K. Hall & L.S.Verplaetse (Eds.), *Second and foreign language learning through classroom interaction* (PP. 287-298). N.J.: Lawrence Erlbaum Associates.

Hall, J. K. (2002). *Teaching and researching language and culture.* London: Longman.

Hall, J. K. & Eggington, W. G. (Eds.). (2000). *The sociolinguistics of English language teaching.* Clevedon: Multilingual Matters.

Hall, J. K. & Verplaetse, L. S. (Eds.). (2000). *Second and foreign language learning through classroom interaction.* N.J.: Lawrence Erlbaum Associates.

Hammersley, M. (1990). *Reading ethnographic research: A critical guide.* London: Longman.

Hammersley, M. & Atkinson, P. (1995). *Ethnography: Principles in practice.* (2nd ed.). London: Routledge.

Hargreaves, D. H. (1972). *Interpersonal relations and education.* London: Routledge & Kegan Paul.

Harmer, J. (1983). *The practice of English language teaching.* London: Longman.

Harmer, J. (1998). *How to teach English: An introduction to the practice of English language teaching.* England: Longman.

Harmer, J. (2001). *The practice of English language teaching.* Essex: Pearson Education.

Harrison, B. (Ed.). (1990). *Culture and the language classroom.* Hong Kong: Modern English Publications.

Hart, C. (1998). *Doing a literature review: Releasing the social science research imagination.* London: Sage.

Hawkins, M. (2005). Becoming a student: identity work and academic literacies in early schooling. *TESOL Quarterly, 39*(1), 59-82.

Hatch, E. (1992). *Discourse and language education.* Cambridge: Cambridge University Press.

Hayhoe, R. (1989). *China's universities and the open door.* N.Y.: M. E. Sharpe.

He, A. W. (2004). CA for SLA: Arguments from the Chinese language classroom. *The Modern Language Journal, 88,* 568-582.

Hedge, T. (2000). *Teaching and learning in the language classroom.* Oxford: Oxford University Press.

Hein, G. E. (1991). *Constructivist learning theory.* Jerusalem: CECA conference.

Heritage, J., Atkinson, J. M. (Eds.). (1984). *Structures of social action: Studies in conversation analysis.* Cambridge: Cambridge University Press.

Heritage, J. (1997). Conversation analysis and institutional talk: Analyzing data. In D. Silverman (Ed.), *Qualitative analysis: Issues of theory and method* (pp. 161-182). London: Sage.

Hicks, D. (1995). Discourse, learning and teaching. *Review of Research in Education, 21,* 49-95.

Hilleson, M. (1996). "I want to talk with them, but I don't want them to hear": An introspective study of second language anxiety in an English-medium school. In K.M. Bailey & D. Nunan (Eds.), *Voices from the language classroom* (pp. 248-275). Cambridge: Cambridge University Press.

Hillage, J. (1998). *Excellence in research on schools.* London: DfEE.

Hinkel, E. (1999). *Culture in second language teaching and learning.* Cambridge: Cambridge University Press.

Ho, J. & Crookall, D. (1995). Breaking with Chinese cultural traditions: Learner autonomy in English language teaching. *System, 23*(2), 235-243.

Hodkinson, P., Biesta, G., James, D., Gleeson, D & Postlethwaite, K. (2005). *Improving learning cultures in further education: A new cultural approach.* TLRP research briefing 12. London: TLRP.

Hoepfl, M. C. (1997). Choosing qualitative research: A primer for technology education Researchers. *Journal of Technology Education. 9*(1). Retrieved on June 6, 2006, from http://scholar.lib.vt.edu/ejournals/JTE/v9n1/hoepfl.html.

Holec, H. (1981). *Autonomy and foreign language learning.* Oxford: Pergamon.

Holliday, A. (1994). *Appropriate methodology and social context.* Cambridge: Cambridge University Press.

Holliday, A. (1999). "Small cultures". *Applied Linguistics, 20*(2), 237-264.

Holliday, A. (2002). *Doing and writing qualitative research.* London: Sage.

Hollis, M. (1994). *The philosophy of social science.* Cambridge: Cambridge University Press.

Hu, G. (2003). English language teaching in China: Regional differences and contributing factors. *Journal of Multilingual and Multicultural Development, 24,* 290-318.

Hu, G. (2005). CLT is best for China-an untenable absolutist claim. *ELT Journal 59*(1), 65-68.

Hutchby, I., & Wooffitt, R. (1998). *Conversation analysis.* Cambridge: Polity Press.

Hwang, C. (2005). Effective EFL education through popular authentic materials. *Asian EFL Journal, 7* (1). Article 6.

Hymes, D. (1982). What is ethnography? In H. T. Trueba, G. P. Guthrie & A. A. Glatthorn (Eds.), *Children in and out of school: Ethnography and education* (pp. 33-58). Washington, D.C.: Center for Applied Linguistics.

Ira Shor, (n.d.). Retrieved on February 6, 2007, from http://www.campbaltimore.org/freire.htm.

Jaworski, A. & Coupland, N. (1998). *The discourse reader.* London: Routledge.

Jepson, K. (2005). Conversations-and negotiated interaction-in text and chat rooms. *Language Learning & Technology, 9*(3), 79-98.

Jin, L. & Cortazzi, M. (2002). English language teaching in China: A bridge for the future. *Asia Pacific Journal of Education, 22*(2), 53-64.

Johnson, D. M. (1992). *Approaches to research in second language learning.* New York: Longman.

Johnson, K. E. (1995). *Understanding communication in second language classrooms.* Cambridge: Cambridge Language Education.

Johnson, B. & Chhetri, N. (2002). Exclusionary policies and practices in Chinese minority education: The case of Tibetan education. *Current Issues in Comparative Education, 2*(2), 142-153.

Joiner, E. G. & Westphal, P. B. (1978). *Developing communication skills: General considerations and specific techniques.* MA: Newbury House Publishers.

Jorgenson, D. L. (1989). *Participant observation: A methodology for human studies.* London: Sage.

Kamberelis, G. (2001). Producing heteroglossic classroom (micro) cultures through hybrid discourse practice. *Linguistics and education, 12,* 85-125.

Kaplan, A. (1997). Public life: A contribution to democratic education. *Curriculum Studies, 29*(4), 431-453.

King, E. J. (1970). *The education of teachers, a comparative analysis.* Surrey: Bartholomew Press.

King, G., Keohane, R. O., Verba, S. (1994). *Designing social inquiry.* Princeton: Princeton University Press.

Klein, W. (1986). *Second language acquisition.* Cambridge: Cambridge University Press.

Kolarik, K. (2004). *Loosening the grip on the communicative ideal-a cultural perspective.* 17th educational conference Adelaide.

Kosnick, C. & Beck, C. (2000). The action research process as a means of helping student teachers understand and fulfil the complex role of the teacher. *Educational Action Research, 8*(1), 115-136.

Kramsch, C. J. (1981). *Discourse analysis and second language teaching.* Washington: Center for Applied Linguistics.

Kramsch, C. (1993). *Context and culture in language teaching.* Oxford: Oxford University Press.

Krashen, S. D. ((1981). *Second language acquisition and second language learning.* Oxford: Pergamon.

Krashen, S. D. (1982). *Principles and practice in second language acquisition.* Oxford: Pergamon.

Krashen, S. D. (1985). *The input hypothesis: Issues and implications.* London: Longman.

Krashen, S. (1994). The Input Hypothesis and its rivals. In N., Ellis (Ed.), *Implicit and Explicit Learning of Languages* (pp. 45-77). London: Academic press.

Krashen, S. D. (1998). Comprehensible output. *System, 26,* 175-182.

Krashen, S. D. & Terrell, T. D. (1983). *The natural approach: Language acquisition in the classroom.* Oxford: Pergamon.

Kuhn, T. S. (1962). *The structure of scientific revolutions.* Chicago: The University of Chicago Press.

Kumaravadivelu, B. (1993). Maximizing learning potential in the communicative classroom. *ELT Journal, 47*(1), 12-21.

Kumaravadivelu, B. (1999). Critical classroom discourse analysis. *TESOL Quarterly, 33,* 453-483.

Kumaravadivelu, B. (2006). TESOL methods: Changing tracks, challenging trends. *TESOL Quarterly, 40*(1), 59-81.

Kozulin, A. (Ed.). (2003). *Vygotsky's Educational Theory in Cultural Context.* Cambridge: Cambridge University Press.

Kvale, S. (1996). *InterViews: An introduction to qualitative research interviewing.* Thousand Oaks: Sage.

Lapadat, J. C. (2003). Teachers in an online seminar talking about talk: Classroom discourse and school change. *Language and Education, 17*(1), 21-41.

Lantolf, J. P. & Pavlenko, A. (1995). Sociocultural theory and second language acquisition. *Annual Review of Applied Linguistics, 15,* 108-124.

Lantolf, J. P. & Pavlenko, A. (2001). In M. P. Breen (Ed.), *Learner contributions to language learning. New directions in research.* Harlow: Longman.

Lantolf, J. P. & Pavlenko, A. (1995). Sociocultural theory and second language acquisition. *Annual Review of Applied Linguistics, 15,* 108-124.

Larsen-Freeman, D. (1986). *Techniques and principles in language teaching.* Oxford: Oxford University Press.

Lather, P. (1991). *Getting smart: Feminist research and pedagogy within the postmodern.* New York: Routledge.

Lave, J. & Wenger, E. (1991). *Situated learning: Legitimate peripheral participation.* Cambridge: Cambridge University Press.

Lazaraton, (2003). Incidental displays of cultural knowledge in the Nonnative-English-Speaking teacher's classroom. *TESOL Quarterly, 37*(2), 213-247.

Lecompte, M. D. & Preissle, J. (1993). *Ethnography and qualitative design in educational research.* San Diego: Academic Press.

Lemke, J. L. (1990). *Talking science: Language, learning and values.* Norwood: Ablex Publishing Company.

Leontiev, A. A. (1981). *Psychology and the language learning process.* Oxford: Pergamon.

Lerner, G. H. (2002). Turn sharing: The choral co-production of talk in interaction. In C. E. Ford, B. A. Fox, & S. A. Thompson (Eds.), *The language of turn and sequence* (pp. 225-256). Oxford: Oxford University Press.

Liao, X. (2004). The need for communicative language teaching in China. *ELT Journal, 58*(3), 270-273.

Lightbown; P. M.; Spada, N. (1990). Focus on form and corrective feedback in communicative language teaching. *Studies in Second Language Acquisition, 12*(4), 429-448.

Lightbown, P. M. & Spada, N.(2001). Factors affecting second language acquisition. In C. N. Candlin & N, Mercer (Eds.), English language teaching in its social context (pp. 28-43). London: Routledge.

Lin, Y. (1935). *My country and my people.* N.Y.: Reynal & Hitchook.

Lin, A. M. Y. (1999). Doing-English-lessons in the reproduction or transformation of social worlds? *TESOL Quarterly, 33,* 393-412.

Liszka, S. (2005). *The inclusive language classroom: Dyslexia and the foreign language learner.* Annual Report (2004-2005): University of London Institute in Paris.

Littlewood, W. (1981). *Communicative language teaching: An introduction.* Cambridge: Cambridge University Press.

Littlewood, W. (1993). *Developing autonomy in the foreign language classroom.* Paper presented at the 10th AILA Congress, Amsterdam, Netherlands.

Littlewood, W. (1996). "Autonomy": An anatomy and a framework. *System, 24,* 427-435.

Lernke, J. L. (1989). *Using language in the classroom.* Oxford: Oxford University Press.

Lightbown, P. (1985). Great expectations in second language acquisition research and classroom teaching. *Applied Linguistics, 6*, 263-273.

Livingston, J. A. (1996). *Effects of metacognitive instruction on strategy use of college students.* Unpublished manuscript: State University of New York at Buffalo.

LoCastro, V. (1994). Teachers helping themselves: Classroom research and action research. *The Language Teacher, 18*(2), 4-7.

LoCastro, V. (2001). Teaching English to large classes. *TESOL Quarterly, 35,* 493-496.

Locke, L. F., Silverman, S. J. and Spirduso, W. W. (1998). *Reading and understanding research.* Thousand Oaks: Sage.

Long, M. H. (1983). Native speaker/non-native speaker conversation in the second language classroom. In M.A. Clarke & J. Handscombe (Eds.), *On TESOL 82: Pacific perspectives on language learning and teaching* (pp. 207-225). Washington, D.C.: TESOL.

Long, M. H., Brock, C., Crookes, G., Deicke, C., Potter, L. and Zhang, S. (1984). *The effect of teachers' questioning patterns and wait-time on pupil participation in public high school classes in Hawaii for students of limited English proficiency.* Manoa: Center for Second Language Classroom Research.

Long, M. and Porter, P. (1985). Group work, interlanguage talk and classroom second language acquisition. *TESOL Quarterly, 19*(2), 207-228.

Long M. (1996). *The role of the linguistic environment in second language acquisition.* San Diego: Academic Press.

Love, K. & Sucherdi, D. (1996). The negotiation of knowledge in an adult English as a second language classroom. *Linguistics and Education, 8,* 229-267.

Lowenberg, J. (1993). Interpretive research methodology: Broadening the dialogue. *Advances in Nursing Science, 16*(2), 57-69.

Luke, A. (1995). Text and discourse in education: An introduction to critical discourse analysis. *Review of Research in Education, 21,* 3- 48.

Lynch, T. (1996). *Communication in the language classroom.* Oxford: Oxford University Press.

Mason, T. (n.d.). Retrieved on May 1, 2006, from http:// www.timothyjpmson.com/WebPages/LangTeach/Licence/CM/Old Lectures/L4_Experiments.htm.

McDonough, J. & Shaw, C. (1993). *Materials and methods in ELT: A teacher's guide.* Oxford: Blackwell.

McDonough, K. (2004). Learner-learner interaction during pair and small group activities in a Thai EFL context. *System, 32,* 207-224.

Macintyre, C. (2000). *The art of action research in the classroom.* London: David Fulton Publishers.

Marcus, G. and Fischer, M. (1986) *Anthropology as cultural critique: An experimental moment in the human sciences.* Chicago: University of Chicago Press.

Markee, N. (2000). *Conversation analysis.* NJ: Lawrence Earlbaum Associates.

Markova, I. (1982). *Paradigms, thought, and language.* Chichester: John Wiley & Sons.

Massey, A. (1998). *"The way we doing things around here": The culture of ethnography.* Paper presented at the Ethnography and Education Conference, Oxford University Department of Educational Studies (OUDES).

Mayo, M. & Pica, T. (2000). Interaction among proficient learners: Are input, feedback and output needs addressed in a foreign language context? *Studia Linguistica 54*(2), 272-279.

McBurney, N. S. & Morrell, S. A. (2001). Insights for interns: Democracy in a whole language classroom. *The English Journal, 90*(5), 23-27.

McDonough, J. & Shaw. C. (1933). *Materials and Methods in ELT.* Oxford: Blackwell.

McDonough, K. (2004). Learner-learner interaction during pair and small group activities in a Thai EFL context. *System, 32,* 207-224.

McEnroe, A. M. (2001). *Confucius's Educational Theory.* Retrieved on May 28, 2006, from http://www.newfoundations.com/GALERY/Confucius.html.

Mehan, H. (1979). *Learning lessons: Social organization in the classroom.* Cambridge: Harvard University Press.

Mehan, H. (1981). Ethnography of bilingual education. In H. Trueba, G. Guthrie and K. Au (Eds.), *Culture and the bilingual classroom.* Rowley: Newbury House Publishers, Inc.

Mercer, N. (1995). *The guided construction of knowledge: Talk amongst teachers and learners.* Clevedon: Multilingual Matters.

Michael, H. (2001). *Textual interaction: An introduction to written discourse analysis.* London: Routledge.

Miles, M. B. & Huberman, A. M. (1994). *An expanded sourcebook: Qualitative data analysis.* Thousand Oaks: Sage.

Millen, D. R. (2000). *Rapid ethnography: Time deepening strategies for HCI field research.* New York City: ACM.

Ministry of Education (2003). Retrieved on November 29, 2004 from http://www.moe.edu.cn.

Mission Statement of the School of Foreign Languages, (n.d.). Retrieved on November 20, 2004, from http://210.30.208.159/cflweb/schoolintro/schoolln.htm.

Mitchell, R. (1988). *Communicative language teaching in practice.* London: Centre for Information on Language Teaching and Research.

Mitchell, R. & Lee, J. H. (2003). Sameness and difference in classroom learning cultures: Interpretations of communicative pedagogy in the UK and Korea. *Language Teaching Research, 7,* 35-63.

315

Moerman, M. (1988). *Talking culture: Ethnography and conversation analysis*. Philadelphia: University of Pennsylvania Press.

Morgan, B. (1997). Identity and intonation: Linking dynamic processes in an ESL classroom. *TESOL Quarterly, 31*(3), 431-450.

Moskowitz, G. (1967). The attitudes and teaching patterns of co-operaing teachers and student teachers trained in interaction analysis. In E. J. Amidon & J. B. Hough (Eds.), *Interaction analysis: Theory, research and application*. Reading: Addison-Wesley.

Murray, G. L. (1999). Autonomy and language learning in a simulated environment. *System, 27,* 295-308.

Nakahama, Y., Tyler, A., and Van Lier (2001). Negotiation of meaning in conversational and information gap activities: A comparative discourse analysis. *TESOL Quarterly, 35*(3), 377-405.

Nash, R. (1976). *Teacher expectations and pupil learning*. Henley and Boston, Routledge & Kegan Paul.

Nassaji H. & Wells, G. (2000). What's the use of "triadic dialogue"?: An investigation of teacher-student interaction. *Applied Linguistics, 21,* 376-406.

NCEC (2004). Retrieved on September 12, 2006, from http://www. bfsu.edu.cn/chinese/site/gxyyzyxxw/zywj/tyyjxdg.htm.

Newman, D., Griffin, P., & Cole, M. (1989). *The construction zone: Working for cognitive change in school*. New York: Cambridge University Press.

Newman, W. L. (1997). *Social research methods: Qualitative and quantitative approaches*. MA: Allyn & Bacon.

Nolasco, R. & Arthur, L. (1988). *Large classes*. Hong Kong: Macmillan Publishers Ltd.

Norton, B. 2000). *Identity and language learning: gender, ethnicity and educational change*. Harlow: Pearson Education.

Nunan, D. (1987) Communicative language teaching: Making it work. *ELT Journal, 41*(2), 136-145.

Nunan, D. (1988). *The learner-centred curriculum.* Cambridge: Cambridge University Press.

Nunan, D. (1989). *Understanding language classrooms.* Hemel Hempstead: Prentice Hall.

Nunan, D. (1990). *Second language classroom research. ERIC digest.* Washington D.C.: ERIC Clearinghouse on Languages and Linguistics.

Nunan, D. (1992). *Research methods in language learning.* Cambridge: Cambridge University Press.

Nunan, D. (1993). *Discourse analysis.* London: Penguin Books.

Nunan, D. (1996). Issues in second language acquisition research: Examining substance and procedure. In W. Ritchie & T. Bjatia (Eds.), *Handbook of Second Language Acquisition.* New York: Academic Press.

Nunan, D. & Bailey, K. (Eds.). (1996). *Voices from the language classroom: Qualitative research in second language education.* Cambridge: Cambridge University Press.

Nunan, D. (2004). *Research methods in language learning.* Cambridge: Cambridge University Press.

Nunes, A. (2004). Portfolios in the EFL classroom: Disclosing an informed practice. *ELT Journal, 58*(4), 327-35.

Oppenheim, A. N. (1996). *Questionnaire design, interviewing and attitude measurement.* London: Continuum.

Oxford, R. (1992/1993). Language learning strategies in a nutshell: Update and ESL suggestions. *TESOL Journal, 2*(2), 18-22.

Oxford, R. L. (2001). The bleached bones of a story: Learners' constructions of language teachers. In Breen, M. (Ed.), *Learner contribu-*

tions to language learning: New directions in research. Harlow: Pearson.

Paine, L. W. (1992). Teaching and modernization in contemporary China. In R. Hayhoe (Ed.), *Education and modernization: The Chinese experience* (pp. 183-209). Oxford: Pergamon Press.

Painter, C. (1989). *Learning the mother tongue.* Oxford: Oxford University Press.

Palys, T. (1997). *Research decisions: Quantitative and qualitative perspectives* (2nd ed.).Toronto: Harcourt Brace.

Patton, M. Q. (1990). *Qualitative evaluation and research methods.* (2nd ed.). C.A.: Sage.

Paul, B. D. (1953). Interview techniques and field relationships. In S. Tax (Ed.), *Anthropology today: Selections.* Chicago: Chicago University Press.

Perrement, M. (2005). Action research revolutionizes the classroom. *China Development Brief, Volume IX*(4), 3-6.

Phillips, D. C. & Burbules, N. C. (2000). *Postpositivism and educational research.* Lanham: Rowman & Littlefield Publishers.

Pica, T. (1994). Research on negotiation: What does it reveal about second-language learning conditions, processes and outcomes? *Language Learning, 44,* 493-527.

Pica, T. (2000). Tradition and transition in English language teaching methodology. *System, 28,* 1-18.

Pica, T., Young, R, & Doughty, C. (1987). The impact of interaction on comprehension. *TESOL Quarterly, 21*(4), 737-758.

Pintrich P. R., Cross, D. R., Kozma, R. B., & McKeachie, W. J. (1986). Instructional psychology. *Annual Review of Psychology, 37,* 611-651.

Pike, K. (1967). *Language in relation to a unified theory of the structure of human behaviour.* The Hague: Mouton.

Pitt, K. (2005). *Debates in ESOL teaching and learning: Culture, communities and classrooms.* London: Routledge.

Platt, R. J. & Platt, H. (1992). *Dictionary of language teaching and applied linguistics.* (2nd ed.). Essex: Longman.

Postiglione, G. (1999). *China's national minority education: Culture, schooling and development.* New York: Falmer.

Popper, K. R. (1972). *Objective knowledge: An evolutionary approach.* Oxford: University of Oxford Press.

Powney, J. & Watts, M. (1987). *Interviewing in educational research.* London: Routledge & Kegan Paul.

Prabhu, N. S. (1992). The dynamics of the language lesson. *TESOL Quarterly, 26,* 225-241.

Preece, P. F. W. (1994). *Basic quantitative data analysis.* Exeter: The Research Support Unit.

Price, T. W. (2003). Action research investigating the amount of teacher talk in my classroom. *Classroom Research and Research Methods:* The University of Birmingham.

Pring, R. (2000). *Philosophy of educational research.* London/New York: Continuum.

Psathas, G. (1995). *Conversation analysis: The study of talk-in- interaction.* Thousand Oaks: Sage.

Radnor, H. (2002). *Researching your professional practice.* Buckingham: Open University Press.

Rampton, B. Roberts, C. Leung, C. & Harris, R. (2002). Methodology in the analysis of classroom discourse. *Applied Linguistics, 23*(3), 373-392.

Rao, Z. (2002). Chinese students' perceptions of communicative and non-communicative activities in EFL classroom. *System, 30,* 85-105.

Reason, P. & Bradbury, H. (2001). *Handbook of action research: Participative inquiry and practice.* London: Sage.

Reynolds, J. & Skilbeck, M. (1976). *Culture and the classroom.* London: Open Books.

Richards, J. & Rodgers, T. (2001). *Approaches and methods in language teaching.* (2nd ed.). Cambridge, Cambridge University Press.

Richards, K. (2003). *Qualitative inquiry in TESOL.* Basingstoke: Palgrave Macmillan.

Richards, J. & Renandya, W. A. (2002). *Methodology in language teaching: An anthology of current practice.* Cambridge: Cambridge University Press.

Richardson, V (Ed.). (1997). *Constructivist teacher education: Building new understanding.* Washington, D. C.: Falmer.

Ritchie, J. & Lewis, J. (2003). *Qualitative research practice.* London: Sage.

Roberts, C., et al. (2004). *English for Speakers of Other Languages (ESOL) - Case studies of provision, learners' needs and resources.* London: NRDC.

Robson, C. (1993). *Real world research.* Oxford: Blackwell.

Rolin-Ianziti (2005). *Introducing changes in the tertiary language classroom: report on an action research project.* Paper presented to the social change in the 21st century conference: Center for social change research. Queensland university of Technology.

Rosenberg, B. (2004). Editorial. *New Zealand Journal of Tertiary Education Policy. 1* (1), 3.

Rosenthal, R., & Jacobson, L. (1968). *Pygmalion in the classroom: Teacher expectation and pupils' intellectual development.* New York: Holt, Rinehart and Winston.

Rubin, J. & Thompson, I. (2nd ed.). (1994). *How to be a more successful language learner: Toward learner autonomy.* Boston: Heinle & Heinle Publishers.

Rudestam, K. E. and Newton, R. R. (1992). *Surviving your dissertation: A comprehensive guide to content and process.* Newbury Park: Sage.

Sacks, H., Shegloff, E. A., & Jefferson, G. (1974). A simplest systematic for the organization of turn-taking for conversation. *Language, 50,* 696 - 735.

Sage, R. (2000). *Class talk: Successful learning through effective communication.* Leicester: Network Educational Press.

Salili, F. (1999). Teacher-student interaction: Attributional implications and effectiveness of teachers' evaluative feedback. In D. A. Watkins & J. B. Biggs (Eds.), *Teaching the Chinese learner: Psychological and pedagogical perspectives* (pp. 77-99). Comparative Education Research Centre: The University of Hong Kong.

Salmon, P. (1992). *Achieving a PhD: Ten students' experience.* Chester: Trentham books.

Sardar, Z. (2000). *Thomas Kuhn and the science wars.* Cambridge: Icon Books.

Savignon, S. J. (2001). Communicative language teaching for the twenty-first century. In Celce-Murcia (Ed.), *Teaching English as a second or foreign language* (3rd ed., pp. 13-28). Boston: Heinle & Heinle.

Savignon, S. J. (2002). *Interpreting communicative language teaching: Contexts and concerns in teacher education.* New Haven: Yale University Press.

Savilole-Troike, M. (1982). *The ethnography of communication: An introduction.* Oxford: Basil Blackwell.

Scheffler, I. (1965). *Conditions of knowledge: An introduction to epistemology and education.* Chicago: the University of Chicago Press.

Schegloff, E. A. (1987). Between micro and macro: Contexts and other connections. In J. Alexander (Ed.), *The micro-macro link* (pp. 207-234). Berkeley and Los Angeles: University of California Press.

Schiffrin, D. (1994). *Approaches to discourse.* Oxford: Blackwell.

School of Foreign Languages, SYNU, (2004). Retrieved on June 6, 2005, from http://www.synu.edu.cn/1024/index_1024.html.

Schreck, R. (2005). *Classroom culture shock.* Retrieved on June 4, 2007 from http://dudao.szpt.edu.cn/Showcontent.asp?ID=298.

Scollon, S. (1999). Not to waste words or students: Confucian and Socratic discourse in the tertiary classroom. In: E. Hinkel. (Ed.), *Culture in Second Language Teaching and Learning* (pp.13-27). Cambridge: Cambridge University Press, 13-27.

Scollon, R. & S. W. Scollon. (2000). *Intercultural communication: a Discourse approach.* Oxford: Blackwell Publishers.

Scott, D. & Usher, R. (1999). *Researching education: Data, methods and theory in educational enquiry.* London: Cassell.

Scott, D. & Usher, R. (1999). *Researching education: Data, methods and theory in educational enquiry.* London: Cassell.

Seedhouse, P. (2004). *The interactional architecture of the language classroom: A conversation analysis perspective.* Oxford: Blackwell Publishing.

Seliger, H. W., & Long, M. H. (Eds.). (1983). *Classroom-oriented research on second language acquisition.* Mass.: Newbury House.

Senior, R. M. (2002). A class-centred approach to language teaching. *ELT Journal 56*(4), 397-403.

Shannon F. (n.d.). *Blog.* Retrieved on June 12, 2006, from http://fredshannon.blogspot.com/2005/11/input-hypothesis.html.

Sharan, S. (1990). Cooperative learning: A perspective on research and practice. In S. Sharan (Ed.), *Cooperative learning: Theory and research* (pp. 285-300). N.Y.: Praeger.

Shaw, M. E. (1981). *Group dynamics: The psychology of small group behavior.* (3rd ed.). New York: McGraw-Hill.

Shehadeh, A. (2001). Self- and other-initiated modified output during task-based interaction. *TESOL Quarterly, 35*(3), 433-457.

Sherman, R. & Webb, R. (1988). (Eds.). *Qualitative research in education: Focus and methods.* London: Falmer.

Showler, J. (2000). Case study of classroom practice: a "quiet form of research". *The Qualitative Report, 5.* Retrieved on August 25, 2006, from http://www.nova.edu/ssss/QR/QR5-3/showler.html.

Sinclair, J. M., & Couthard, R.M. (1975). *Towards an analysis of discourse: The English used by teachers and pupils.* London: Oxford University Press.

Silverman, D. (1985). *Qualitative methodology in sociology.* Aldershot: Gower.

Silverman, D. (1997). *Qualitative research: Theory, method and practice.* London: Sage.

Silverman, D. (2001). *Interpreting qualitative data: Methods for analysing talk, text and interaction.* London: Sage.

Slavin, R. F. (1980). Cooperative Learning. *Review of Educational Research, 50*(2), 315-342.

Slee, R., Weiner, G., Tomlinson, S. (1998). *School effectiveness for whom? Challenges to the school effectiveness and school improvement movements.* London: Falmer Press.

Slembrouck, S. (2001). *Explanation, interpretation and critique in the analysis of discourse.* Cambridge: Cambridge University Press.

Slimani, A. 2001. Evaluation of classroom interaction. In C. N. Candlin & N. Mercer (Eds.), *English language teaching in its social context: A reader.* London: Routledge.

Snell, J. (1999). Improving teacher-student interaction in the EFL Classroom: An Action Research Report. *The Internet TESL Journal, Volume V, Number 4.*

Snow, M. A., Hyland, J., Kamhi-Stein, L., & Yu, J. H. (1996). U.S. language minority students: voices from the junior high classroom. In K. Bailey & D. Nunan (Eds.), *Voices from the language classroom: Qualitative research in second language education.* Cambridge: Cambridge University Press.

Sparkes, A. C. (1992). *Research in physical education and sport: Exploring alternative visions.* London: Falmer Press.

Spradley, J. (1980). *Participant observation.* New York: Holt, Rinehart and Winston.

Stenhouse, L. (1975). *An introduction to curriculum research and development.* London: Heinemann.

Stephen, L. Schensul, J. & LeCompte, M. (1999). *Essential ethnographic methods: Observations, interviews, and questionnaires.* Walnut Creek: Altamira Press.

Sternberg, R. J. (1986). Inside intelligence. *American Scientist, 74,* 137-143.

Stewart, A. (1998). *The ethnographer's method.* Thousand Oaks: Sage.

Storch, N. (2002). Patterns of interaction in ESL pair work. *Language learning, 52,* 119-158.

Stronach, I. & Maclure, M. (1997). *Educational research undone: The post-modern embrace.* Buckingham: Open University Press.

Strauss, A., & Corbin, J. (1990). *Basics of qualitative research.* Thousand Oaks, CA: Sage.

Stubbs, M. (1983). *Discourse analysis: The sociolinguistic analysis of natural language.* Chicago: University of Chicago Press.

Sullivan, P. (2000). Playfulness as mediation in communicative language teaching in a Vietnamese classroom. In J. P. Lantolf (Ed.), *Sociocultural theory and second language learning.* Oxford: Oxford University Press.

Swain. M. (1985). Communicative competence: Some roles of comprehensible input and comprehensible output in its development In S. Gass & C. Madden (Eds.), *Input in Second Language Acquisition* (pp. 235-253). M.A.: Newbury House.

Swain, M. (1995). Three functions of output in second language learning. In G. Cook and B. Seidlhofer (Eds.) *Principle and practice in applied linguistics.* Oxford: Oxford University Press.

Swain, M., & Lapkin, S. (1995). Problems in output and the cognitive processes they generate: A step towards second language learning. *Applied Linguistics 16*, 371-391.

Swann, J. (2001). Recording and transcribing talk. In C. N. Candlin & N. Mercer (Eds.), *English language teaching in its social context: A reader.* London: The Open University.

Tarone, E. (2006). Language lessons: A complex, local co-production of all participants. In S. Gieve & I. K. Miller (Eds.), *Understanding the language classroom* (pp.163-175). Palgrave: Macmillan.

Tang, D. & Absalom, D. (n.d.). Retrieved on October 6, 2006 from http://sunzi1.lib.hku.hk/hkjo/view/5/500050.pdf.

Ten Have (1999). *Doing conversation analysis: A practical guide.* London: Sage.

Tharp, R. G., & Gallimore, R. (1988). *Rousing minds to life: Teaching, learning, and schooling in social context.* Cambridge, England: Cambridge University Press.

Thornhill, S., Ascencio, M., Young, C. (2002). *Video streaming: A guide for educational development.* Manchester: The JISC Click and Go Video Project.

Thomas, D. R. (n.d.). *Qualitative research methods: Data gathering & data analysis.* Retrieved on November 27, 2003, from http://www.health.auckland.ac.nz/.

Thomas, J. (1993). *Doing critical ethnography.* London: Sage.

Thorne, S. (1997). The art (and science) of critiquing qualitative research. In J.M. Morse (Ed.), *Completing a qualitative project: Details and dialogue* (pp.117-132). Thousand Oaks: Sage.

Tierney, W. (2002). Get real: Representing reality. *Qualitative Studies in Education, 15,* 385-398.

Trochim, W. M. K. (2006). *Qualitative methods.* Retrieved on August, 25, 2006 from http://www.socialresearchmethods.net/kb/quameth.htm.

Tseng, M. L. & Ivanic, R. (2006). Recognizing complexity in adult literacy research and practice. In S. Gieve & I. K. Miller (Eds.), *Understanding the language classroom* (pp.136-163). Palgrave: Macmillan.

Tsui, A. B. (1995). *Introducing classroom interaction.* London: Penguin Books.

Tsui, A. (1996). In Nunan & Bailey (Eds.), *Voices from the language classroom: Qualitative research in second language education.* Cambridge: Cambridge University Press.

Tudor, I. (2001). *The dynamics of the language classroom.* Cambridge: Cambridge University Press.

Tyk, I. (1996). *Culture in the classroom: A personal view.* London: Centre for Policy Studies.

Van Lier, L. (1988). *The classroom and the language learner.* London: Longman.

Van Lier, L. (1990). Ethnography: Bandaid, bandwagon, or contraband. In B. Christopher & M. Rosamond (Eds.), *Research in the language classroom.* London: Macmillan modern English in association with the British Council.

Van Lier, L. (1991). Inside the classroom: Learning procedures and teaching procedures. *Applied Language Learning, 2* (1), 29-70.

Van Lier, L (1996). *Interaction in the language curriculum: Awareness, autonomy & authenticity.* London: Longman.

Van Lier, L. (1998). The relationship between consciousness, interaction and language learning. *Language Awareness, 7*(2&3), 128-145.

Van Lier, L., & Matsuo, N. (2000). Varieties of conversational experience looking for learning Opportunities. *Applied Language Learning, 11*(2), 265-287.

Van Lier, L. (2001). In C. N. Candlin & N. Mercer, N. (Eds.), *English language teaching in its social context: A reader.* London: The Open University.

Van Maanen, J. (1988). *Tales of the field: On writing ethnography.* Chicago: Chicago guides to writing, editing and publishing.

Verplaetse, L. S. (2000). Mr. Wonder-ful: Portrait of a dialogic teacher. In J. K. Hall & L. S. Verplaetse (Eds.), *Second and foreign language learning through classroom interaction* (pp. 221-243). N.J.: Lawrence Earlbaum Associates.

Vygotsky, L S. (1978). *Mind in Society: The development of higher psychological processes.* Cambridge: Harvard University Press.

Vygotsky, S. L.(1987). Thinking and speech. In R.W. Riber & A.S. Carton (Eds.), *The collected works of S. L. Vygotsky, Volume 1: Problems of general psychology.* New York: Plenum.

Wallace, M. (1998). *Action research for language teachers.* Cambridge: Cambridge University Press.

Wallen, N. E. & Fraenkel, J. R. (2001). *Educational research: A guide to the process.* N.J.: Lawrence Erlbaum Associates, Inc.

Walliman, N. (2001). *Your research project: A step-by-step guide for the first-time researcher.* London: Sage.

Walsh, S. (2006). *Investigating classroom discourse.* Abingdon: Routledge.

Watkins, D. A. & Biggs, J. B. (1999). *The Chinese learner: Cultural, psychological and contextual influences.* Hong Kong: Comparative Education Research Centre.

Waxman, H. C. & Tellez, K. (2002). *Spotlight on student success.* The laboratory for student success, the mid-Atlantic regional educational laboratory.

Watkins, D. A. & Biggs, J. B. (2001). *Teaching the Chinese learner: Psychological and pedagogical perspectives.* Hong Kong: Comparative Education Research Centre.

Watson-Gegeo, K. A. (1988). Ethnography in ESL: Defining the essentials. *TESOL Quarterly, 22*(4), 575-592.

Weiner, G. (1994). *Feminisms in education: An introduction.* Buckingham: Open University Press.

Weinstein, C. (1981). Classroom design as an external condition for learning. *Educational Technology, 8,* 12-19.

Wellington, J. (2000). *Educational research: Contemporary issues and practical approaches.* London: Continuum.

Wells, G. (1981). *Learning through interaction.* Cambridge: Cambridge University Press.

Wells, G. (1985). *Language development in the pre-school years.* Cambridge: Cambridge University Press.

Wells, G. (1993) Reevaluating the IRF Sequence: A proposal for the articulation of theories of activity and discourse for the analysis of teaching and learning in the classroom. *Linguistics and Education, 5*(1), 1-38.

Wells, G. (1995). Language and the inquiry-oriented curriculum. *Curriculum Inquiry, 25*(3), 233-269.

Wengraf, T. (2001). *Qualitative research interview.* London: Sage.

Whetherell, M., Taylor, S., and Yates, S. (Eds.). (2001). *Discourse as data: A guide for analysis.* London: Sage.

Widdowson, H. G. (1978). *Teaching language as communication.* Oxford: Oxford University Press.

Widdowson, H. G. (1987). The Roles of Teacher and Learner. *ELT Journal, 41*(2), 83-84.

Wikipedia, the online encyclopedia. Retrieved November 16, 2005, from http://www.wikipedia.org/.

Wilkinson, A. (1975). *Language and education.* Oxford: Oxford University Press.

Williams, M. & Burden, R. (1997). *Psychology for language teachers. A social constructivist approach.* Cambridge: Cambridge University Press

Willis, J. (1996). Consciousness-raising activities in the language classroom. In J. Willis & D. Willis (Eds.), *Challenge and change in language teaching.* Oxford: Heinemann ELT.

Wills, R. H. (1998). *Human instincts, everyday life, and the brain: A paradigm for understanding behaviour.* Charlottetown: The Book Emporium.

Wittrock, M. C. (1977). Learning as a generative process. In M. C. Wittrock (Ed.), *Learning and instruction.* C.A.: McCutchan Publishing Corporation.

Wittrock, M. (Ed.). (1986). *Handbook of research on teaching.* New York: Macmillan.

Wodak, R. & Meyer, M. (2001). *Methods of critical discourse analysis.* London: Sage.

Wolcott, H. F. (1988). Ethnographic research in education. In R. M. Jaeger (Ed.), *Complementary methods for research in education* (pp. 26-35). Washington. D. C.: American Educational Research Association.

Wolcott, H. F. (1994). *Transforming qualitative data.* Thousand Oaks: Sage.

Wolf, R. M. (2005). *Judging educational research based on experiments and surveys.* Paris: International institute for educational planning/UNESCO.

Woods, P. (1986). *Inside schools: Ethnography in educational research.* London: Routledge & Kegan Paul.

Woods, P. (1996). *Researching the art of teaching: Ethnography for educational use.* London: Routledge.

Woolgar, S. (1988). *Science: The very idea.* Chichester: Ellis Horwood Ltd.

Wragg, E. 1979. *Classroom interaction.* Milton Keynes: The Open University.

Wragg, E. C. (1994). *An introduction to classroom observation.* London: Routledge.

Wright, T. (1987). *Roles of teachers & learners.* Oxford: Oxford University Press.

Wright, T. (2005). *Classroom management in language education.* Basingstoke: Palgrave Macmillan.

Wright, T. (2006). Managing classroom life. In S., Gieve & I., Miller (Eds.), *Understanding the language classroom* (pp.64-87). Macmillan: Palgrave.

Wright, T. & Bolitho, R. (1993). Language awareness, a missing link in language teacher education? *ELT Journal ,47*(2), 292-304.

Wringe, C. (1984). *Democracy, schooling and political education.* London: Allen & Unwin.

Wu, (2004). *Speech made at the Tertiary English Education Reform Video Conference.* Beijing: China.

Yin, R. K. (2003). *Case study research, design and methods.* (3rd ed.). Newbury Park: Sage.

Yu, E. K. W. (n.d.). Communicative English teaching, critical literacy, and the possibility of cultivating a participatory citizenry. *CUHK Journal of Humanities.* Retrieved on April 23, 2006 from http://sunzi1.lib.hku.hk/hkjo/view/9/900042.pdf.

Yu, L. (1990). The comprehensible output hypothesis and self- directed learning: A learner's perspective. *TESL Canada Journal, 8*(1), 9-26.

Yu, E. K. W. (n.d.). Communicative English teaching, critical literacy, and the possibility of cultivating a participatory citizenry. *CUHK Journal of Humanities.* Retrieved on April 23, 2006, from http://sunzi1.lib.hku.hk/hkjo/view/9/900042.pdf.

Zamel, V. (1997). Toward a model of transculturation. *TESOL Quarterly, 31*(2), 341-352.

Zhang, L. (2004). CLT in China: Frustrations, misconceptions, and clarifications. *Hwa Kuang Journal of TEFL.*

Zhong, Y.X. & Shen, H. Z. 2002. Where is the technology-induced pedagogy? Snapshots from 2 multimedia EFL classrooms. *British Journal of Educational technology. 33*(1), 39-52.

Zhu, H. (2006). Teaching quieter students. *English Teaching Professional, 42,* 37-39.

Zou, H. & Cai, Z. (2006). CLT in China: A re-examination. *US-China Foreign language, 4*(1), 68-74.

社會科學類　AF0124

Classroom Culture and the Construction of Learning Opportunities: An Ethnographic Case Study of Two EFL Classrooms in a Higher Education Setting in China

作　　者 / 李英春
發 行 人 / 宋政坤
執行編輯 / 藍志成
圖文排版 / 黃莉珊
封面設計 / 陳佩蓉
數位轉譯 / 徐真玉　沈裕閔
圖書銷售 / 林怡君
法律顧問 / 毛國樑　律師
出版印製 / 秀威資訊科技股份有限公司
　　　　　台北市內湖區瑞光路 583 巷 25 號 1 樓
　　　　　電話：02-2657-9211　　　　傳真：02-2657-9106
　　　　　E-mail：service@showwe.com.tw
經 銷 商 / 紅螞蟻圖書有限公司
　　　　　台北市內湖區舊宗路二段 121 巷 28、32 號 4 樓
　　　　　電話：02-2795-3656　　　　傳真：02-2795-4100
　　　　　http://www.e-redant.com

2009 年 12 月 BOD 一版
定價：420 元

讀 者 回 函 卡

感謝您購買本書，為提升服務品質，煩請填寫以下問卷，收到您的寶貴意見後，我們會仔細收藏記錄並回贈紀念品，謝謝！

1. 您購買的書名：_____

2. 您從何得知本書的消息？

　　□網路書店　□部落格　□資料庫搜尋　□書訊　□電子報　□書店

　　□平面媒體　□ 朋友推薦　□網站推薦　□其他_____

3. 您對本書的評價：(請填代號　1.非常滿意 2.滿意 3.尚可 4.再改進)

　　封面設計____　版面編排____　內容____　文/譯筆____　價格____

4. 讀完書後您覺得：

　　□很有收獲　□有收獲　□收獲不多　□沒收獲

5. 您會推薦本書給朋友嗎？

　　□會　□不會，為什麼？_____

6. 其他寶貴的意見：_____

_____

_____

_____

讀者基本資料

姓名：_____　年齡：_____　性別：□女 □男

聯絡電話：_____　E-mail：_____

地址：_____

學歷：□高中(含)以下　　□高中　　□專科學校　　□大學

　　　□研究所(含)以上 □其他_____

職業：□製造業 □金融業 □資訊業 □軍警 □傳播業 □自由業

　　　□服務業 □公務員 □教職　□學生 □其他_____

To：114

台北市內湖區瑞光路 583 巷 25 號 1 樓

秀威資訊科技股份有限公司　　　收

寄件人姓名：

寄件人地址：□□□

(請沿線對摺寄回,謝謝!)

秀威與 BOD

BOD（Books On Demand）是數位出版的大趨勢，秀威資訊率先運用 POD 數位印刷設備來生產書籍，並提供作者全程數位出版服務，致使書籍產銷零庫存，知識傳承不絕版，目前已開闢以下書系：

一、BOD 學術著作—專業論述的閱讀延伸
二、BOD 個人著作—分享生命的心路歷程
三、BOD 旅遊著作—個人深度旅遊文學創作
四、BOD 大陸學者—大陸專業學者學術出版
五、POD 獨家經銷—數位產製的代發行書籍

BOD 秀威網路書店：www.showwe.com.tw
政府出版品網路書店：www.govbooks.com.tw

永不絕版的故事・自己寫・永不休止的音符・自己唱